JAPANESE FROM ZERO! 5

George Trombley
Yukari Takenaka

Japanese From Zero! Book 3
Proven Methods to Learn Japanese with integrated Workbook

PREFACE

Japanese From Zero! is a Japanese language book series built on Japanese grammar that makes sense! Each book is crafted page by page and lesson by lesson to have relevant (and sometimes fun) Japanese conversation and sentence structure patterns that enhance the Japanese learner's ability to speak Japanese faster and understand the small nuances of Hiragana and everyday Japanese speech.

DEDICATION

This book is dedicated and made for:

Japanese culture lovers, Japanese language learners, Japanese anime and drama watchers, Japanese beginners, JPOP music fans, people of Japanese heritage connecting to their history, and anyone planning travel to Japan!

I lived in Japan for 9 years and have been married to my Japanese wife, Yukari, for 20 years. When we began writing the Japanese From Zero series, it was out of frustration with current Japanese books on the market. I felt they were either too fast, too slow, or too complicated. Japanese has enriched my life so much and writing this series was a way to express my sincere appreciation to all that the country of Japan and the Japanese language can offer.

All of us on the Japanese From Zero! team wish you success on your road to Japanese fluency and hope this book is a solid first step!

COPYRIGHT

DISTRIBUTION

Distributed in the UK & Europe by:
Bay Foreign Language Books Ltd.
Unit 4, Kingsmead, Park Farm,
Folkestone, Kent. CT19 5EU, Great Britain
sales@baylanguagebooks.co.uk

Distributed in the USA & Canada by:
From Zero LLC.
10624 S. Eastern Ave. #A769
Henderson, NV 89052, USA
sales@fromzero.com

Thanks for the nice comments! We love feedback!

These books and this website remain my nihongo bible!
Ray_San – YesJapan.com

The books are great! I like the way everything is explained, the examples, the lessons and the reviews.
Eijioo – YesJapan.com

Japanese From Zero Book 1 and 2 are amazing books for beginners! Having tried other ways of learning Japanese from the beginning, I find that the Japanese from Zero series are incredibly user friendly.
Kurisuti.Chan – YesJapan.com

I love JFZ, because it's so so so easy to use compared to others I've tried! It's clear you put a lot of work into it and I'm very grateful. Even though I lead a busy life and can't find too much time to learn, JFZ makes it easy for me to pick up where I left off and revise what I might have forgotten. THANKS!! ☺
J. Brooks – Facebook

THANK-YOU JFZ!!!!!! I think Everything JFZ does is wonderful! It is the most helpful book I've come across!
Rukia Kuchiki – YesJapan.com

Thank you, I just finished the 2nd book and can't wait to start with the 3rd! Soon am getting my hands on the 4th!
religionflag – YesJapan.com

JFZ! is perfect. If you're a complete beginner, this book takes you through the bare basics and really helps you progress quickly. I highly recommend this.
F. Morgan – Good Reads review

The perfect Japanese textbook for young learners. One of the benefits of this book, which also slows it down, are the tangents it takes to explain the nuances of Japanese that a beginner might encounter.
Michael Richey – Tofugu.com

You really learn Japanese from zero – no prior knowledge at all required. The grammar is easy to understand.
Karl Andersson - karlandersson.se

As someone who owns the first three books, I can say the books are great.
Mastema – YesJapan.com

feedback@fromzero.com

Japanese From Zero! 3
— CONTENTS —

Lesson 3 Level ③

My Loud Mother

the て forms

Kanji Lesson 4

休上下左右

Lesson 4 Level ③

The Concert
expressing opinion

Kanji Lesson 5

大中小円人目

Kanji Lesson 7

立男女子生

Lesson 7 Level ③

Two Chickens

a Japanese tongue twister

Kanji Lesson 8

天空気雨山川

Kanji Lesson 10   村田夕赤青白見

Lesson 10 Level ③   **Yumiko's Cavity**
using とき

- ■ Translation
- ■ Question and answer
- ■ Useful Expressions

Kanji Lesson
1

一二三四五六 and the basics

一 **Kanji Basics かんじの きほん**

❑ Why kanji are important

Welcome to kanji, and congratulations for coming this far in your quest to learn Japanese. Many students ask, "Is it really necessary to learn the kanji?" The answer is *yes*. The kanji are not just phonetic symbols like hiragana and katakana. Each kanji has meaning. By learning the kanji you will be able to make sense of how words are related to each other, and your ability to understand Japanese will increase substantially as you learn new characters.

The kanji 食 can be read as しょく or た, depending on the word. The kanji 食 means "food," and words with this kanji in them tend to have meanings related to food. Even if you didn't know the word, you would know that it is related to food if this kanji were in it. Consider the following words that use this kanji:

食堂	しょくどう	cafeteria
食卓	しょくたく	dinner table
食欲	しょくよく	appetite
食品	しょくひん	food products
夕食	ゆうしょく	dinner
食中毒	しょくちゅうどく	food poisoning
夜食	やしょく	midnight snack

As you can see, all of the words have 食 in them and are somehow related to food.

❑ Listening for kanji

Kanji are great because they give you a level of comprehension not available from hiragana and katakana alone. For example, if you hear the word にほんしょく, even though you have never heard the word before you might be able to understand what it means based on the kanji you have "heard." Because you know that にほん means Japan, and you know that しょく is one of the readings for the kanji "food," you could assume that the word means "Japanese food." Of course, it is possible that the しょく portion of にほんしょく was not the kanji for food but the kanji for color, 色, which can also be read as しょく. You can rule out other kanji possibilities by the context of the conversation.

Knowing how words are written in kanji will help your comprehension because you will be able to guess what something means based on what the possible kanji are. Learning kanji is not as easy as learning hiragana or katakana, but the benefits of knowing kanji make the effort worthwhile.

❏ Different readings

Unlike hiragana and katakana, kanji can have more than one reading. The best way to learn the different readings is to learn a word that uses the particular reading. The kanji section of the lesson will provide you with sample words for each reading.

There are two types of readings:
くんよみ is the Japanese reading of the kanji. It is normally unique to the Japanese language.

おんよみ is the Chinese reading of the kanji. If you ever study Chinese, you will notice the similarity in the way the kanji is read in both languages. Sometimes the おんよみ of the kanji sounds *nothing* like it does in Chinese.

❏ Reading instinct

Many students struggle with kanji because they are not sure whether the kanji in the word should be read with the おんよみ or くんよみ. Although there is no foolproof way to know which reading to use, you will usually be correct if you follow this simple guideline: most kanji in words using a combination of hiragana and kanji use the Japanese reading, くんよみ. On the other hand, if the word is composed of two or more kanji without any hiragana, then normally the おんよみ is used. When the kanji is all by itself, your first inclination should be to use the くんよみ reading.

― New Kanji あたらしい かんじ

Make sure you learn the correct stroke order. Correct stroke order will mean neater symbols when writing quickly. Also, take time to learn the new words for each kanji – these will help you memorize the different readings.

1 ―	くんよみ	ひとつ				
	おんよみ	イチ、イツ				
	<u>いち</u>	<u>いち</u>・ど	<u>ひと</u>・つ	<u>いち</u>・がつ	<u>つい</u>・たち	<u>いっ</u>・ぱん
	一	一度	一つ	一月	一日	一般
1 stroke	one	one time	one thing	January	first day of the month	normal; general

2 二	くんよみ	ふたつ				
	おんよみ	ニ				
	<u>に</u>	<u>ふた</u>・つ	<u>に</u>・がつ	<u>ふつ</u>・か	<u>に</u>・かい	<u>に</u>・じ
	二	二つ	二月	二日	二階	二時
2 strokes	two	two things	February	second day of the month	second floor	two o'clock

三 [1 2 3]	くんよみ	みっつ				
	おんよみ	サン				
	さん 三	さん・がつ 三月	みっ・か 三日	さん・かく 三角	みっ・つ 三つ	さん・じげん 三次元
3 strokes	three	March	third day of the month	a triangle	three things	third dimension

四	くんよみ	よっつ				
	おんよみ	シ、ヨン				
	よん、し 四	し・がつ 四月	よっ・か 四日	し・かく 四角	よっ・つ 四つ	し・き 四季
5 strokes	four	April	fourth day of the month	a square	four things	four seasons

五	くんよみ	いつつ				
	おんよみ	ゴ				
	ご 五	ご・がつ 五月	いつ・か 五日	いつ・つ 五つ	ご・かん 五感	ご・ふん 五分
4 strokes	five	May	fifth day of the month	five things	five senses	five minutes

六	くんよみ	むっつ、むい				
	おんよみ	ロク、ロッ				
	ろく 六	むい・か 六日	ろく・がつ 六月	むっ・つ 六つ	ろく・じゅう 六十	ろっ・ぴゃく 六百
4 strokes	six	sixth day of the month	June	six things	60	600

一 Writing Points かくポイント

❑ Numbers in kanji versus "1, 2, 3…"

In modern Japan, kanji numbers is not used as frequently as in the past. More commonly, numbers are written with Arabic numerals (1, 2, 3…). One factor that probably influenced this was the limitation of early computers. Written Japanese employs many more characters than English and accordingly requires a more sophisticated computer code. It would have been more convenient to use Arabic numerals for computing, and the practice probably stuck.

Although there is still a place for kanji numbers in Japan, they aren't used as frequently today. In Japan today you will see the Arabic numbers you are used to on TV, clocks, license plates and just about anything that uses numbers. However you do need to know the number kanji since many words and phrases integrate these kanji into them.

▬ Kanji Activities

❑ **Stroke order**
   Trace the light gray symbols for practice. Pay attention to stroke order and stroke type.

❑ **Words you can write**

Write the following words using the kanji that you just learned. This is a great way to increase your Japanese vocabulary.

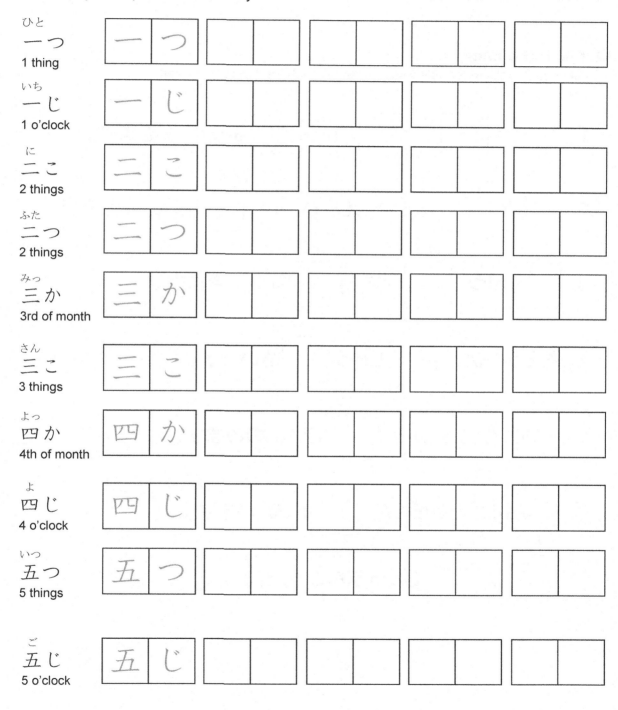

ひと
一つ
1 thing

いち
一じ
1 o'clock

に
二こ
2 things

ふた
二つ
2 things

みっ
三か
3rd of month

さん
三こ
3 things

よっ
四か
4th of month

よ
四じ
4 o'clock

いつ
五つ
5 things

ご
五じ
5 o'clock

<ruby>六<rt>むい</rt></ruby>か
6th of month

| 六 | か | | | | | | | | |

❏ Fill in the kanji

Fill in the blanks in the following sentences with the appropriate kanji.

1. あした ☐(ろく)じ ☐(よん)じゅう ☐(ご)ふんに おきます。

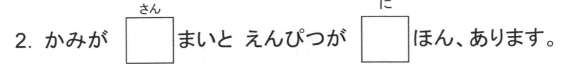

2. かみが ☐(さん)まいと えんぴつが ☐(に)ほん、あります。

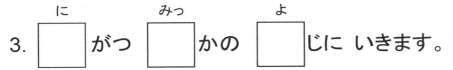

3. ☐(に)がつ ☐(みっ)かの ☐(よ)じに いきます。

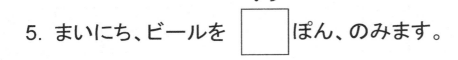

4. おとうさんは ☐(ろく)じゅう ☐(いっ)さいです。

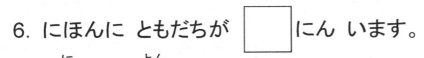

5. まいにち、ビールを ☐(いっ)ぽん、のみます。

6. にほんに ともだちが ☐(ご)にん います。

7. ☐(に)じ ☐(よん)じゅっぷんごろ、きます。

WRITING PRACTICE

Use these sheets as extra writing practice for the kanji you have learned up to this point. Recently you have learned: 一二三四五六

VOCABULARY GROUPS ———————————— set 1

Throughout this book we will introduce groups of words that are important to everyday Japanese speaking. You don't have to try to memorize them all at once. Just familiarize yourself with the each group as they will be showing up in subsequent lessons.

There are two versions of each word for your future convenience. As you learn kanji throughout the lessons the progressive version will slowly replace the hiragana that can be represented in kanji.

A   geography

English	Progressive	Kanji +
Asia	アジア	アジア
Europe	ヨーロッパ	ヨーロッパ
Oceania	オセアニア	オセアニア
Middle East	ちゅうとう	中東
Africa	アフリカ	アフリカ
North Pole	ほっきょく	北極
South Pole	なんきょく	南極
equator	せきどう	赤道
Atlantic Ocean	たいせいよう	大西洋
Pacific Ocean	たいへいよう	太平洋
Japan Sea	にほんかい	日本海
national border	こっきょう	国境
United Nations	こくれん	国連

Lesson
1
Level ③

Masumi and Me
counting time spans

1   About this Lesson このレッスンについて

Before The Lesson

1. know how to read and write 一二三四五六
2. review vocabulary set 1

Lesson Goals

1. learn to count time spans of hours, days, weeks, months and years
2. learn to say something happened in the past

From The Teachers

1. Memorize the time spans. They will be important for the next few lessons.

1   New Words あたらしい ことば

Take the time to memorize the new words in this lesson. Move on to the next section only after you know these words. If you are having a hard time memorizing the words, try writing each word ten times, repeating the word to yourself as you write it.

Progressive	Kanji +	English
どれぐらい、どのぐらい	どれぐらい、どのぐらい	how long; how much (time, money)
どれぐらいまえ	どれぐらい前	(about) how long ago
かんごふ(さん)	看護婦さん	a nurse
このあいだ	この間	the other day
でんわだい	電話代	telephone bill
もしもし	もしもし	hello (telephone only)
いまから	今から	from now (starting from now)
これから	これから	starting now (from now on)
また あとで	また あとで	again later
ページ	ページ	page
ロス	ロス	short for ロサンゼルス (LA)

1 New Adjectives あたらしい けいようし

Progressive	Kanji +	English	Type
すごい	凄い	amazing, great, wow	い adjective

1 New Verbs あたらしい どうし

As you learn new verbs you can learn more about them in the Verb Usage section. Use the verb type to figure out each verbs conjugations.

Dictionary	Kanji +	た-form	English	Type
もどる	戻る	もどった	to go or come back, return	regular
がんばる	頑張る	がんばった	to do your best	regular
とまる	泊まる	とまった	to stay (overnight)	regular
はたらく	働く	はたらいた	to work	regular
はなす	話す	はなした	to speak or talk	regular

1 Verb Usage どうしの つかいかた

☐ **もどる (to come back, return)**

もどる uses particles just like いく、くる and かえる. This verb is very similar to かえる, but there are some subtle differences. かえる is usually used only when you are going to return to the place of origin. もどる can be used when returning to the place of origin or any point along the way. Also, もどる can be used when referring to non-physical places such as さいしょに もどる (returning to the beginning).

> [*place*] に もどる
>
> return to [*place*]

Example Sentences

1. なんじに もどりますか。 — What time will you come back?
2. 五ページに もどってください。 — Please go back to page five.
3. あした、もどります。 — I will be back tomorrow.
4. きのう、アフリカから もどりました。 — I came back from Africa yesterday.

❏ がんばる (to do your best)

がんばる is used a lot in Japan. Whenever you are determined to do something, you will がんばる. No matter how tough it gets, you will がんばる. The particle を marks the thing that you are going to do your best at.

> ### [*something*] を がんばる
> ### do your best at [*something*]

Example Sentences

1. しごとを がんばります。
2. しゅくだいを がんばりましょう。
3. かおりちゃんは がんばりました。

I will do my best at work.
Let's do our best at homework.
Kaori did her best.

❏ とまる (to stay over, spend the night)

に is used to mark the place where you are staying.

> ### [*place*] に とまる
> ### stay over at [*place*]

Example Sentences

1. かようびに ともだちの いえに とまりました。
   I spent the night at a friend's house on Tuesday.

2. あした ホテルに とまります。
   I will stay in a hotel tomorrow.

❏ はたらく (to work)

で marks the place where one is working.

> ### [*place*] で はたらく
> ### work at [*place*]

Example Sentences

1. らいしゅうから ここで はたらきます。
2. なんじまで はたらきましたか。
3. きのう、はたらいたの？

I will work here from next week.
Until what time did you work?
Did you work yesterday? (informal)

❏ **はなす (to speak, talk with)**

```
┌─────────────────────────────────┐
│          to talk with           │
├─────────────────────────────────┤
│                                 │
│     [person] と はなす          │
│                                 │
│     talk with [person]          │
│                                 │
└─────────────────────────────────┘
```

Example Sentences

1. せんしゅう、のぶよちゃん<u>と</u> はなしました。
   I spoke <u>with</u> Nobuyo last week.

2. だれ<u>と</u> はなしましたか。
   <u>With</u> whom did you speak?

3. がっこうの ともだち<u>と</u> あんまり はなしません。
   I don't talk that much <u>with</u> my school friends.

```
┌─────────────────────────────────┐
│             to tell             │
├─────────────────────────────────┤
│                                 │
│     [person] に はなす          │
│                                 │
│     tell/inform [person]        │
│                                 │
└─────────────────────────────────┘
```

Example Sentences

1. あさって、しまださん<u>に</u> はなします。
   I will tell Mr. Shimada the day after tomorrow.

2. ともだちに はなしません。
   I won't tell my friends.

```
┌─────────────────────────────────┐
│          to talk about          │
├─────────────────────────────────┤
│                                 │
│     [thing]の ことを はなす     │
│                                 │
│     talk about [thing]          │
│                                 │
└─────────────────────────────────┘
```

Example Sentences

1. おばあさんに くるま<u>の ことを</u> はなします。
   I will tell my grandmother <u>about</u> the car.

2. なんで わたしに しゅくだいの ことを はなさなかったの？
   How come you didn't tell me about the homework?

3. おとうさんに かれの ことを はなした。
   I told my father about my boyfriend. (informal)

1 Time Spans じかん

The time spans below, like the other counters you have learned, continue past twelve units in a pattern similar to the first ten.

When counting time spans for days, months, and years, sometimes the suffix かん is added at the end. かん literally means "period of time" or "interval," but it does not always have to be used.   When counting しゅうかん (weeks) and じかん (hours), かん can never be removed.

How many?	Hours じかん なんじかん？	Days にち (かん optional) なんにち？	Weeks しゅう なんしゅうかん？
1	いちじかん	いちにち (never add かん)	いっしゅうかん
2	にじかん	ふつか	にしゅうかん
3	さんじかん	みっか	さんしゅうかん
4	よじかん	よっか	よんしゅうかん
5	ごじかん	いつか	ごしゅうかん
6	ろくじかん	むいか	ろくしゅうかん
7	ななじかん	なのか	ななしゅうかん
8	はちじかん	ようか	はっしゅうかん
9	くじかん	ここのか	きゅうしゅうかん
10	じゅうじかん	とおか	じゅっしゅかん
11	じゅういちじかん	じゅういちにち	じゅういっしゅうかん
12	じゅうにじかん	じゅうににち	じゅうにしゅうかん

How many?	Months つき (かん optional) なんかげつ？	Years ねん (かん optional) なんねん？
1	いっかげつ	いちねん
2	にかげつ	にねん
3	さんかげつ	さんねん
4	よんかげつ	よねん
5	ごかげつ	ごねん
6	ろっかげつ	ろくねん
7	ななかげつ	しちねん、ななねん
8	はちかげつ	はちねん
9	きゅうかげつ	きゅうねん
10	じゅっかげつ	じゅうねん
11	じゅういっかげつ	じゅういちねん
12	じゅうにかげつ	じゅうにねん

1 Grammar ぶんぽう

❑ Using まえ to mean "ago"

Previously you learned that まえ means "before" and "in front of." For example けっこんまえ means "before marriage," and がっこうのまえ means "before school" or "in front of school." When used with time spans, まえ means "ago." の is not needed to connect まえ to the time spans.

> **[*time span*] + まえ(に)**
>
> **[*time span*] ago**

Examples		
	一ねん<u>まえ</u>	one year <u>ago</u>
	二しゅうかん<u>まえ</u>	two weeks <u>ago</u>
	三かげつ<u>まえ</u>	three months <u>ago</u>
	よっか<u>まえ</u>（四か<u>まえ</u>）	four days <u>ago</u>
	五じかん<u>まえ</u>	five hours <u>ago</u>
	六ぷん<u>まえ</u>	six minutes <u>ago</u>

In the following Q&A, notice that because we are using time spans, the time particle に is used after "ago."

Example Q&A	
1. いつ けっこんしましたか。	When did you get married?
二ねん<u>まえに</u> けっこんしました。	I got married two years <u>ago</u>.
三しゅうかん<u>まえに</u> けっこんしました。	I got married three weeks <u>ago</u>.
2. なんじかん<u>まえに</u> きましたか。	How many hours <u>ago</u> did you come?
六じかん<u>まえに</u> きました。	I came six hours <u>ago</u>.
一じかん<u>まえに</u> きました。	I came one hour <u>ago</u>.

❑ Using はん to half any timespan

Previously you learned that はん means "half past" when saying times. You can do the same thing with any other time span.

Examples		
	一ねん<u>はん</u>	one year and a <u>half</u>
	二しゅうかん<u>はん</u>	two weeks and a <u>half</u>
	三かげつ<u>はん</u>	three months and a <u>half</u>
	よっか<u>はん</u>（四か<u>はん</u>）	four days and a <u>half</u>

❑ Counting pages

This is very easy. In English we say, for example, "page five." In Japanese, "page" comes after the number: 五ページ. The ページ counter can also be used to say the amount of pages, as in "150 pages" (150 ページ).

page 1 いちページ 1 ページ	page 2 にページ 2 ページ	page 3 さんページ 3 ページ	page 4 よんページ 4 ページ	page 5 ごページ 5 ページ
page 6 ろくページ 6 ページ	page 7 ななページ 7 ページ	page 8 はちページ 8 ページ	page 9 きゅうページ 9 ページ	page 10 じゅっページ 10 ページ
How many pages? なんページ			What page? なんページ	

Remember that when ページ is used to say the number of pages in a book, it is a counter and does not require any particles but, when you are refering to a specific page (such as "page ten"), the respective particle must be used.

Example Q&A

1. このほんは なんページ、ありますか。   How many pages does this book have?
   136 ページ、あります。   It has 136 pages.

2. しゅくだいは なんページに ありますか。   What page is the homework on?
   51 ページに あります。   It is on page 51.

Important: Be careful with your particles, as they will change the meaning of the sentence. Without any particles, ページ becomes a counter, and when the location particle に is used, it becomes a location (in a book).

Example Sentences

1. 10 ページ あります。   There are ten pages.
2. 10 ページに あります。   It is on page ten.

❑ The difference between これから and いまから

これから and いまから mean the same thing. They both mean "from now" or "starting now" and can refer to things that occur in the future. They are both used to express that the present time is being used as a starting point when speaking about the future.   However, only いまから can be used in expressions like 「いまから 三ねんまえに」 (three years ago from now) which refer to events in the past. Other than this difference they are used in the same way.   Note that いまから and これから can mean a variety of similar phrases such as "from this point," etc.

Example Q&A

1. <u>いまから</u> なにを しますか。
   <u>いまから</u> しごとを します。

   What will you do (from) <u>now</u>?
   I will work from <u>now</u>.

2. <u>これから</u> どこに いきますか。
   <u>これから</u> アフリカに いきます。

   Where are you going <u>from this point</u>?
   I am going to Africa <u>from this point</u>.

1 Q&A しつもんと こたえ

1. なんねん ほっきょくに いましたか。
   How many years were you at the North Pole?

   三ねん いました。
   I was there for three years.

   ほっきょくに いきませんでした。
   I didn't go to the North Pole.

2. なんにち べんきょうしましたか。
   How many days did you study?

   三かかんぐらいです。
   About three days.

   べんきょうしませんでした。
   I didn't study.

3. たいせいようの しゃしんは なんページに ありますか。
   What page is the picture of the Pacific Ocean on?

   144 ページに あります。
   It's on page 144.

4. なんじかん かいものを しましたか。
   How many hours did you shop?

   五じかん かいものを しました。
   I shopped for five hours.

   二じかんぐらい、しました。
   I shopped for about two hours.

5. いつ アメリカに かえりましたか。
    When did you return to America?

    四かげつまえに かえりました。
    I came back four months ago.

    せんしゅう かえりました。
    I came back last week.

    三しゅうかんまえに かえりました。
    I came back three weeks ago.

6. ここから ロスまで なんじかん ありますか。
    How many hours are there to LA from here?

    ここから 四じかんはんです。
    It's four-and-a-half hours from here.

1 Mini Conversations ミニかいわ J-E

Using a piece of paper cover up the entire English portion of the conversations below. Read the Japanese conversation several times until you understand it. Only then should you move the paper to compare your comprehension to the English translation.

1. Polite conversation between new friends
    A: じゅう二さいから スペインに いました。
    B: なんねんかん いましたか。
    A: 四ねんかん いました。

    A: I was in Spain since the age of twelve.
    B: How many years were you there?
    A: I was there for four years.

2. Polite conversation between two people in a golf shop
    A: わたしは ゴルフが だいすきです。まいしゅう にちようびに します。
    B: いつも なんじかん しますか。
    A: 一じかんはんぐらいです。あなたは？
    B: わたしは ときどき どようびに します。

    A: I really like golf. I play every Sunday.
    B: How many hours do you always play?
    A: About an hour and a half. How about you?
    B: I sometimes play on Saturday.

3. Polite conversation between friends

A： いつ アメリカに いきますか。
B： らいしゅうの きんようびに いきます。
A： よく いきますか。
B： はい、まいとし いきます。
A： いつも どれぐらい いますか。
B： 二かげつぐらい います。

A： When are you going to America?
B： I am going on Friday of next week.
A： Do you go there often?
B： Yes, I go every year.
A： How long do you always stay there?
B： I am there for about two months.

4. Polite conversation between a mother and a daughter

A： きょう、なにを しましたか。
B： ともだちと テニスを しました。
A： どれぐらい しましたか。
B： たぶん 二じかんぐらいです。
A： あしたの テストのべんきょうを どれぐらい しましたか。
B： べんきょう しませんでした。

A： What did you do today?
B： I played tennis with friends.
A： How long did you play?
B： Probably about two hours.
A： How long did you study for tomorrow's test?
B： I didn't study.

5. Polite conversation between friends

A： きょねんの 四がつに カナダに りょこうを しました。
B： どれぐらい いましたか。
A： 三しゅうかんと 五か、いました。

A： Last April I took a trip to Canada.
B： About how long were you there?
A： I was there for three weeks and five days.

1 Mini Conversations ミニかいわ E-J

Using a piece of paper, cover up the entire Japanese portion of the conversations below. Translate the English conversation to Japanese. Only after you have translated the entire conversation should you move the paper to check your work.

1. Mixed conversation between friends
A: When did you come back from Africa?
B: Two weeks ago.
A: How long were you there?
B: About three weeks.

A: いつ アフリカから もどったの？
B: 二しゅうかんまえです。
A: どれぐらい いたの？
B: 三しゅうかんぐらいです。

2. Informal conversation between classmates
A: There is a lot of homework today!
B: When are you going to do it?
A: I don't know. Maybe I'll do it tomorrow.
B: Do your best.
A: Okay. I will do my best.

A: きょう しゅくだいが おおいよ。
B: いつ するの？
A: わからない。たぶん あした する。
B: がんばって。
A: わかった。がんばる。

3. Formal conversation between aquaintances
A: I work everyday until eleven o'clock.
B: That is hard, isn't it!
A: It is. Sometimes I stay (overnight) at my office!
B: Really?!

A: まいにち じゅういちじまで はたらきます。
B: たいへんですね。
A: はい。ときどき オフィスに とまります。
B: ほんとうですか？！

1 Reading Comprehension どっかい

Read the sentences below. Use the information to answer the reading comprehension questions later in this lesson.

① わたしの かのじょは 二じゅう六さいの かんごふです。
② にほんじんです。
③ なまえは ますみです。
④ ますみさんは じゅう二がつ 五かに はじめて アメリカに きます。
⑤ じゅう二がつ じゅう三にちまで わたしの いえに とまります。
⑥ じゅう三にちの あさに にほんに かえります。
⑦ かのじょは まいにち よるの しちじまで はたらきます。
⑧ かのじょは しごとの あとに よく わたしに でんわを します。
⑨ わたしは まいしゅう げつようびの よるに かのじょに でんわをします。
⑩ いつも 二じかんぐらい、はなします。
⑪ でも、このあいだは 四じかんぐらい、はなしたから、もう おかねが ありません。
⑫ せんげつの でんわだいは 四ひゃく 五じゅう きゅうドルでした。

❑ Short dialogue

Here is a phone call that Chris had with Masumi in Japan.

おかあさん:　はい、たかはらです。

クリスさん:　もしもし、クリスです。ますみさんは いますか。

おかあさん:　はい、ちょっと まってください。

ますみさん:　はい、もしもし。

クリスさん:　もしもし、クリスです。

ますみさん:　ああ、クリス！ いま、アメリカは なんじ？

クリスさん:　あさの 五じだよ。にほんは？

ますみさん:　よるの くじ。 きょうは なにを するの？

クリスさん:　しちじはんに しごとに いく。 いつ アメリカに くるの？

ますみさん:　じゅう二がつ 五かに いく。 三じ 四じゅう五ふんの ひこうきだよ。

クリスさん:　うれしいな。はやく きてね。 ひとりだから、さびしいよ。

ますみさん: わたしも…。 あっ、ごめん。いまから ごはんを たべるから、また あとで

でんわするね。

クリスさん: わかった。じゃ、あとで。バイバイ。

ますみさん: しごと、がんばってね。バイバイ。

New words and expressions in the dialogue

Progressive	**Kanji +**	**English**
はやく きてね。	早く着てね。	Come here soon.
がんばってね。	頑張ってね。	Do your best.

1   Activities

❑ **Reading comprehension questions**
Answer the following questions about the reading comprehension in this lesson.

1. クリスの かのじょの なまえは なんですか。

   _____

2. ますみさんは いつ アメリカに きますか。

   _____

3. ますみさんは アメリカで ホテルに とまりますか。

   _____

4. いつ にほんに かえりますか。

   _____

5. ますみさんの しごとは なんですか。

   _____

6.　なんじまで　はたらきますか。

_____

7.　かのじょは　クリスに　いつ　でんわしますか。

_____

8.　クリスは　いつ　ますみさんに　でんわを　しますか。

_____

9.　クリスは　ふつう　なんじかんぐらい　でんわで　ますみさんと　はなしますか。

_____

10.　クリスは　なんで　おかねが　ありませんか。

_____

❑ Substitution drill

Compose new sentences as shown in the example by replacing the appropriate section.

> **Ex.** あした　アメリカから　もどります。
> → the day after tomorrow　　あさって アメリカから　もどります。
> → the day before yesterday　おととい アメリカから　もどりました。
> → from Japan　　　　　　　おととい にほんから　もどりました。

1.　きのう　四じかん　べんきょうしました。

→ two hours　　_____

→ watched TV　_____

→ read a book　_____

→ about three hours　_____

2. 二じから しごとを します。

   → from four o'clock   _____

   → from now on   _____

   → listen to music   _____

3. 三しゅうかんまえに けっこんしました。

   → one year ago   _____

   → six months ago   _____

   → came to America   _____

   → went to Japan   _____

4. なんねん とうきょうに いましたか。

   → how many days   _____

   → how many weeks   _____

   → how many months   _____

❑ Question and answer

Answer the following questions as if they were directly asked to you using the words and patterns in this lesson.

1. よく だれと でんわで はなしますか。

   _____

2. いつも なんじかん／なんぷんぐらい はなしますか。

   _____

3. なんねんまえ／なんかげつまえに ここに きましたか。
   (where you live right now)

   _____

4. まいにち しごと／がっこうは なんじから なんじまでですか。

_____

5. まいにち なんじかん はたらきますか／べんきょうしますか。

_____

6. ときどき にほんごで はなしますか。

_____

7. ともだちの いえに とまりますか。

_____

Kanji Lesson
2

七八九十百千 **9**

ニ New Kanji あたらしい かんじ

Make sure you learn the correct stroke order. Correct stroke order will mean neater symbols when writing quickly. Also, take time to learn the new words for each kanji – these will help you memorize the different readings.

七	くんよみ	なな、なの				
	おんよみ	シチ				
	<u>なな</u> 七	<u>しち</u>・がつ 七月	<u>なの</u>・か 七日	じゅう・<u>なな</u> 十七	<u>なな</u>・つ 七つ	<u>しち</u>・じ 七時
2 strokes	seven	July	7th day of the month	17	seven things	seven o'clock

八	くんよみ	や、やっ、よう				
	おんよみ	ハチ				
	<u>はち</u> 八	<u>よう</u>・か 八日	<u>やっ</u>・つ 八つ	<u>はっ</u>・ぴゃく 八百	<u>はち</u>・じ 八時	<u>はち</u>・がつ 八月
2 strokes	eight	eigth day of the month	eight things	800	eight o'clock	August

九	くんよみ	ここのつ、				
	おんよみ	キュウ、ク				
	<u>きゅう</u> 九	<u>く</u>・がつ 九月	<u>ここの</u>・か 九日	<u>く</u>・じ 九時	<u>きゅう</u>・ひゃく 九百	<u>きゅう</u>・じゅう 九十
2 strokes	nine	September	ninth day of the month	nine o'clock	900	90

十	くんよみ	とお、と				
	おんよみ	ジュウ、ジッ				
	<u>じゅう</u> 十	<u>じゅっ</u>・かい 十回	<u>とう</u>・か 十日	<u>じゅう</u>・がつ 十月	<u>とお</u> 十	せき・<u>じゅう</u>・じ 赤十字
2 strokes	ten	ten times	tenth day of the month	October	10 things	the Red Cross

		くんよみ	none				
百		おんよみ	ヒャク				
		ひゃく **百**	ひゃっ・か・てん **百貨店**	さん・びゃく **三百**	ろっ・ぴゃく **六百**	ひゃく・ねん **百年**	ひゃっ・こ **百個**
6 strokes		100	department store	300	600	100 years	100 things

		くんよみ	ち				
千		おんよみ	セン				
		せん **千**	せん・ねん **千年**	せん・えん **千円**	さん・ぜん **三千**	ち・ぎる **千切る**	ち・ば・けん **千葉県**
3 strokes		1000	1000 years	1000 yen	3000	to tear into pieces	Chiba Prefecture

二 Writing Points かくポイント

❑ Combining kanji to make じゅくご

じゅくご means "compound kanji." Any word composed of two or more kanji is considered じゅくご. Many times, when two kanji are combined, the second kanji's reading is slightly modified by adding だくてん to the reading. For example, the word 花火 (はなび) has the kanji 火 (ひ) in it, but it is read as び. This happens with many じゅくご, so it should be the first thing you do when guessing a reading of a word. Here is a summarization of this rule:

> When kanji are combined into じゅくご, in many cases the reading of the second kanji is modified by adding だくてん to the first hiragana in the reading.

$$ \underset{\text{誕生}}{\text{たんじょう}} + \underset{\text{日}}{\text{ひ}} = \underset{\text{誕生日}}{\text{たんじょうび}} $$

❏ Kanji Activities

❏ Stroke order

Trace the light gray symbols for practice. Pay attention to stroke order and stroke type.

七	七	七	七	七	七					
八	八	八	八	八	八					
九	九	九	九	九	九					
十	十	十	十	十	十					
百	百	百	百	百	百					
千	千	千	千	千	千					

❑ Words you can write

Write the following words in the boxes four times each. This is a great way to practice the new kanji and review the words at the same time.

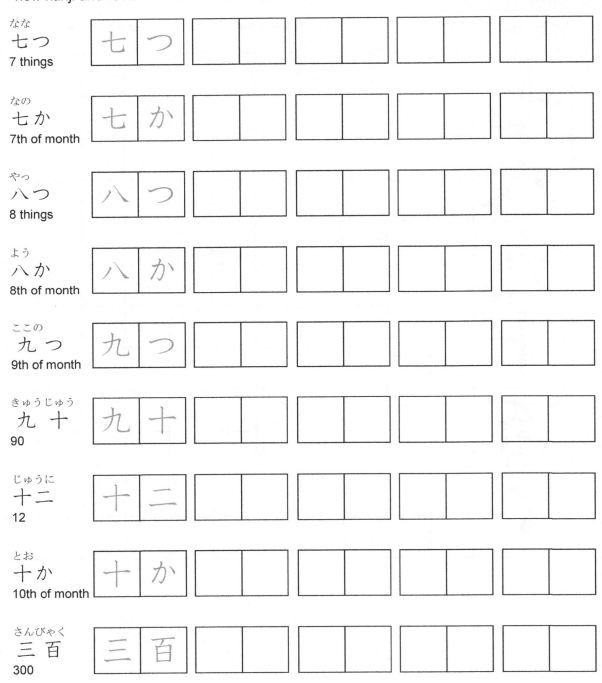

なな
七つ
7 things

なの
七か
7th of month

やっ
八つ
8 things

よう
八か
8th of month

ここの
九つ
9th of month

きゅうじゅう
九十
90

じゅうに
十二
12

とお
十か
10th of month

さんびゃく
三百
300

<table>
<tr><td>ひゃっ
百 こ
100 items</td><td>百 こ</td><td></td><td></td><td></td><td></td></tr>
</table>

<table>
<tr><td>よんせん
四千
4,000</td><td>四千</td><td></td><td></td><td></td><td></td></tr>
</table>

<table>
<tr><td>さんぜん
三千
3,000</td><td>三千</td><td></td><td></td><td></td><td></td></tr>
</table>

❑ **Fill in the kanji**

Fill in the blanks in the following sentences with the appropriate kanji.

1. にほんに ［じゅう｜よ］ねんはん いました。

2. ［に｜じゅう］ ねんまえに アメリカに きました。

3. ［ご］がつ ［よう］かの ［しち］じに きてください。

4. おばあさんは ［はち｜じゅう｜さん］ さいです。

5. このシャツは ［きゅう｜せん｜はっ｜ぴゃく］ えん です。

6. ひとが ［しち］にんと ねこが ［ろっ］ぴき います。

7. チケットを ［に｜せん｜きゅう｜ひゃく］ まい、かいます。

❑ **Writing review: Katakana countries**

Write the following countries' names in katakana. Some of these have not been covered in the lessons, so do your best! The correct katakana for each country can be found in the answer key in the back of the book.

1. America ☐☐☐☐

2. England ☐☐☐☐

3. France ☐☐☐☐

4. Italy ☐☐☐☐

5. Belgium ☐☐☐☐

6. Vietnam ☐☐☐☐

7. Switzerland ☐☐☐

8. Russia ☐☐☐

9. Brazil ☐☐☐☐

10. Spain ☐☐☐☐

11. Canada ☐☐☐

12. Mexico ☐☐☐☐

13. Scotland ☐☐☐☐☐☐☐

14. Australia ☐☐☐☐☐☐☐

15. New Zealand ☐☐☐☐☐☐☐☐

WRITING PRACTICE

Use these sheets as extra writing practice for the kanji you have learned up to this point.
Recently you have learned: 一二三四五六七八九十百千

VOCABULARY GROUPS ──────────── set 2

B	in the house

English	Progressive	Kanji +
electricity	でんき	電気
wall	かべ	壁
emergency exit	ひじょうぐち	非常口
door	ドア	ドア
curtains	カーテン	カーテン
carpet	カーペット	カーペット
roof	やね	屋根
floor	ゆか	床
ceiling	てんじょう	天井
rooftop	おくじょう	屋上
basement	ちかしつ	地下室
shower	シャワー	シャワー
electric outlet	コンセント	コンセント
hanger	ハンガー	ハンガー
iron	アイロン	アイロン
radio	ラジオ	ラジオ
washing machine	せんたくき	洗濯機

Lesson
2
Level ③

Mikami Sensei
by which means

---

2 About this Lesson このレッスンについて

Before The Lesson

1. be able to write and read 七八九十百千
2. review vocabulary group 2

Lesson Goals

1. learn to say the amount of times you have done something in a period of time
2. use the particle で to show by which means something was done.

From The Teachers

1. Make sure that you fully understand the last lesson or you will be confused in this lesson.

---

2 New Words あたらしい ことば

Progressive	Kanji +	English
あるいて	歩いて	by foot
タクシー	タクシー	taxi
プール	プール	swimming pool
カップラーメン	カップラーメン	cup ramen (instant ramen)
ミニスカート	ミニスカート	mini skirt
ストロー	ストロー	straw
ドイツ	ドイツ	Germany
はじめて	初めて	first time
げんきん	現金	cash
じょうだん	冗談	a joke

2 New Verbs あたらしい どうし

Dictionary	Kanji	た form	English Verb	Verb Type
かかる	掛かる	かかった	to cost money; take time	regular
かいもの(を)する	買い物する	かいもの(を)した	to shop	する
はらう	払う	はらった	to pay	regular

2 Verb Usage どうしの つかいかた

❏ **かかる (to cost money, to take time)**

かかる uses が by default when a particle is necessary. Remember that amounts of time and money are considered counters and do not require particles.

> [time, money] が かかる
>
> to cost [money];
>
> to take [time]

Example Sentences

1. おかね<u>が</u> かかりません。
   It doesn't cost money.

2. いくら かかりますか。
   How much does it cost?

3. どれぐらい かかりますか。
   How long will it take?

4. ちかしつから おくじょうまで なんぷん かかりますか。
   How many minutes is it from the basement to the rooftop?

❏ **かいものをする (to shop)**

Remember that shopping and buying are entirely different things. Many students get this mixed up. If you want to say that you bought a car, then you would use かいました, not かいものをしました.

Example Sentences

1. きょう、かいものを しました。
   I did (went) shopping today.

2. きょうは いそがしいから、かいものを しません。
   I am not going to shop because I am busy today.

3. おかあさんは まい日、かいものを します。
   My mother goes shopping everyday.

❑ はらう (to pay)

The thing that is being paid is marked with を. As you will learn later on in this lesson, the method of payment (credit, cash) is marked with で.

> **[*thing*] を はらう**
>
> **to pay [*thing*]**

> **[*method*]で はらう**
>
> **to pay with [*method*]**

Example Sentences

1. やちんを はらってください。	Please pay the rent.
2. クレジットカードで はらいます。	I will pay with a credit card.
3. でんわだいを げんきんで はらいました。	I paid the phone bill with cash.

2 Grammar ぶんぽう

❑ The "by which means" marker で

The particle で means with, by, or on. It marks the item that is being used to do something. It is also used to mark modes of transportation.

Example Sentences

1. スプーンで たべます。	I will eat <u>with</u> a spoon.
2. げんきんで かいます。	I will buy <u>with</u> cash.
3. ストローで のみます。	I will drink <u>with</u> a straw.
4. ひこうきで いきます。	I will go <u>by</u> airplane.
5. タクシーで かえります。	I will return <u>by</u> taxi.
6. なにで きますか。	<u>How</u> will you come?

Note that when saying "by foot," あるいて not あしで is used.

7. あるいて いきます。	I will go <u>by foot</u>.
8. あるいて きました。	I came <u>by foot</u>.

❑ Event frequency

What "event frequency" means is how often or how many times an event occurs. The counter for frequency is かい.

How many times? なんかい				
once いっかい 一回	twice にかい 二回	three times さんかい 三回	four times よんかい 四回	five times ごかい 五回
six times ろっかい 六回	seven times ななかい 七回	eight times はちかい 八回	nine times きゅうかい 九回	ten times じゅっかい 十回

You can use event frequency in a sentence with a time span to say how many times something has been done in a certain period of time.

> [time span に] + [number of times] + [action]
>
> I [action] + [number of times] in + [time span]

Example Q&A

1. あなたは 一ねんに なんかい アメリカに きますか。
   How many times a year do you come to America?

   一ねんに 四かい いきます。
   I go four times a year.

   二ねんに 一かい いきます。
   I go once every two years.

2. 一にちに にほんごを どれぐらい べんきょうしますか。
   About how long do you study Japanese a day?

   一にちに 五じかんぐらい べんきょうします。
   I study for about five hours a day.

   あんまり べんきょうしません。
   I don't study that much.

3. にほんに よく きますか。
   Do you come to Japan often?

   六かげつに 一かい きます。
   I come once every six months.

❑ **The expense of**…

In the previous lesson you learned the word でんわだい (telephone bill). だい can be added to many other words in Japanese to mean the cost of whatever it is added to. だい can mean "cost of," "bill," and other similar words.

Examples	ホテル<u>だい</u>	hotel expenses
	タクシー<u>だい</u>	cost of taxi
	バス<u>だい</u>	cost of bus
	でんき<u>だい</u>	electric bill

❑ **The difference between** どれぐらい **and** どのぐらい

These words both mean how much or how many (distances, times or amounts). They are both used in the same way. It's up to you which one to use.

2 Q&A しつもんとこたえ

1. **How long did it take?**
   どれぐらい かかりましたか。

   It took three hours.
   三じかん かかりました。

   It took about two months.
   二かげつぐらい かかりました。

2. **How many minutes does it take by train?**
   でんしゃで なんぷん かかりますか。

   It takes twenty minutes by train.
   でんしゃで 二十ぷん かかります。

   It takes about four and a half hours by train.
   でんしゃで 四じかんはんぐらいです。

3. **How many more minutes will it take?**
   あと なんぷん かかりますか。

   It will take fifteen minutes more.
   あと 十五ふん かかります。

   It will take about five more minutes.
   あと 五ふんぐらい かかります。

4. **How will you go to Germany?**
   ドイツに なにで いきますか。

   I will go by airplane.
   ひこうきで いきます。

   I will go by bicycle.
   じてんしゃで いきます。

5. **How long does it take by foot?**
   あるいて どれぐらい かかりますか。

   It takes a half-hour by foot.
   あるいて 三十ぷん かかります。

   It takes about five hours by foot.
   あるいて 五じかんぐらい かかります。

6. **How long does it take you to get to school by foot?**
   がっこうまで あるいて どれぐらい かかりますか。

   It takes twenty five minutes to school by foot.
   がっこうまで あるいて 二十五ふん かかります。

7. **What did you pay the electric bill with?**
   でんきだいを なにで はらいましたか。

   I paid in cash.
   げんきんで はらいました。

2 Mini Conversations ミニかいわ J-E

Cover up the entire English portion of the conversations below. Read the Japanese conversation several times until you understand it. Only then should you move the paper to compare your translation to the English translation.

1. **Polite conversation between friends on the phone**
   A: もしもし、いま どこに いますか。
   B: まだ、がっこうの まえです。
   A: あと どれぐらい かかりますか。
   B: あと 十ぷん かかります。

   A: Hello, where are you now?
   B: I am still in front of the school.
   A: How much longer will it take?
   B: It will take ten more minutes.

2. Polite conversation between people who have met recently
A: 一にちに 五かいぐらい プールに いきます。
B: なんでですか。
A: しごとだからです。
B: いえから プールまで どれぐらい かかりますか。
A: あるいて 五ふんぐらい かかります。
B: いいですね。

A: I go to the pool five times a day.
B: Why?
A: Because it's my job.
B: How long does it take from your house to the pool?
A: It takes about five minutes by foot.
B: That's nice.

3. Polite conversation between a boat captian and another person
A: にほんまで ふねで どれぐらい かかりますか。
B: 十二にちぐらい かかります。
A: なぜ ふねで いきますか。
B: うみが すきだからです。

A: How long does it take by boat to Japan?
B: It takes about twelve days.
A: Why are you going by boat?
B: Because I like the ocean.

2 | Mini Conversations ミニかいわ E-J

Using a piece of paper, cover up the entire Japanese portion of the conversations below. Translate the English conversation to Japanese. Only after you have translated the entire conversation should you move the paper to check your work.

1. Polite conversation between two friends planning on going to the shopping mall
A: How will we go to the shopping mall?
B: Let's go by bus.
A: Since taxis are cheap in America, let's go by taxi.
B: All right, then let's go by taxi.

A: ショッピングモールに なにで いきますか。
B: バスで いきましょう。
A: アメリカは タクシーが やすいから、タクシーで いきましょう。
B: じゃ、タクシーで いきましょう。

2. **Conversation between co-workers. Who do you think is higher up in the company?**
   A: I am going to return to Chicago tomorrow by bus.
   B: It will take eight hours by bus. Why aren't you going by plane?
   A: I am scared of planes.

   A: あした、バスで シカゴに かえります。
   B: バスで 八じかん かかるよ。なんで、ひこうきで いかないの？
   A: ひこうきが こわいです。

3. **Polite conversation between a friend who lives in Japan and one who will be visiting soon**
   A: Is Japan hot now?
   B: Yes, it is very hot. When are you coming?
   A: I will go on the six o'clock flight.
   B: How long will it take?
   A: It will take twelve hours.

   A: にほんは いま あついですか。
   B: はい、とても あついですよ。いつ きますか。
   A: あした 六じの ひこうきで いきます。
   B: どれぐらい かかりますか。
   A: 十二じかん かかります。

4. **Informal conversation between friends in line at a movie theater**
   A: Who is going to pay?
   B: It's okay. I will pay.
   A: Really? You sure are kind!
   B: I'm just kidding.
   A: You're not kind at all.

   A: だれが はらうの？
   B: いいよ。ぼくが はらうよ。
   A: ほんとうに？ やさしいね！
   B: じょうだんだよ！
   A: ぜんぜん やさしくない！

5. **Informal conversation between co-workers of equal status**
   A: Who paid the cost of the hotel?
   B: Murata paid with the company credit card.

   A: だれが ホテルだいを はらったの？
   B: むらたさんが かいしゃの クレジットカードで はらったよ。

2 Reading Comprehension どっかい

Read the sentences below. Use the information to answer the reading comprehension questions later in this lesson.

みかみせんせいへ

①こんにちは、おひさしぶりです。②みなさんは げんきですか。③ここは みんな げんきです。

④きょう、ラスベガスは とても あついです。⑤きのうも とても あつかったです。⑥わたしたち は ラスベガスが はじめてです。⑦三かまえに にほんから きました。⑧ラスベガスまで ひこうきで 十一じかん かかりました。

⑨おかあさんは まいにち かいものします。⑩おとといのよるは おねえさんと ショッピング モールで かわいい ミニスカートと くつを かいました。⑪とても やすかったです。⑫おとうさんは ギャンブルが だいすきです。⑬わたしは おかね があんまり ないから すきじゃない です。⑭あし たにほんに かえります。⑮じゃあ、おからだに きを つけてください。

くどう まりこ より

2 Activities

❑ **Reading comprehension questions**
Answer the following questions about the reading comprehension in this lesson.

1. まりこさんは いま どこに いますか。

   _____

2. ラスベガスは きょう、さむいですか。

   _____

3. きのうは さむかったですか。

   _____

4. にほんから ラスベガスまで ひこうきで なんじかん かかりますか。

   _____

5. まりこさんは おととい なにを かいましたか。

   _____

6. どこで かいましたか。

   _____

7. だれと ショッピングモールに いきましたか。

   _____

8. まりこさんの おとうさんは ギャンブルが すきですか。

   _____

9. まりこさんは ギャンブルが きらいですか。

   _____

10. なんで まりこさんは ギャンブルが すきじゃないですか。

    _____

11. まりこさんは いつ にほんに かえりますか。

    _____

❑ **Substitution drill**

Compose sentences according to the example.

> **Ex.**   ここまで 三じかん、かかりました。
>   → thirty minutes   ここまで 三十ぷん、かかりました。
>   → five hours   ここまで 五じかん、かかりました。
>   → an hour and half   ここまで 一じかんはん、かかりました。

1. おはしで ごはんを たべます。

   → with a spoon   _____

   → with a fork   _____

   → with the hand   _____

   → with a fork and a knife _____

2. 一ねんに 一かい にほんに いきます。

   → twice a year   _____

   → return to America   _____

   → once in two years   _____

   → often   _____

3. にほんごの クラスに タクシーで きました。

   → by bus   _____

   → by car   _____

   → by train   _____

   → by foot   _____

4. こぎってで でんわだいを はらいました。

    → with a credit card   _____

    → with cash   _____

    → electric bill   _____

    → hotel expenses   _____

❑ Question and answer

Answer the following questions using the words and patterns in this lesson.

1. スプーンで ピザを たべますか。

_____

2. なにで おすしを たべますか。

_____

3. しごと／がっこうに くるまで いきますか。

_____

4. スーパーに なにで いきますか。

_____

5. 一ねんに なんかい りょこうしますか。

_____

6. 一にちに にほんごを どれぐらい べんきょうしますか。

_____

7. いえから ともだちの いえまで くるまで どのぐらい かかりますか。

_____

8. にほんごの ほんは いくらでしたか。

_____

❑ **Practice**

How often do you do the following activities? Use the pictures to make your own sentences.

Ex

わたしは いっしゅうかんに いっかい、かいものをします。

I go shopping once a week.

かいものを する
to go shopping

1

ほんを よむ
to read a book

2

てがみを かく
to write a letter

3

ねる
to sleep

Kanji Lesson

3

日月火水木金土

☰ New Kanji あたらしい かんじ

Make sure you learn the correct stroke order. Correct stroke order will mean neater symbols when writing quickly. Also, take time to learn the new words for each kanji – these will help you memorize the different readings.

日	くんよみ	ひ、か					
	おんよみ	ニチ、ジツ					
		<u>ひ</u> **日**	<u>にち・よう・び</u> **日曜日**	<u>はつ・か</u> **二十日**	<u>きゅう・じつ</u> **休日**	<u>たん・じょう・び</u> **誕生日**	<u>きょう</u> **今日**
4 strokes		day	Sunday	20th day of the month	day off, holiday	birthday	today

月	くんよみ	つき					
	おんよみ	ゲツ、ガツ					
		<u>つき</u> **月**	<u>こん・げつ</u> **今月**	<u>しょう・がつ</u> **正月**	<u>つき・み</u> **月見**	<u>げつ・よう・び</u> **月曜日**	<u>げつ・まつ</u> **月末**
4 strokes		moon	this month	New Years	moon viewing	Monday	end of month

火	くんよみ	ひ					
	おんよみ	カ					
		<u>ひ</u> **火**	<u>か・ようび</u> **火曜日**	<u>はな・び</u> **花火**	<u>か・じ</u> **火事**	<u>か・せい</u> **火星**	<u>か・りょく</u> **火力**
4 strokes		fire	Tuesday	fireworks	a fire	Mars	thermal power

水	くんよみ	みず					
	おんよみ	スイ					
		<u>みず</u> **水**	<u>すい・よう・び</u> **水曜日**	<u>すい・りょく</u> **水力**	<u>かい・すい</u> **海水**	<u>すい・せい</u> **水星**	<u>みず・いろ</u> **水色**
4 strokes		water	Wednesday	hydraulic power	seawater	Mercury	light blue color

木	くんよみ	き、こ					
1 2 3 4	おんよみ	ボク、モク					
	き **木**	もく・よう・び **木曜日**	こ・だち **木立**	もく・せい **木星**	ざい・もく **材木**	うえ・き **植木**
4 strokes	tree, wood	Thursday	grove of trees	Jupiter	lumber	potted plant garden plant

金	くんよみ	かね、かな					
	おんよみ	キン、コン					
	きん **金**	お・かね **お金**	きん・ぞく **金属**	かな・もの **金物**	きん・よう・び **金曜日**	きん・せい **金星**
8 strokes	gold	money	metal	ironware	Friday	Venus

土	くんよみ	つち					
	おんよみ	ド、ト					
	つち **土**	と・ち **土地**	あか・つち **赤土**	こく・ど **国土**	ど・よう・び **土曜日**	ど・せい **土星**
3 strokes	soil, earth	land	red clay	territory, country	Saturday	Saturn

三 Fun Kanji たのしい かんじ

❏ Kanji and the planets

You may have noticed that some of the example words in this section were planets. The second kanji in these words is the kanji for star, which is 星 (ほし). It is interesting to note that planet Earth doesn't have 星 in it, but instead uses the kanji for "sphere." Here is a list of all the planets:

Mercury	すいせい	水星	water planet
Venus	きんせい	金星	gold planet
Earth	ちきゅう	地球	earth, soil sphere
Mars	かせい	火星	fire planet
Jupiter	もくせい	木星	wood, tree planet
Saturn	どせい	土星	soil planet
Uranus	てんのうせい	天王星	heaven king planet
Neptune	かいおうせい	海王星	ocean king planet
Pluto	めいおうせい	冥王星	dark king planet

☰ Kanji Activities

❑ Stroke order

Trace the light gray symbols for practice. Pay attention to stroke order and stroke type.

日	日	日	日	日	日			
月	月	月	月	月	月			
火	火	火	火	火	火			
水	水	水	水	水	水			
木	木	木	木	木	木			
金	金	金	金	金	金			
土	土	土	土	土	土			

❑ **Words you can write**

Write the following words in the boxes four times each. This is a great way to practice the new kanji and review the words at the same time.

よっか
四日   四 日
4th of month

ようか
八日   八 日
8th of month

じゅうがつ
十 月   十 月
October

ろくがつ
六 月   六 月
June

げつ　　び
月 よ う 日   月 よ う 日
Monday

か　　び
火 よ う 日   火 よ う 日
Tuesday

すい　　び
水 よ う 日   水 よ う 日
Wednesday

もく　び
木 よう 日
Thursday

| 木 | よ | う | 日 |

きん　び
金 よう 日
Friday

| 金 | よ | う | 日 |

ど　び
土 よう 日
Sunday

| 土 | よ | う | 日 |

みず
水
water

| 水 |

き
木
tree

| 木 |

かね
お 金
money

| お | 金 |

❏ Fill in the kanji

Fill in the blanks in the following sentences with the appropriate kanji.

1. お 〔かね〕 が 〔ご〕〔せん〕〔さん〕〔びゃく〕 えん、あります。

2. 〔ろく〕〔がつ〕〔なの〕〔か〕 に 〔に〕 ほんに いきます。

3. 〔か〕 よう 〔び〕 は 〔よ〕 じから しごとです。

4. あそこに 〔き〕 が 〔に〕〔じゅっ〕 ぽん、あります。

5. 〔みず〕 を 〔よっ〕 つと メニューを おねがいします。

6. らいしゅうの 〔げつ〕 よう 〔び〕 は 〔とお〕〔か〕 です。

VOCABULARY GROUPS — set 3

C — kitchen and bath

English	Progressive	Kanji +
brush	ブラシ	ブラシ
safety pin	あんぜんピン	安全ピン
toilet paper	トイレットペーパー	トイレットペーパー
flower vase	かびん	花瓶
pots and pans	なべ	鍋
kitchen knife	ほうちょう	包丁
frying pan	フライパン	フライパン
cutting board	まないた	まな板
kettle	やかん	やかん
candle	ろうそく	蝋燭

D — Christmas words

English	Progressive	Kanji +
Christmas tree	クリスマスツリー	クリスマスツリー
Santa Claus	サンタクロース	サンタクロース
reindeer	トナカイ	トナカイ
fireplace	だんろ	暖炉
snowman	ゆきだるま	雪だるま
bell	ベル / すず	ベル / 鈴
Merry Christmas	メリークリスマス	メリークリスマス

Lesson
3
Level ③

My Loud Mother
the て forms

---

3 | About this Lesson このレッスンについて

Before The Lesson

1. be able to write and read 日月火水木金土
2. review vocabulary group set 3

Lesson Goals

1. learn how the positive and negative command verb form (て-form) is used

From The Teachers

1. This lesson is not so difficult if you know how to conjugate verbs into the た-form. If you do not know, you should learn. Learn the song in the *Cool Tools* section.

---

3 | New Words あたらしい ことば

Progressive	Kanji +	English
ばん	晩	evening
こうこく	広告	advertisement
かぜ	風	wind
かぜ	風邪	a cold
ソファー	ソファー	sofa
トースト	トースト	toast
しゃしん	写真	photograph
やすみ	休み	day off, a break
ティーシャツ	ティーシャツ	T-shirt
あほ	あほ	fool; idiot
ちゃんと	ちゃんと	properly
ごぜんちゅう	午前中	in the morning time

3 New Adjectives あたらしい けいようし

Progressive	Kanji +	English	Type
しずか	静か	quiet	な adjective

3 New Phrase あたらしい フレーズ

よかった。   Good. / What a relief.

よかった literally, this means "was good."   This is a very common phrase and can be used in place of a variety of commonly used English phrases, such as "Thank God!" or "What a relief"

3 Grammar ぶんぽう

❑ **Changing verbs into the positive て form (the "do it" form)**

In this lesson, the command/request verb form (also called the て form) is introduced. There is a pattern for figuring out the て form of any particular verb.

Conjugating verbs into the て form is based on the ending hiragana of the dictionary form of the verb. The て form formula is only used for regular verbs, since for いる/える verbs you simply switch the last る to a て.

You will notice that the て form formula is exactly like the た form formula introduced in Lesson 9 of Japanese From Zero! Level 2.

(+)て form Formula ("do it" form) for REGULAR verbs	
dictionary form ending with	**changes into**
ぶ、む、ぬ	んで
う、つ、る	って
く	いて、って（いて is most common）
ぐ	いで
す	して

Most of the time verbs ending in く change to いて, for example かく (to write) changes to かいて. One of the exceptions is いく (to go), which changes to いって.

❑ Changing verbs into the negative て form (the "don't do it" form)

This is the pattern to use when making the "don't do it" form:

> **Regular Verbs**
> あ form + ないで

> **いる/える Verbs**
> drop the る + ないで

❑ Sample conjugations into the て forms

The verbs in the following list have been conjugated into their て-forms. Cover up the conjugations and see if you can figure out what they should be by using the patterns above.

Regular Verbs		
Dictionary form	**て form (do it)**	**て form (don't do it)**
to drink の<u>む</u>	drink it の<u>ん</u>で	don't drink it の<u>まないで</u>
to write か<u>く</u>	write it か<u>いて</u>	don't write it か<u>かないで</u>
to talk はな<u>す</u>	talk はな<u>して</u>	don't talk はな<u>さないで</u>
to pay はら<u>う</u>	pay はら<u>って</u>	don't pay はら<u>わないで</u>

いる／える Verbs		
Dictionary form	**て form (do it)**	**て form (don't do it)**
to eat たべ<u>る</u>	eat it たべ<u>て</u>	don't eat it たべ<u>ないで</u>
to go to bed, sleep ね<u>る</u>	go to bed ね<u>て</u>	don't go to bed ね<u>ないで</u>
to get up, wake up おき<u>る</u>	get up おき<u>て</u>	don't get up おき<u>ないで</u>

The irregular verbs する and くる do not follow any pattern that you know to conjugate them into the て form. Just take the time and memorize the conjugations.

Irregular Verbs		
Dictionary form	**て form (do it)**	**て form (don't do it)**
to do する	do it して	don't do it しないで
to come くる	come きて	don't come こないで

❑ Verbs that end in う

When the dictionary form actually ends with an う, the う changes to a わ and then ない で is added to it when creating the negative て form. Here are some verbs that you may or may not know that end in う.

Dictionary form	**て form (do it)**	**て form (don't do it)**
to buy かう	buy it かって	don't buy it かわないで
to say いう	say it いって	don't say it いわないで

❑ Making things polite with ください

By adding ください after the て forms you make things sound nice by adding please.
The same particle and sentence structure rules of other verb forms are applied when using the て form. Examine the sample sentences below.

Example Sentences

1. たべてください。 — Please eat.
2. この おんがくを きいてください。 — Please listen to this music.
3. ミルクを かってください。 — Please buy some milk.
4. このくるまを かってください。 — Please buy this car.
5. ここに きてください。 — Please come here.

6. ビールを あんまり のまないでください。 — Please don't drink that much beer.
7. ギャンブルを しないでください。 — Please don't gamble.
8. いかないでください。 — Please don't go.
9. なにも のまないでください。 — Please don't drink anything.
10. しごとに おくれないでください。 — Please don't be late to work.

3 | Cool Tool クール　ツール

❑ The shortcut for making the positive て form (do it)

As you know, all the た forms follow a similar pattern introduced in Level 2, Lesson 9 of *Japanese From Zero!*. If you have memorized the pattern, or are familiar with the た forms (the "did do" form) you know that they all end in た or だ. To make the positive tense of the て form (the "do it" form), you just change the た on the end of た forms to て or the だ to で. Look at the following chart.

Dictionary form	た form (did)	て form (do it)
いく to go	いった went	いって （ください） (please) go
くる to come	きた came	きて （ください） (please) come
たべる to eat	たべた ate	たべて （ください） (please) eat it
のむ to drink	のんだ drank	のんで （ください） (please) drink it

❑ The shortcut for making the negative て form (don't do it)

There is also a pattern to making the negative て-form (the "don't do it!" form). You simply just add で to the ない (the informal "won't do it" form).   This should be easy since you already know the ない-form from *Japanese From Zero! Book 2*.

> ### ない form + で

Verb	ない form (won't / don't)	negative て form (don't do it)
いく to go	いかない won't go	いかないで（ください） (please) don't go
くる to come	こない won't come	こないで（ください） (please) don't come
たべる to eat	たべない won't eat	たべないで（ください） (please) don't eat it
のむ to drink	のまない won't drink	のまないで（ください） (please) don't drink it

❑ The GREATEST cool tool for remembering the て and た forms

Here is the *best* way to remember how to conjugate the verbs into the て and た forms. Just memorize this song. It should work to help you recall how to convert the verbs into the て and た forms. For the た forms you change て to た and で to だ.

The て and た song (sung to the melody of *Silver Bells*)
ぶ、む、ぬ んで う、つ、る って
く いて ぐ いで
す して are the て and た-forms

---

3 Mini Conversations ミニかいわ J-E

A WORD OF ADVICE: You will notice that as you understand more and more Japanese, sometimes the literal translation of the sentence into English doesn't make much sense. It is at this point that you should concentrate on translating sentences into the *equivalent* sentence rather then the literal sentence. Remember, your job when translating or interpreting is to make the listener understand what the point of the conversation is and not to confuse them with useless direct translations.

Because the meaning of so many Japanese words change depending on the context of the dialogue, you must also remember to keep track of the past dialogue and try not to translate sentences independently of other sentences in the dialogue. In the following ミニかいわ, pay attention to the whole of the conversation and not just the current sentence when translating.

1. Informal conversation between a boyfriend and girlfriend

A： ゆびわを かって！
B： おかねが あんまり ないよ。
A： きのう、しんぶんの こうこくで やすいのが あったよ。
B： わかった。じゃあ、かうよ。

A： Buy me a ring!
B： I don't have that much money.
A： Yesterday, there were cheap ones in the newspaper ads.
B： OK. Well then, I will buy it.

2. Polite conversation between two roommates

A: もう マヨネーズが ありません。
B: いまから、おみせに いきますよ。かいましょうか。
A: よかった。じゃ、おねがいします。
B: どんなのが いいですか。
A: おおきいマヨネーズを かってください。
B: はい。

A: We don't have any more mayonnaise.
B: I am going to the store right now. Shall I buy some?
A: Good. Well, then get some please. (literally: "I request it.")
B: What kind would you like?
A: Please buy the large size mayonnaise. (literally "a big mayonnaise")
B: Okay

3. Polite conversation between two classmates

A: いっしょに しゅくだいを しましょう。
B: いいですよ。どこで しますか。
A: わたしの いえで しましょう。
B: いいですね。なんじが いいですか。わたしは ごぜんちゅうは だめです。
A: じゃ、二じに きてください。

A: Let's do the homework together.
B: Okay. Where will we do it?
A: Let's do it at my house.
B: That sounds good. What time is good? I'm tied up (busy) in the morning.
A: Well then, come at two o'clock.

4. Polite conversation between friends

A: 水よう日に じかんが ありますか。
B: はい、すこし あります。
A: じゃ、わたしの いえに きてください。
B: なんじが いいですか。
A: 四じに きてください。

A: Do you have time on Wednesday?
B: Yes, I have a little.
A: Okay then come to my house.
B: What time is good?
A: Come at four.

3   Mini Conversations ミニかいわ E-J

Using a piece of paper, cover up the entire Japanese portion of the conversations below. Translate the English conversation to Japanese. Only after you have translated the entire conversation should you move the paper to check your work.

1. Informal conversation between friends
A: Why aren't you coming on Friday?
B: I am busy at work. Please understand!

A: なんで 金よう日に こないの？
B: しごとが いそがしい。わかって！

2. Polite conversation between acquaintances on the telephone. B is higher in status.
A: Hello. Do you have any Japanese dictionaries?
B: Yes we do. Would you like to see them?
A: Yes. Please. I'll be there at six o'clock. Is that all right?
B: Six o'clock is no good. Please come at five.
A: Okay.
B: Don't be late.

A: もしもし、にほんごの じしょが ありますか。
B: ありますよ。みますか。
A: はい。おねがいします。六じに いきます。いいですか。
B: 六じは だめです。五じに きてください。
A: わかりました。
B: おくれないでください。

3. Polite conversation with a friend who is sleeping over
A: How many beds do you have?
B: One.
A: Well then, I will sleep on the sofa.
B: I will sleep on the sofa. You sleep on the bed.
A: Thanks.

A: ベッドは いくつ ありますか。
B: 一つ です。
A: じゃ、わたしは ソファーで ねます。
B: わたしが ソファーで ねます。あなたは ベッドで ねてください。
A: ありがとう。

4. Polite conversation between co-workers

A: Do you have work the day after tomorrow?
B: No, I am off.
B: Won't you eat at McDonald's with me?
A: Okay. What time is good?
B: Five o'clock is good.
A: Okay then, please be in front of the bank at four forty.
B: Okay.

A: あさって しごとが ありますか。
B: いいえ、やすみです。
B: わたしと マクドナルドで たべませんか。
A: いいですよ。なんじが いいですか。
B: 五じが いいです。
A: じゃ、四じ 四十ぷんに ぎんこうの まえに いてください。
B: わかりました。

3   Reading Comprehension どっかい

Read the sentences below. Use the information to answer the reading comprehension questions later in this lesson.

① わたしの なまえは よしえです。
② おかあさんの なまえは しずかです。
③ えいごで しずかの いみは 「quiet」です。
④ でも、わたしの おかあさんは とても うるさいです。
⑤ あさから ばんまで うるさいです。
⑥ みなさん、きいてください。
⑦ たとえば あさの かいわは これです。

おかあさん：	よしえ、おきて。もう、はちじよ。
よしえさん：	ええ、もう はちじ？ かいしゃに おくれる！
おかあさん：	あさごはんを たべてね。
よしえさん：	じかんが ないから もう いく。このりんごは くるまの なかで たべる。
おかあさん：	だめだめ、ミルクも のんで！
よしえさん：	はい、はい。いってきます。
おかあさん：	いってらっしゃい。

3 | Activities

❑ Reading comprehension questions
Answer the following questions about the reading comprehension in this lesson.

1. よしえさんの おかあさんの なまえは なんですか。

   _____

2. えいごで しずかの いみは なんですか。

   _____

3. よしえさんの おかあさんは しずかですか。

   _____

4. よしえさんは なんじに おきましたか。

   _____

5. よしえさんは どんな あさごはんを たべましたか。

   _____

6. よしえさんは どこで あさごはんを たべましたか。

   _____

7. よしえさんは なにを のみましたか。

   _____

8. 「いってきます」は えいごで なんですか。

   _____

9. 「いってらっしゃい」は えいごで なんですか。

   _____

❑ Substitution Drill

Compose sentences according to the example.

> **Ex.** ミルクを かってください。
> → to drink　　ミルクを <u>のんで</u>ください。
> → juice　　　<u>ジュース</u>を のんでください。
> → water　　　<u>みず</u>を のんでください。
> → don't　　　みずを <u>のまないでください</u>。

1. にほんに いってください。

　　→ to return　　_____

　　→ to come　　 _____

　　→ America　　 _____

　　→ don't　　　　_____

2. そこで でんわしてください。

　　→ to shop　　　_____

　　→ to eat　　　 _____

　　→ over there　 _____

　　→ don't　　　　_____

3. にほんごを べんきょうしてください。

　　→ to read　　　_____

　　→ to write　　 _____

　　→ to listen to　_____

　　→ don't　　　　_____

4. この CD を きいてください。

    → to buy   _____

    → this dictionary   _____

    → that magazine   _____

    → don't   _____

❏ **Practice**

Look at the pictures below and give them some advice using ～てください or ～ないで ください.

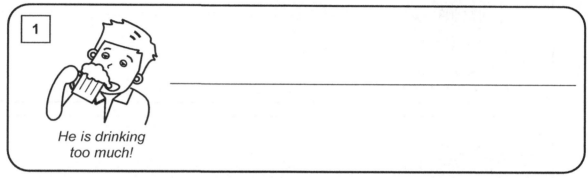

1

*He is drinking
too much!*

2

He is very late!

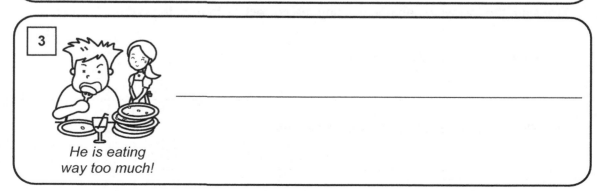

3

*He is eating
way too much!*

4

She didn't hear her alarm!

5

He is nervous about the first day.

6

He is maxing out his credit cards!

❏ Translation

Translate the following sentences using the correct て form of the verb.

1. Please ask a question in Japanese.

   _____

2. Please don't go to that restaurant over there.

   _____

3. Please buy (me) this ring.

    _____

4. Please don't sell my car.

    _____

5. Please come to my house at five.

    _____

6. Please don't come to class on Wednesday.

    _____

7. Please read this Japanese newspaper.

    _____

8. Please go to bed now (already).

    _____

Kanji Lesson **4**   休上下左右

四 New Kanji あたらしい かんじ

Make sure you learn the correct stroke order. Correct stroke order will mean neater symbols when writing quickly. Also, take time to learn the new words for each kanji – these will help you memorize the different readings.

休 6 strokes	くんよみ	やす				
	おんよみ	キュウ				
	やす・み **休み**	きゅう・けい **休憩**	やす・む **休む**	なつ・やす・み **夏休み**	ねん・じゅう・む・きゅう **年中無休**	
	day off, holiday	a break	to take a break	summer vacation	open all year	

上 3 strokes	くんよみ	うえ、うわ、かみ、あ、のぼ				
	おんよみ	ジョウ、ショウ				
	うえ **上**	うわ・ぎ **上着**	のぼ・る **上る**	かみ・はん・き **上半期**	あ・がる **上がる**	じょう・ひん **上品**
	up, above	jacket, overcoat	to climb up	first half of the year	to go up	elegant

下 3 strokes	くんよみ	した、しも、もと、さ、くだ、お				
	おんよみ	カ、ゲ				
	した **下**	げ・すい **下水**	か・りゅう **下流**	くだ・さい **下さい**	さ・げる **下げる**	お・ろす **下ろす**
	down, below	sewage	down stream	please	to lower	to take down

左 5 strokes	くんよみ	ひだり				
	おんよみ	サ				
	ひだり **左**	さ・せつ **左折**	ひだり・て **左手**	ひだり・がわ **左側**	ひだり・うえ **左上**	さ・ゆう **左右**
	left	left turn	left hand	left side	upper left	left and right

右	くんよみ	みぎ				
1↓ 2 4→ 3↓ 5→	おんよみ	ウ、ユウ				
	みぎ **右**	みぎ・がわ **右側**	みぎ・て **右手**	う・せつ **右折**	みぎ・した **右下**	みぎ・きき **右利き**
5 strokes	right	right side	right hand	right turn	lower right	right-handed

---

Writing Points かくポイント

❏ Memorizing 左 and 右 stroke order

You may have noticed that the kanji for "left" and "right" are very similar. It is hard to remember which one of them has the first stroke across and which one is down. Getting the stroke order wrong will not be accepted on the Kanji Proficiency Test (Kanji Kentei). If you memorize the next phrase, you shouldn't have any more trouble remembering the stroke order:

Downright Leftovers

Hopefully this makes sense to you. The kanji for "right" starts with the stroke going down and the kanji for "left" starts with the horizontal line going to the right (or over).

❏ Which one is left and which one is right?

It is common for students of kanji to mistake the kanji for "right" and "left" since they are so similar. There is a sneaky way to remember which one is which. This trick involves using the katakana ロ (ro). Since the katakana ロ starts with an "R" sound, it is easy to remember that the kanji with the small ロ in it means "**r**ight."

The kanji for *right* has a katakana ロ (*ro*) in it. Use this to distinguish it from the kanji for *left*. *Ro* starts with *R* for *right*.

四 **Kanji Activities**

❑ **Stroke order**
Trace the light gray symbols for practice. Pay attention to stroke order and stroke type.

休	休	休	休	休	休			
上	上	上	上	上	上			
下	下	下	下	下	下			
左	左	左	左	左	左			
右	右	右	右	右	右			

❑ **Words you can write**
Write the following words in the boxes. This is a great way to practice the new kanji, review the words, and learn new words at the same time.

やす
休む
to rest

休	む							

きゅうじつ
休日
holiday

休	日							

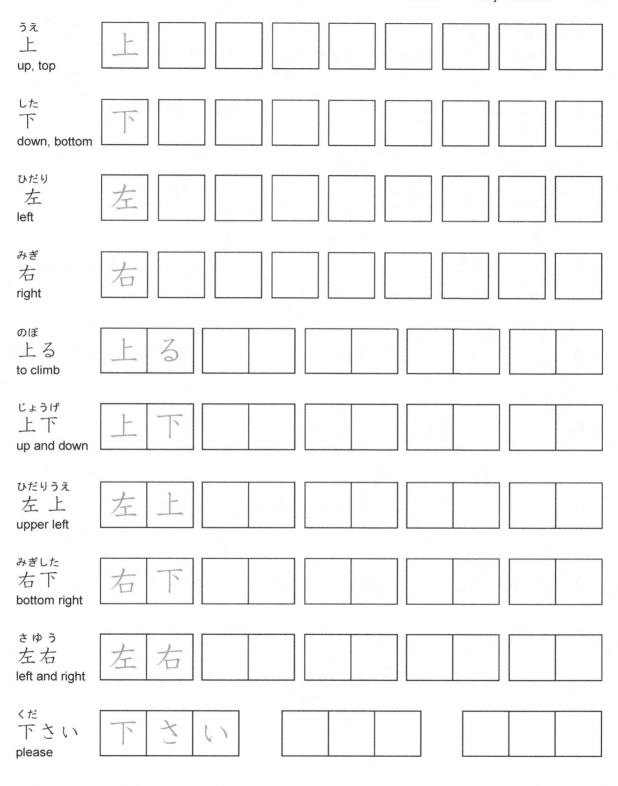

うえ
上
up, top

した
下
down, bottom

ひだり
左
left

みぎ
右
right

のぼ
上る
to climb

じょうげ
上下
up and down

ひだりうえ
左上
upper left

みぎした
右下
bottom right

さゆう
左右
left and right

くだ
下さい
please

❑ Fill in the kanji

Fill in the blanks in the following sentences with the appropriate kanji.

1. き☐ の した☐ に ひとが じゅう☐ にん、います。

2. じゅう☐ いち☐ がつ☐ みっ☐ か☐ は やす☐ みです。

3. ど☐ よう び☐ は じゅう☐ に☐ じに ひるごはんを たべる。

4. テーブルの うえ☐ に かみが よん☐ じゅう☐ まい あります。

5. ひだり☐ に いすが むっ☐ つ あります。

6. じょう☐ げ☐ さ☐ ゆう☐ を よく みて くだ☐ さい。

7. らいしゅうの きん☐ よう び☐ に やす☐ まないで くだ☐ さい。

WRITING PRACTICE

Use these sheets as extra writing practice for the kanji you have learned up to this point.
Recently you have learned: 日月火水木金土、休上下左右

VOCABULARY GROUPS — set 4

E — scary words

English	Progressive	Kanji +
grave	（お）はか	墓
bat	こうもり	こうもり
devil	あくま	悪魔
skeleton	がいこつ	骸骨
ghost	おばけ	お化け
blood	ち	血

F — marriage words

English	Progressive	Kanji +
wedding ring	けっこんゆびわ	結婚指輪
bouquet	ブーケ	ブーケ
wedding cake	ウエディング・ケーキ	ウエディング・ケーキ
wedding dress	ウエディング・ドレス	ウエディング・ドレス
divorce	りこん	離婚
lawyer	べんごし	弁護士
heart	ハート	ハート
wine	ワイン	ワイン
red wine	あかワイン	あかワイン
rose wine	ロゼワイン	ロゼワイン
white wine	しろワイン	しろワイン
champagne	シャンパン	シャンパン

Lesson
4
Level ③

The Concert
expressing opinion

4 About this Lesson このレッスンについて

Before The Lesson

1. be able to write and read 休上下左右
2. review vocabulary groups set 4

Lesson Goals

1. learn how to express your opinion and relay what someone else has said.

4 New Words あたらしい ことば

Progressive	Kanji +	English
どう	どう	how, what
みかみ	三上	(common Japanese last name)
コンサート	コンサート	concert
ファン	ファン	a fan
うた	歌	song
かいじょう	会場	(concert) hall
りょうほう	両方	both (items or objects)
たくさん	たくさん	a lot, many, much
ぜんぶ	全部	all
なにも	何も	anything, nothing

4 New Verbs あたらしい どうし

Dictionary	Kanji +	た-form	English Verb	Verb Type
おもう	思う	おもった	to think	regular
いう	言う	いった	to say, speak, tell	regular
まつ	待つ	まった	to wait	regular

4   Verb Usage どうしの つかいかた

❏ おもう (to think)

おもう uses a particle that we have not discussed: と. This と is totally unrelated to the "and" and the "with" meanings of と. We will call it the thought-, opinion-, quotation-marker, for lack of a better name. Anything that is thought or said is marked with と. The と *must* come *after* the thought.

[*thought, opinion, quotation*] と おもう
(he/she/I) think(s) [*thought/opinion*]

In sentences using おもう, the phrase that makes up the thought must be in informal form. Even です should be conjugated to だ. Look at the following examples to see how this verb is used:

Example Sentences
1. あしたは 金よう日だと おもいます。   I think tomorrow is Friday.
2. きょうの しごとは なんだと おもいますか。   What do you think today's work is?
3. あなただと おもわなかった。   I didn't think it was you. (informal)

❏ いう (to say)

いう is used exactly as おもう is used. Any phrase being quoted is followed by the と particle, and normally the phrase being quoted is stated in the informal form.

[*phrase*] と いう
say [*phrase*]

Remember that even です is converted to it's informal form だ. If it was でした it could convert to だった.

Example Sentences
1. かれは くみこさんが すきだと いいました。
   He said that he likes Kumiko.

2. らい月、とうきょうに いくと いいました。
   (She) said she was going to Tokyo next month.

3. こうえんに いぬが 三びき いると いいました。
   (They) said that there were three dogs in the park.

❏ まつ (to wait)

The thing or person you are waiting for is marked with the object marker を. The place you are waiting at is marked with the event location marker で.

> **[*thing/person*] を まつ**
> **wait for [*thing/person*]**

> **[*place*] で まつ**
> **wait at [*place*]**

Example Sentences

1. かなえさんを まちましょう。
   Let's wait for Kanae.

2. がっこうの まえで さんじかん、まちました。
   I waited for three hours in front of the school.

4 Grammar ぶんぽう

❏ Japanese quotation marks

Japanese quotation marks look like 「this」 and are used in the same way as English quotation marks. They are generally only used when you are quoting someone's words, and are not usually used for ideas.

❏ The "quote and thought" marker と

When you are including a thought, idea, or quote in a sentence, it must be following with the particle と. The particle と, from now on referred to as the thought-marker, opinion marker, or quotation-marker, is often used with the verbs おもう (to think), いう (to say), and きく (to hear).

❏ The particle と with the verb いう (to say, tell)

When using 「something」 と いいます, anything can be inside the quotation marks.

> **「*thing that was said*」 + と いいました。**
> **[*someone*] said "thing that was said"**

The sentence that is being quoted sounds more natural if the verb in it is changed to its informal version. For example, いきます should be changed to いく, and たべました should be changed to たべた.

Example Sentences

1. ハンズさんは 「ドイツにかえる」と いいました。
   Hans said he was going to return to Germany.

2. まりかさんは 「きのう ビールを たくさん のんだ」と いいました。
   Marika said she drank a lot of beer yesterday.

3. わたしのおとうさんは 「アメリカに いかないで」と いいました。
   My father said, "Do not go to America."

4. なんと いいましたか。
   What did you say?

❏ The particle と with the verb おもう (to think)

When using 「*something*」と おもいます, all verbs in the quotations should also be used in their informal versions. In the following examples we are assuming that the speakers are referring to themselves. Quotation marks may or may not be used in sentences that are expressing thoughts, opinions, or quotations.

「*thought / opinion*」 + と おもいます。

[*someone*] thinks "*thought/opinion*"

Example Sentences

1. トムと ジェニーは りこんすると おもいます。
   I think Tom and Jenny will divorce.

2. ピザを たべると おもいます。
   I think I will eat pizza.

3. ひこうきを かうと おもいます。
   I think I will buy an airplane.

4. お金が ないから けっこんゆびわを うると おもいます。
   Since I have no money, I think I will sell my wedding ring.

❑ **The particle と with the verb きく (to hear)**

When saying 「*something*」と ききました, all verbs in the quotations should be used in their informal versions. In the following examples we are assuming that the speakers are referring to themselves. Again, quotation marks may or may not be used in sentences that are expressing the thoughts, opinions, and quotations.

> 「*thing that was heard*」+ と ききました。
>
> [*someone*] heard "*thing that was heard*"

Example Sentences

You can use the particle から or に to mean "from" in sentences like "I heard from…"

1. きょうの よる、七じに しごとが ある<u>と</u> ききました。
   I heard there was work from seven tonight.

2. きょう、わたしの ボス<u>から</u> しごとが ない<u>と</u> ききました。
   I heard from my boss that there is no work today.

3. こばやしさん<u>に</u> ジェフさんと さよこさんが けっこんする<u>と</u> ききました。
   I heard from Kobayashi that Jeff and Sayoko are going to get married.

❑ **When です ends the sentence being quoted or idea**

When the sentence being quoted ends in です, don't forget to change です to the informal だ. Similiarly, if the sentence ends in でした, it should be changed to the informal だった.

Examples Sentences

1. わたしは いいくるま<u>だ</u>と おもいます。
   I think it's a nice car.

2. たなかさんは すしが きらい<u>だ</u>と いいました。
   Tanaka said that he dislikes sushi.

3. きのうは あなたの たんじょう日<u>だった</u>と ききました。
   I heard that yesterday was your birthday.

4. せんせいは 三十五さい<u>だ</u>と おもいます。
   I think our teacher is 35 years old.

❑ Using adjectives with いう、おもう and きく

In sentences where an adjective exists, です is removed from the sentence.

Examples Sentences

1. わたしは いいと おもいます。   I think it is good.
2. これは おいしいと おもいます。   I thinks this tastes good.
3. たなかさんは やさしいと おもいます。   I think Mr. Tanaka is kind.
4. たださんは あついと いいました。   Mr. Tada said it is hot.
5. きのう ロンドンは さむかったと ききました。   I heard London was cold yesterday.
6. そのワインは おいしくないと ききました。   I heard that wine doesn't taste good.

❑ Using なにも

なにも is always used with negative verbs or adjectives. In the following examples we are assuming that the speakers are referring to themselves:

Example Sentences

1. なにも かいません。   I won't buy anything.
2. なにも わからない。   I don't understand anything.
3. なにも うりませんでした。   I didn't sell anything.
4. なにも ない。   There isn't anything. / It's nothing.
5. なにも いわないでください。   Don't say anything please.
6. なにも のまないでください。   Don't drink anything please.
7. なにも あたらしくないです。   Nothing is new.
8. なにも よくないです。   Nothing is good.

❑ The question word どう

どう means "how" or "what," depending on the context. It is also very commonly used when asking someone's opinion.

Example Sentences

9. どう おもいますか。   What do you think?
10. あした、どうしますか。   What will you do tomorrow?
11. しごとは どうですか。   How is work?

❑ **Did you think that Japanese had no plurals?**

Initially you learned that Japanese doesn't have any plurals. That is *mostly* true.
But there are plurals that are made using たち after certain words. たち is normally used with people and is only used with non-living things when they're being given human characteristics like ほしたちが ほほえみました (stars smiled). The most common plurals:

Examples	わたし<u>たち</u>	us, we
	あなた<u>たち</u>	you (guys)
	せいと<u>たち</u>	students
	せんせい<u>たち</u>	teachers

❑ **たち after names**

When たち comes after a name, as in たなかさん<u>たち</u>, it means that たなか is part of a group and he is being used to describe that group or is a representative of that group.

4 Mini Conversations ミニかいわ J-E

Using a piece of paper cover up the entire English portion of the conversations below. Read the entire Japanese conversation several times until you understand it. Only then should you move the paper to reveal the English and check your translation.

1. Polite conversation between friends

A： これは いくらですか。
B： 千二百えんです。
A： たかいですね。
B： いいえ、やすいと おもいます。

A： How much is this?
B： It's ¥1200.
A： It is expensive.
B： No, I think it is cheap.

2. Polite conversation between friends at a car lot

A： このくるまを どう おもいますか。
B： いろが いいと おもいます。
A： わたしは あんまり すきじゃないですね。

A： What do you think of this car?
B： I think the color is good.
A： I don't like it very much.

3. Polite conversation between friends

A： いま、なんと いいましたか。
B： あなたが きらいだと いいました。
A： えっ！ なに！
B： いいえ、なにも…

A： What did you say just now?
B： I said I dislike you.
A： What!?
B： No, nothing…

4. Polite conversation between classmates

A： きのう、せんせいは なんと いいましたか。
B： ハちから テストが あると いいました。
A： テストが だいきらいです。
B： わたしも…

A： What did the teacher say yesterday?
B： (He) said there is a test from eight o'clock.
A： I hate tests.
B： Me too.

4 Mini Conversations ミニかいわ E-J

Using a piece of paper, cover up the entire Japanese portion of the conversations below. Translate the English conversation to Japanese. Only after you have translated the entire conversation should you move the paper to check your work.

1. Polite conversation with a friend who may or may not be hard of hearing

A： You're a fool.
B： What did you say?
A： I said I am hungry.
B： I thought that you said I was a fool.
A： I didn't say that!

A： あほですね。
B： なんと いいましたか。
A： おなかが すいたと いいました。
B： あほだと いったと おもいました。
A： いいませんでしたよ。

2. Polite conversation between friends
   A: Please wait here.
   B: About how long will I wait?
   A: Please wait about three minutes.
   B: Okay, I understand.

   A: ここで まって下さい。
   B: どれぐらい まちますか。
   A: 三ぷんぐらい、まって下さい。
   B: はい、わかりました。

3. Polite conversation between friends
   A: Which one do you think is good?
   B: I think this one is good. What about you?
   A: I like both of them.

   A: どれが いいと おもいますか。
   B: これが いいと おもいます。 あなたは？
   A: わたしは りょうほうが すきです。

4 Reading Comprehension どっかい

Read the sentences below. Use the information to answer the reading comprehension questions later in this lesson.

① きょう、わたしは ともだちと 三上けんの コンサートに いきます。
② わたしは 三上けんの うたが だいすきです。
③ CD が ぜんぶ ほしいです。
④ 三上けんは ファンが とっても おおいから、三か月まえに チケットを かいました。
⑤ チケットは 五千八百えんでした。
⑥ ともだちは たかいと いったけど、わたしは たかくないと おもいます。
⑦ コンサートは 九じからです。
⑧ わたしたちは 八じから かいじょうの まえで まちます。
⑨ ともだちの いえから かいじょうまで くるまで 一じかん、かかります。
⑩ ともだちは いえに 六じ五十ぷんまで いると いいました。
⑪ わたしは ともだちの くるまで いきます。

4 Activities

❏ Reading comprehension questions

Answer the following questions about the reading comprehension in this lesson.

1. きょう、わしゃ (see note above)は どこに いきますか。

　　_____

2. なぜ、みかみけんの コンサートに いきますか。

　　_____

3. いつ チケットを かいましたか。

　　_____

4. チケットは いくらでしたか。

　　_____

5. だれが チケットは たかいと いいましたか。

　　_____

6. わしゃは チケットが たかいと おもいましたか。

　　_____

7. コンサートは なんじからですか。

　　_____

8. わしゃは 八じから 九じまで なにを しますか。

　　_____

9. ともだちの いえから かいじょうまで、くるまで どのぐらい かかりますか。

　　_____

10. ともだちは いえに なんじまで いますか。

　　_____

❑ Substitution Drill

Compose sentences according to the example.

> **Ex. おとうさんは 「アメリカにいかないで」と いいました。**
>
> → don't drink beer   おとうさんは 「ビールをのまないで」と いいました。
> → please eat breakfast   おとうさんは 「あさごはんをたべて」と いいました。
> → please return to Japan   おとうさんは 「にほんにかえって」と いいました。
> → don't go to the concert   おとうさんは 「コンサートにいかないで」と いいました。

1. あさって、テレビを かうと おもいます。

→ sell my computer   _____

→ read this book   _____

→ sleep until noon   _____

→ won't watch a movie _____

→ won't go to school _____

2. まりこさんが けっこんすると ききました。

→ will go to China   _____

→ drank a lot of beer _____

→ bought a new car   _____

→ shops at that store _____

→ wrote a book   _____

3. なにも わかりません。

→ won't buy anything   _____

→ won't eat anything   _____

→ didn't do anything   _____

→ didn't read anything   _____

→ didn't hear anything   _____

❑ Translation

Fill in the blanks and translate the resulting sentences into Japanese.

Ex. I think <u>I will study tonight.</u>   I think <u>I won't study tonight.</u>

<u>こんや、 べんきょう**する**と おもいます。</u>   <u>こんや、べんきょう**しない**と おもいます。</u>

---

1. I think my Japanese class is _____

    Translation: _____

2. I think _____ is beautiful.

    Translation: _____

3. I think _____ doesn't taste good.

    Translation: _____

4. I think I will _____ this Saturday.

    Translation: _____

5. I think I won't _____ this Sunday.

    Translation: _____

6. I think my mom likes _____

    Translation:

7. I heard _____ dislikes fish.

    Translation:

8. I heard there are lots of _____ in Japan.

    Translation: _____

╭COMMENTARY╮———————— When will I be fluent?

Originally Posted on YesJapan.com
George Trombley Jr.

When will I be fluent?

This is the magic question, and normally the first question that I am asked by a new student. Of course it is impossible to answer this question with an exact date, since all students are different in terms of study habits and access to Japanese influences.

The answer to this question lies in the definition of fluency. I easily qualify as fluent. I can understand just about any Japanese thrown my way and even earn a very nice living as an interpreter. But since when was I fluent? The honest answer is that I don't remember. I remember not being able to speak Japanese but I cannot recall the magical day when I qualified as fluent – which leads us to the answer to this question.

Fluency is not something that you can earn like a black belt in karate. You won't all of a sudden be given a certificate that says, "Congratulations! You are now fluent." Instead, fluency is built little by little, just as a hill is slowly pushed upwards until it grows into a mountain. After some point the hill is no longer referred to as a hill. But after a while, no matter how tall it gets, it is always a mountain. You can be partially fluent in Japanese from the first day of study. If you hear the Japanese word "neko" and, without flinching, know that it means "cat," you are fluent with that word. The more words you know, the more fluent you become.

In Japanese they have a saying: Chiri mo tsumoreba yama to naru – even specks of dust become a mountain. I like this saying so much that it is on the cover of our first level book. Every time you learn a new word or grammar point you add to your fluency hill. Before you know it your mountain will be huge. It all depends on how much dust you add.

So what do I do to be fluent?

No book or website exists that will single-handedly give you total fluency. There isn't even a teacher on the entire planet than can achieve this feat. You need to study, speak, and interact with the Japanese language as much as possible.

For me, Japanese music, comic books and TV were major influences on my ability. I had every Asaka Yui album! You might not know who she is... She is not really around anymore, but without her, I would be flipping hamburgers for a living. If you have access to Japanese videos, start watching them. If there is a Japanese music group that you like, start taking apart the lyrics of the songs and learn what the song means. Keep on adding to your mountain. Studying alone will not make you fluent. You need to use your Japanese. Use it or lose it! If you live in a fairly large town you might find that there is a local Japanese Friendship club where Japanese people get together. If there is a major college in your town you can bet that there are Japanese exchange students enrolled.

Learning Japanese is a major project. Put all your efforts into it and I promise you that you too will become fluent.

Kanji Lesson 5

五 New Kanji あたらしい かんじ

Make sure you learn the correct stroke order. Correct stroke order will mean neater symbols when writing quickly. Also, take time to learn the new words for each kanji, as these will help you to memorize the different readings.

大 3 strokes	くんよみ	おお				
	おんよみ	ダイ、タイ				
	おお・きい **大きい**	だい・がく **大学**	かく・だい **拡大**	おお・どおり **大通り**	たい・へん **大変**	たい・りょう **大量**
	big	college	enlargement	main street	terrible, disasterous	a large quantity

中 4 strokes	くんよみ	なか			
	おんよみ	チュウ			
	なか **中**	ちゅう・しん **中心**	ちゅう・がっこう **中学校**	と・ちゅう **途中**	しごと・ちゅう **仕事中**
	inside, in	the middle, the center	junior high school	on the way	on duty

小 3 strokes	くんよみ	ちい（さい）、こ、お				
	おんよみ	ショウ				
	ちい・さい **小さい**	しょう・がっこう **小学校**	お・がわ **小川**	こ・ねこ **小猫**	しょう・せつ **小説**	だい・しょう **大小**
	small	elementary school	brook, stream	small cat	a novel	big and small

円 4 strokes	くんよみ	まる				
	おんよみ	エン				
	まる・い **円い**	ひゃく・えん **百円**	えん・だか **円高**	えん・けい **円形**	だ・えん **楕円**	はん・えん **半円**
	round	100 yen	high value of the yen	round, round shape	ellipse	half circle

人 (2 strokes)	くんよみ	ひと					
	おんよみ	ジン、ニン					
	<u>ひと</u> 人	<u>にん</u>・<u>げん</u> 人間	<u>にほん</u>・<u>じん</u> 日本人	<u>せい</u>・<u>じん</u> 成人	<u>こい</u>・<u>びと</u> 恋人	<u>う</u>・<u>ちゅう</u>・<u>じん</u> 宇宙人
2 strokes	person, people	human	Japanese person	an adult	lover	space alien

目 (5 strokes)	くんよみ	め、ま					
	おんよみ	モク、ボク					
	<u>め</u> 目	<u>もく</u>・<u>てき</u> 目的	<u>め</u>・<u>だつ</u> 目立つ	<u>もく</u>・<u>ぜん</u> 目前	<u>もく</u>・<u>ひょう</u> 目標	<u>みぎ</u>・<u>め</u> 右目
5 strokes	eye	purpose	to stand out	before one's eyes	a goal	right eye

五 Fun Kanji たのしい かんじ

❏ **The kanji of love**

There is a really cool combination of kanji to make up the phrase "love at first sight". The word is ひとめぼれ.

> ### 一目惚れ (ひとめぼれ)
> ### "love at first sight"

This is so straightforward. The first kanji is for *one* and the second for *eye*, and that makes sense logically. The last portion of the word is from the verb 惚れる(ほれる), which means "to fall in love," or "to be charmed".

Continuing on the same idea, if you combine the kanji 自 which means "self" and 惚れる (ほれる) then you end up with the word 自惚れる（うぬぼれる）, which means, "to be conceited," or literally "self love."

> ### 自惚れる(うぬぼれる)
> ### "to be conceited"

❏ **In the middle of something**

The more kanji you learn, the more you will realize how much kanji is tied to your overall fluency level.   Here is a cool thing done with the 中 kanji.

Look at how the meaning of the following words are changed when 中 is added to them.

| べんきょう 勉強 study | べんきょうちゅう 勉強中 studying | | しごと 仕事 work | しごとちゅう 仕事中 working |

Example Sentence

1. いま、べんきょう中です。　　　　　　　　　I am studying.

五　**Kanji Activities**

❑ **Stroke order**

Trace the light gray symbols for practice. Pay attention to stroke order and stroke type.

大	大	大	大	大	大					
中	中	中	中	中	中					
小	小	小	小	小	小					
円	円	円	円	円	円					
人	人	人	人	人	人					
目	目	目	目	目	目					

❑ **Words you can write**

Write the following words in the boxes. This is a great way to practice the new kanji and review the words at the same time.

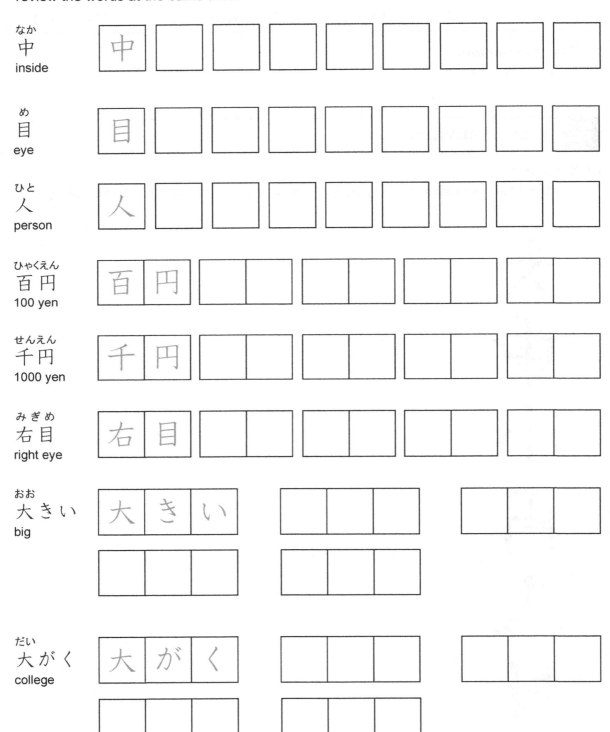

なか
中
inside

め
目
eye

ひと
人
person

ひゃくえん
百円
100 yen

せんえん
千円
1000 yen

みぎめ
右目
right eye

おお
大きい
big

だい
大がく
college

ちい
小さい
small

小	さ	い

ひだりめ
左目
left eye

左	目

ごじゅうえん
五十円
50 yen

五	十	円

に　　　じん
日ほん人
Japanese person

日	ほ	ん	人

❑ Fill in the kanji

Fill in the blanks in the following sentences with the appropriate kanji.

1. あした、[だい]がくで[みっ]つの クラスが あります。

2. へやの[なか]に[ちい]さいテーブルが[ふた]つ あります。

3. [おお]きいりんごは[ろっ][ぴゃく][えん]です。

4. あのおんなの[ひと]は[さん][じゅっ]さいだと ききました。

5. いつも ウィンクは[みぎ][め]で します。

6. このクラスに[ひと]が[に][じゅう][ご][にん]います。

7. いまは しごと[ちゅう]だから、[ご]じに あいましょう。

WRITING PRACTICE

Use these sheets as extra writing practice for the kanji you have learned up to this point. Recently you have learned: 休上下左右、大中小円人目

VOCABULARY GROUPS ───── set 5

G — around town

English	Progressive	Kanji +
parking lot	ちゅうしゃじょう	駐車場
taxi stand	タクシーのりば	乗り場
elevator	エレベーター	エレベーター
escalator	エスカレーター	エスカレーター
bus stop	バスてい	バス停
library	としょかん	図書館
railroad crossing	ふみきり	踏み切り
sidewalk	ほどう	歩道

H — around the office

English	Progressive	Kanji +
calculator	けいさんき	計算機
tape (cellophane)	セロテープ	セロテープ
two-sided tape	りょうめんテープ	両面テープ
stapler	ホッチキス	ホッチキス
file cabinet	ファイル	ファイル　キャビネット
paper clip	（ペーパー）クリップ	（ペーパー）クリップ
folder	フォルダー	フォルダー
ballpoint pen	ボールペン	ボールペン
ink	インク	インク
correction fluid	しゅうせいえき	修正液
hole puncher	パンチ	パンチ
pencil sharpener	えんぴつけずり	鉛筆削り
appointment book	システムてちょう	システム手帳
laptop computer	ラップトップ	ラップトップ
safe (to secure valuables)	きんこ	金庫
piggy bank	ちょきんばこ	貯金箱
tip (for services)	チップ	チップ

Lesson
5
Level ③

Family Vacation

which is better?

---

5 About this Lesson このレッスンについて

Before The Lesson

1. be able to write and read 大中小円人目
2. review vocabulary group set 5

Lesson Goals

1. learn to use the particle か to mean "or"
2. learn *verb + -ing* form of the verbs
3. learn to compare items

From The Teachers

1. The ています form learned in this lesson is *very* important and powerful. Make sure you remember how it is used.

---

5 New Words あたらしい ことば

Progressive	Kanji +	English
どちら	どちら	where, which and who (polite)
こえ	声	voice
なきごえ	鳴き声	animal cry, chirp, roar
みんな	皆	everybody
こどもたち	子供達	children
ピクニック	ピクニック	picnic
ディズニーランド	ディズニーランド	Disneyland
せんとう	銭湯	public bath (artificially heated)
おんせん	温泉	hot spring (natural heat source)
もの	物	thing(s)
けっきょく	結局	after all, in the end
かじ	家事	housework
そうじ	掃除	cleaning

せんたく	洗濯	laundry
中^{ちゅう}かりょうり	中華料理	Chinese cooking (food)
おんなゆ	女湯	women's bath
おとこゆ	男湯	men's bath
こんよく	混浴	men's and women's bath

5 New Verbs あたらしい どうし

Dictionary	Kanji +	た form	English Verb	Verb Type
こたえる	答える	こたえた	to answer	いる/える

5 New Adjectives あたらしい けいようし

Adjective	Kanji +	English	Type
ひどい	酷い	terrible	い adjective
あかるい	明るい	bright	い adjective
くらい	暗い	dark	い adjective

5 Verb Usage どうしの つかいかた

❏ こたえる (to answer)

The と particle is used to mark the answering phrase in the same way that it is used with おもう and いう. The answering phrase sounds better if it is changed to its informal form. The thing being answered is marked with に, and of course the person to whom you are answering is also marked with に.

> [*phrase*] と こたえる
> **to answer with [*phrase*]**

> [*thing*] に こたえる
> **to answer [*thing*]**

Example Sentences

1. せんせいの しつもんに なんと こたえたの？
   How did you answer the teacher's question?

2. しつもんに ぜんぶ こたえてください。
   Please answer all the questions.

3. あしたまでに できないと こたえました。
   I answered that I couldn't do it by tomorrow.

5   Grammar ぶんぽう

❏ The ています verb form

The ています form is the *verb + -ing* form in English. It is used when an action is currently taking place or is ongoing. The ています form of a verb is made by adding います after the positive て-form of the verb.

> **[*positive* て-*form verb*] + います**
> **I am [*verb*]-ing.**

Example Sentences

1. すしを たべています。   I am eating sushi.
2. テレビを みています。   I am watching TV.
3. ビールを のんでいます。   I am drinking beer.

The ています form describes actions that are occurring at the moment. Accordingly, if the います is changed to いません, then the action was not occurring

1. すしを たべていません。   I am not eating sushi.
2. がっこうに いっていません。   I am not going to school.
3. テレビを みていません。   I am not watching TV.

If the います is changed to いました, then obviously the action taken was occurring in the past.

1. すしを たべていました。   I was eating sushi.
2. テレビを みていました。   I was watching TV.
3. ビールを のんでいました。   I was drinking beer.

By now I am sure that you see the pattern. You can say that the action was not occurring in the past by changing the います to いません でした。

1. すしを たべて<u>いませんでした</u>。　　　　I wasn't eating sushi.
2. テレビを みて<u>いませんでした</u>。　　　　I wasn't watching TV.
3. ビールを のんで<u>いませんでした</u>。　　　I wasn't drinking beer.

❏ ています vs. てます

In spoken Japanese, people often drop the い sound in the ています verb form. Typically this shouldn't be done when writing, but when speaking it sounds more relaxed and casual. In some of the future example conversations, you may notice that instead of writing たべています, for example, we will use たべてます. This is to make the conversation sound more natural when you read it aloud.

> **Example Sentences**
> 1. いま、べんきょうしてます。
>   I am studying now.
>
> 2. きのうの よるは えいがを みてました。
>   I was watching a movie last night.

❏ This is better than that

The following sentence structure is used to say that one item is better, newer, older, bigger, more liked, etc., than another item. Depending on the context, より can mean "than, more than, or instead of."

> ITEM 1 is more ADJECTIVE than ITEM 2 .
> ITEM 2 より ITEM 1 のほうが ADJECTIVE です。

Example Sentences
1. はやし<u>より</u> もり<u>のほうが</u> 大きいです。
   The forest is bigger than the woods.

2. このへや<u>より</u> あのへや<u>のほうが</u> あかるいです。
   That room over there is brighter than this room.

3. 土よう日の てんき<u>より</u> 金よう日の てんき<u>のほうが</u> よかったです。
   Friday's weather was better than Saturday's weather.

4. イタリアりょうり<u>より</u> ちゅうかりょうり<u>のほうが</u> おいしいです。
   Chinese food tastes better than Italian food.

5. きょう<u>より</u> あした<u>のほうが</u> いいです。
    Tomorrow is better than today.

❑ Using より alone

より can also be used alone. より means more than, instead of, than, or rather than.

> **Example Sentences**
> 1. ロザンセルス<u>より</u> シアトルに いきましょう。
>   <u>Rather than</u> Los Angeles, let's go to Seattle.
>
> 2. りんご<u>より</u> いちごが すきです。
>   I like strawberries, <u>more than</u> apples.

❑ Using のほうが alone

It is also possible to use のほうが by itself.

> **Example Sentences**
> 1. あした<u>のほうが</u> いいです。
>   Tomorrow is better.
>
> 2. テレビ<u>のほうが</u> おもしろいです。
>   TV is more interesting.

❑ Saying "or" in Japanese using か

か is used between words in a list to say "or." It is optional to have か after the last item.

> **Example Sentences**
> 1. えんぴつ<u>か</u> ペンで かいてください。
>   Please write it with a pencil <u>or</u> a pen.
>
> 2. まいあさ、ミルク<u>か</u> オレンジジュースを のみます。
>   I drink milk <u>or</u> orange juice every morning.
>
> 3. あかいくるま<u>か</u> くろいくるま<u>か</u> どっちが いいと おもいますか。
>   Which one do you think is good, the red car <u>or</u> the black car?

くるま

か

トラック

ハンバーガー

か

ホット・ドッグ

5 Mini Conversations ミニかいわ J-E

1. Informal conversation between a man who cheated and his upset girlfriend

A： わたしか よしえさんか どっちが いいの？
B： ごめん。 よしえさんのほうが すきだ。
A： ひどい人!

A： Me or Yoshie, which (who) is better?
B： Sorry, Yoshie is better (than you).
A： You're a terrible person!

2. Polite conversation between co-workers

A： おひるごはんは なにが いいですか 。
B： イタリアりょうりか 中<small>ちゅう</small>かりょうりが いいです。
A： わたしは きのう 中かりょうりを たべたから、イタリアりょうりのほうが いいです。
B： じゃあ、そうしましょう。

A： What would be good for lunch?
B： Italian or Chinese is good.
A： I ate Chinese yesterday, so Italian is better.
B： Okay, let's do (that).

3. Polite conversation between friends

A： らいしゅうの 日よう日に ぼくと えいがを みませんか。
B： えいがより こうえんで ピクニックを しましょう。
A： うん。 いいですね。 そうしましょう。

A： Won't you see a movie with me next Sunday?
B： Instead of a movie, let's have a picnic in the park.
A： Okay that's good. Let's do it that way.

4. Mixed conversation; A is higher in status than B

A： いま なにを しているの。
B： とりの なきごえを きいています。
A： とりは どこにいるの?
B： あの いえの 上に います。

A： What are you doing now?
B： I am listening to a bird's chirp.
A： Where is the bird?
B： It's on top of that house.

5 Mini Conversations ミニかいわ E-J

1. Polite conversation between friends
A: Let's listen to a CD.
B: Which do you like, Japanese music or American music?
A: Japanese music is better.

A: CD を ききましょう。
B: 日ほんの おんがくか アメリカの おんがくか どっちが すきですか。
A: 日ほんの おんがくのほうが いいです。

2. Polite conversation between co-workers
A: My wife hasn't been here since yesterday.
B: Aren't you sad by yourself?
A: I am very lonely.

A: きのうから かないが いないです。
B: 一人は さびしくないですか。
A: とっても さびしいです。

5 Reading Comprehension どっかい

Read the sentences below. Use the information to answer the reading comprehension questions later in this lesson.

① らい月の 二十日に さとうさんは かぞくと りょこうを します。

② おとうさんは かぞくの みんなに 「どこが いい?」と ききました。

③ おかあさんは 「おんせんが いいよ。おいしいものを たべましょう」と こたえました。

④ おねえちゃんは 「おんせんより ディズニーランドのほうが いい」と いいました。

⑤ おとうとの じゅんくんも ディズニーランドがいいと おもっています。

⑥ おかあさんは いつも いえの そうじと りょうりと せんたくを している から、おとうさんは こどもたちに 「ディズニーランドより おんせんが いいよ」と いいました。

⑦ けっきょく おんせんに いきました。

⑧ 日ほんの おんせんは おとこゆと おんなゆが あります。

⑨ こんよくも あります。

⑩ 日ほん人は おんせんが 大すきです。

⑪ おんせんの しょくじは 日ほんりょうりです。

⑫ こどもたちは ホテルより おんせんのほうが よかったと おもいました。

5 | Activities

❑ Reading comprehension questions

Answer the following questions about the reading comprehension in this lesson.

1. さとうさんは　いつ、りょこうしますか。

   _____

2. おかあさんは　どこが　いいと　いいましたか。

   _____

3. おねえちゃんは　どこが　いいと　いいましたか。

   _____

4. なぜ、おとうさんは　おんせんが　いいと　いいましたか。

   _____

5. みんなは　けっきょく、どこに　いきましたか。

   _____

6. こどもたちは　ホテルと　おんせんと　どっちが　よかったですか。

   _____

❏ What are they doing?

Describe the pictures below using the ています form.

1
writing a letter

2
reading a book

3
eating pizza

4
(drinking) soup

5
waiting for customer

6
buying a book

❏ **Sentence creation**

Make sentences using the pictures below.
Use the sentence pattern「[*item 1*] より [*item 2*] のほうが [*adjective*] です。」

Ex. ___ケーキより アイスクリームの ほうが つめたいです。___

1. _____

2. _____

3. _____

4. _____

❏ **Substitution drill**

Compose sentences according to the example.

Ex. ゆうごはんの あと、しゅくだいを します。
  → want to do   ゆうごはんの あと、しゅくだいを したいです。
  → do not want to do   ゆうごはんの あと、しゅくだいを したくないです。
  → please do   ゆうごはんの あと、しゅくだいを してください。
  → please don't do   ゆうごはんの あと、しゅくだいを しないでください。

1. フランスごを べんきょうしています。

→ studying Japanese _____

→ listening to music _____

→ drinking wine _____

→ not drinking wine _____

2. てがみを よんでいます。

→ writing a letter _____

→ traveling _____

→ calling _____

→ not calling _____

3. りんごより バナナのほうが すきです。

→ like sushi more than sashimi

_____

→ like ice cream more than chocolate

_____

→ like doing laundry more than cleaning

_____

→ like water more than juice

_____

❑ Question and answer

Answer the following questions using the words and patterns in this lesson.

1. いま、テレビを みていますか。

   _____

2. いま、ばんごはんを たべていますか。

   _____

3. まいにち、日ほんごの べんきょうを していますか。

   _____

4. あなたの へやは あかるいですか。

   _____

5. コーラと ジュースと どっちが すきですか。

   _____

6. おんせんと ホテルと どっちが いいですか。

   _____

7. そうじと せんたくと どっちが たのしいですか。

   _____

8. ディズニーランドと マジックマウンテンと どっちが おもしろいですか。

   _____

9. カタカナと ひらがなと どっちが むずかしいですか。

   _____

10. えいがと ピクニックと どっちが すきですか。

   _____

11. 日ほんりょうりと 中かりょうりと どっちを よく たべますか。

   _____

Kanji Lesson 6

耳口手足力

六 New Kanji あたらしい かんじ

Make sure you learn the correct stroke order. Correct stroke order will mean neater symbols when writing quickly. Also, take time to learn the new words for each kanji – these will help you to memorize the different readings.

耳	くんよみ	みみ					
	おんよみ	ジ					
		<u>みみ</u>・なり **耳鳴り**	<u>みみ</u> **耳**	パンの・<u>みみ</u> **パンの耳**	<u>じ</u>・び・か **耳鼻科**	<u>みみ</u>・うち **耳打ち**	ちゅう・<u>じ</u>・えん **中耳炎**
6 strokes		ear-ringing	ear	bread crust	ear, nose doctor	whisper into another's ear	ear infection

口	くんよみ	くち					
	おんよみ	コウ、ク					
		<u>くち</u> **口**	<u>こう</u>・しゅう **口臭**	じん・<u>こう</u> **人口**	で・<u>ぐち</u> **出口**	<u>く</u>・ちょう **口調**	い・り・<u>ぐち</u> **入り口**
3 strokes		mouth	foul breath	population	exit	tone of voice	entrance

手	くんよみ	て、た					
	おんよみ	シュ					
		<u>て</u> **手**	あく・<u>しゅ</u> **握手**	<u>て</u>・がみ **手紙**	<u>た</u>・づな **手綱**	す・<u>で</u> **素手**	から・<u>て</u> **空手**
4 strokes		hand	handshake	a letter	bridle rein, hand ropes	unarmed, bare hands	Karate

足	くんよみ	あし、た					
	おんよみ	ソク					
		<u>あし</u> **足**	<u>あし</u>・くび **足首**	えん・<u>そく</u> **遠足**	<u>あし</u>・おと **足音**	<u>た</u>・りる **足りる**	さん・<u>そく</u> **三足**
7 strokes		leg, foot	ankle	excursion	footsteps	to have enough	three pairs (shoes, socks)

力 ²↓¹	くんよみ	ちから					
	おんよみ	リョク、リキ					
	<u>ちから</u>	でん・<u>りょく</u>	じん・<u>りき</u>・しゃ	ば・<u>りき</u>	<u>ちから</u>・し・ごと	そこ・<u>ぢから</u>	
	力	電力	人力車	馬力	力仕事	底力	
2 strokes	power, energy, force	electric power	rickshaw	horse power	physical work	reserve strength	

六 Fun Kanji　たのしい　かんじ

❑ Kanji on your body

You already know that kanji are often based on picture representations of their meanings. The kanji for number 1, number 2, and number 3 are perfect examples of how kanji was created with deep thought: 一, 二, 三 are pretty easy concepts. If I told you that there is a kanji prominent on everyone's body you might not believe me – but if you look at the palm of your right hand, you will notice a rough version of the kanji for "hand." Of course it isn't going to be a perfect copy of the kanji, but you can see where it can from.

❑ Is it a leg or a foot???

In Japanese 足 (あし) means foot, feet, leg and legs, which can cause some confusion if your feet hurt.　足が いたいです　afterall can mean "my feet hurt" or "my leg hurts". Luckily there is a way to distinguish your feet from your legs.　You can use 足のうら for "feet" and "foot".　足のうら literally means, "bottom of my foot".

六 Kanji Activities

❑ Stroke order

Trace the light gray symbols for practice. Pay attention to stroke order and stroke type.

耳	耳	耳	耳	耳	耳					
口	口	口	口	口	口					
手	手	手	手	手	手					
足	足	足	足	足	足					
力	力	力	力	力	力					

❑ Words you can write

Write the following words in the boxes. This is a great way to practice the new kanji, review vocabulary, and learn new words at the same time.

じんりき
人力しゃ
rick-shaw

人	力	し	ゃ				

みみ
耳
ear

くち
口
mouth

て
手
hand

あし
足
foot, leg

ちから
力
power

じんこう
人口
population

みぎて
右手
right hand

あし
足くび
ankle

て
手がみ
letter

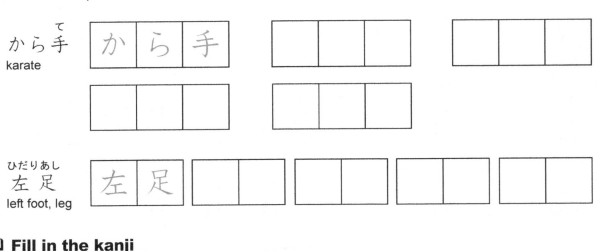

から手 (karate)
て
から手

ひだりあし
左足 (left foot, leg)
左足

❏ Fill in the kanji

Fill in the blanks in the following sentences with the appropriate kanji.

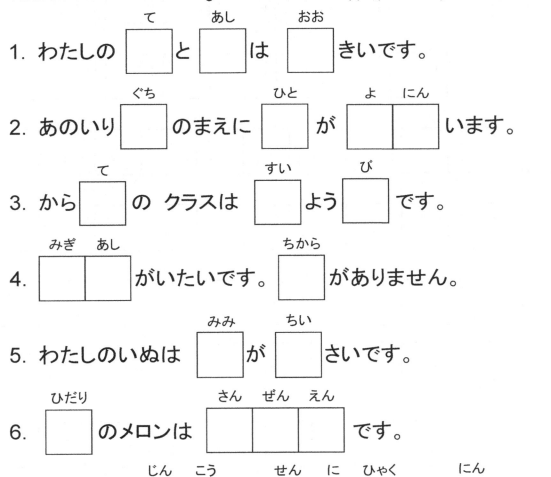

1. わたしの ［て］ と ［あし］ は ［おお］ きいです。

2. あのいり ［ぐち］ のまえに ［ひと］ が ［よ］［にん］ います。

3. から ［て］ の クラスは ［すい］ よう ［び］ です。

4. ［みぎ］［あし］ がいたいです。 ［ちから］ がありません。

5. わたしのいぬは ［みみ］ が ［ちい］ さいです。

6. ［ひだり］ のメロンは ［さん］［ぜん］［えん］ です。

7. とうきょうの ［じん］［こう］ は ［せん］［に］［ひゃく］ まん ［にん］ ぐらいです。

WRITING PRACTICE

Use these sheets as extra writing practice for the kanji you have learned up to this point. Recently you have learned: 休上下左右、耳口手足力

VOCABULARY GROUPS ——————————— set 6

	around the hospital

English	Progressive	Kanji +
handicap	ハンディキャップ	ハンディキャップ
a cold	かぜ	風邪
headache	ずつう	頭痛
injury	けが	怪我
thermometer (for body)	たいおんけい	体温計
x-ray	レントゲン	レントゲン
surgery	しゅじゅつ	手術
shot	ちゅうしゃ	注射
cough	せき	咳
tears	なみだ	涙
bandage, dressing	ほうたい	包帯
balloon	ふうせん	風船
dentures (false teeth)	いれば	入歯
hives, rash	じんましん	蕁麻疹
vitamins	ビタミン	ビタミン
wheelchair	くるまいす	車椅子

Lesson 6 Level ③

Old Friends

Japanese school and もう

6 About this Lesson このレッスンについて

Before The Lesson

1. be able to write and read 耳口手足力
2. review vocabulary group set 6

Lesson Goals

1. learn many verbs and how to say the grades of schooling in Japanese
2. learn how to say more than one い-adjective in a row
3. learn how to turn い-adjectives into object attributes

From The Teachers

1. You should start to notice the benefit of knowing kanji. Look for the kanji in this lesson. There is no grammar in this lesson so take this time to gather your thoughts.

6 New Words あたらしい ことば

Progressive	Kanji +	English
なんねんせい	何年生	what year of school? what grade?
しょう 小 がっこう	小学校	elementary school
ちゅう 中 がっこう	中学校	junior high school
こうこう	高校	high school
だい 大 がく	大学	college, university
しょう 小 がくせい	小学生	elementary school student
ちゅう 中 がくせい	中学生	junior high student
こうこうせい	高校生	high school student

だい 大 がくせい	大学生	college student
なつ 休 み	夏休み	summer break
はる 休 み	春休み	spring break
ふゆ 休 み	冬休み	winter break
ペットショップ	ペットショップ	pet shop
いろいろ	色々	various
だんなさん	旦那さん	one's own husband, another's husband
がいこく人	外国人	a foreigner
どくしん	独身	single, unmarried
しりつ	私立	private
しりつ	市立	municipal (public)

6 Word Usage ことばの つかいかた

☐ しりつ (私立) VS しりつ (市立)

This is one of those coincidental things that will most likely confuse students of Japanese and probably confuses the average Japanese person: しりつ is a homonym (same sound different meaning) for either "private" or "public," depending on which kanji are used.

What makes this complicated is the way schools are named. It is possible to have the same school name and the only difference being the kanji.

東京**市**立中学校　（とうきょう しりつ ちゅうがっこう）　Tokyo <u>Municipal</u> Junior High School
東京**私**立中学校　（とうきょう しりつ ちゅうがっこう）　Tokyo <u>Private</u> Junior High School

6 New Adjectives あたらしい けいようし

Progressive	Kanji +	English	Type
おもい	重い	heavy	い-adjective
かるい	軽い	light	い-adjective

6 Culture Clip: The Japanese School Year

The division of Japanese school grades might be slightly different from what you're familiar with. Consider the following chart. While American school systems may vary depending on state or school, the Japanese school system is unified throughout Japan.

Level	Japan	America
しょうがっこう elementary school	6 years	6 years
ちゅうがっこう junior high school	3 years	2 years
こうこう high school	3 years	4 years

In America we have labeled the grades from 1st grade to 12th grade. Japan uses the following labels for their grades.

Level	Grade	Long Name	Short Name
しょうがっこう	1st	しょうがっこう 一ねん	小一 （しょういち）
しょうがっこう	2nd	しょうがっこう 二ねん	小二 （しょうに）
しょうがっこう	3rd	しょうがっこう 三ねん	小三 （しょうさん）
しょうがっこう	4th	しょうがっこう 四ねん(よねん)	小四 （しょうよん）
しょうがっこう	5th	しょうがっこう 五ねん	小五 （しょうご）
しょうがっこう	6th	しょうがっこう 六ねん	小六 （しょうろく）
ちゅうがっこう	7th	ちゅうがっこう 一ねん	中一 （ちゅういち）
ちゅうがっこう	8th	ちゅうがっこう 二ねん	中二 （ちゅうに）
ちゅうがっこう	9th	ちゅうがっこう 三ねん	中三 （ちゅうさん）
こうこう	10th	こうこう一ねん	こう一
こうこう	11th	こうこう二ねん	こう二
こうこう	12th	こうこう三ねん	こう三

You can say "first year elementary school student" by adding 生 (せい) (student) after the grade. This of course can be done for each grade year.

6　New Verbs　あたらしい　どうし

Dictionary	Kanji	た-form	English Verb	Type
あう	会う	あった	to meet	regular
あそぶ	遊ぶ	あそんだ	to play	regular
すむ	住む	すんだ	to live (in a place)	regular
ちがう	違う	ちがった	to be wrong to be different	regular
ホームステイ(を)する		ホームステイ(を) した	to stay at someone's house	する verb
アルバイト(を)する		アルバイト(を) した	to work part-time	する verb

6　Verb Usage　どうしの　つかいかた

❏ あう (to meet)

When meeting someone, the person being met with is marked by the particle に. If you are meeting with a person to discuss something, then と should be used instead of に.

> ### [*person*] に あう
> ### to meet [*person*]

> ### [*person*] と あう
> ### to meet with [*person*]

Example Sentences

1. だれと あいますか。
2. ともだちと あいます。
3. きのう ともだちの おかあさんと あいました。
4. 二十日に あいましょう。

With whom will you meet?
I will meet with a friend.
Yesterday I met a friend's mother.
Let's meet on the twentieth.

❏ あそぶ (to play)

あそぶ is not used for playing sports – that is covered by する.

> ### [*person/thing*] と あそぶ
> ### to play with [*person/thing*]

Example Sentences

1. こどもは そとで あそんでいます。
2. あした さちこちゃんと あそびます。

The children are playing outside.
I will play with Sachiko tomorrow.

❑ すむ (to live, to reside)

When saying that you live somewhere, the location particle に is used. で is not used. Also, the ています form is used when saying that you are currently living somewhere.

> **[place] に すむ**
> **to live in [place]**

Example Sentences

1. ラスベガスに すんでいます。   I am living in Las Vegas.
2. にほんに すんでいました。   I was living in Japan.
3. どこに すんでいますか。   Where do you live?

❑ ちがう (to be wrong, be different)

When saying that something is different, one uses the marker と to mark the object that is being compared. This might take some time to get used to. Look at the two patterns below. Notice how just changing the order of particles changes the nuance of the sentence.

> **[item 1]は [item 2]と ちがう**
> **[item 1] is different than [item 2]**

> **[item 1]と [item 2]は ちがう**
> **[item 1] and [item 2] are different**

Example Sentences

1. 日ほんと アメリカは ちがいます。
   Japan and America are different.

2. きょうの てんきは きのうのと ちがいます。
   Today's weather is different from yesterdays.

3. きょうの すしは ちがうね。
   Today's sushi is different, isn't it?

❑ ホームステイをする (to home stay)

In Japanese this verb means that a foreigner is staying in a Japanese person's home during a visit to Japan. It can also mean that a Japanese person is staying in a foreigner's home in another country. It is not considered a home stay if the host and the guest are of the same nationality. The location marker で is used.

> **[place]で ホームステイをする**
> **to home stay at [place]**

Example Sentences

1. 日ほん<u>で</u> ホームステイを しました。
    I stayed with my host family in Japan.

2. らいねんの はるから 大さか<u>で</u> ホームステイを します。
    I am going to home stay at Osaka from spring of next year.

☐ アルバイトをする (to work part-time)

There is nothing tricky about this verb phrase. Have a look at the example sentence, and it should be pretty clear.

Example Sentences

1. 二か月まえから マクドナルドで アルバイトを しています。
    I have been working (part time) at McDonald's since two months ago.

2. 二ねんまえ、きんじょで アルバイトを していました。
    I was working part time in the neighborhood two years ago.

6 Grammar ぶんぽう

☐ Turning adjectives into attributes

For lack of a better word I have chosen the word "attribute" – a property of an object, such as height, length, weight, etc. Attributes can be made out of most of the い-adjectives by dropping the い and adding さ.

Once you have created the attribute you can use it just as you would use any noun in a sentence to say things like, "The **length** is two feet."

> (い adjective) minus い + さ

Examples	ひろさ	width	あつさ	heat
	たかさ	height	さむさ	coldness

Example Sentences

1. このビルは たかさが あります。
This building is high.

2. きょうは さむさが ありますね。
It is cold today, isn't it?

❏ Stringing い adjectives in a row

In English, if we want to say "little, white car," we just simply string the adjectives in a row and it works. In Japanese, the adjectives must be changed into what we will call the くて form. The い is dropped and くて is added. Every adjective in the row must be in the くて form *except* for the very last one, which should be normal

> (い adjective) minus い + くて

Example Sentences

1. かるくて、かわいい けいたいでんわが ほしいです。
   I want a light, cute cell phone.

2. にほんごは おもしろくて、むずかしいです。
   The Japanese language is interesting and difficult.

3. あたらしくて、やすいれいぞうこを かいましょう。
   Let's buy a new, reasonable refridgerator.

❏ Using ています to describe a state of being

In the previous lesson you learned that the ています form is used to describe an ongoing event. It is also used to describe a "state of being." This is usually the result of an action, and you are left with whatever state you are in. Have a look at the examples:

Example Sentences

1. けっこんを します。
   I will get married.

   けっこん しています。
   I am married.

2. 日本に すみます。
   I will live in Japan.

   日本に すんでいます。
   I live in Japan.

3. おなかが すきました。
   I got hungry.

   おなかが すいています。
   I am hungry.

6　Mini Conversations ミニかいわ J-E

Using a piece of paper cover up the entire English portion of the conversations below. Read the Japanese conversation several times until you understand it. Only then should you move the paper to compare your comprehension to the English translation.

1. Polite conversation between acquaintances
A：きょねん　どこに　すんでいましたか。
B：サンフランシスコに　いました。
A：とおいですね。ここから　くるまで　どれぐらい　かかりますか。
B：あんまり　とおくないです。くるまで　二じかんぐらい　かかります。

A：Where did you live last year?
B：I was in San Francisco.
A：That sure is far away. How long does it take to get there from here by car?
B：It's not that far. It takes about two hours by car.

2. Polite conversation between two people working in the same company
A：どくしんですか。
B：いいえ、けっこんしています。
A：ええ！　ほんとうに？　いつ　けっこんしましたか。
B：五ねんまえの　三がつです。

A：Are you single?
B：No, I am married.
A：What!? Really? When did you get married?
B：Five years ago in March.

4. Informal conversation between friends
A：あなたの　いもうとさんは　なんねんせいですか。
B：中がっこう　一ねんせいです。わたしは　こうこう　二ねんせいです。
A：がっこうで　えいごを　べんきょうしていますか。
B：はい、がいこく人の　ともだちも　います。

A：What grade is your younger sister in?
B：She is in the seventh grade (first year of junior high). I am in the eleventh grade (second year of high school).
A：Are you studying English in school?
B：Yes, I even have a foreign friend.

3. Informal conversation between friends
  A： どこで アルバイトしてるの？
  B： 中がっこうの となりの ペットショップで。
  A： どうぶつが すきだね。
  B： すきじゃないよ。お金が いいから、してる。

  A： Where are you working part-time?
  B： At the pet shop next to the junior high school.
  A： You must like animals.
  B： I don't like them. I do it because the money is good.

---

6 Mini Conversations ミニかいわ E-J

Using a piece of paper, cover up the entire Japanese portion of the conversations below. Translate the English conversation to Japanese. Only after you have translated the entire conversation should you move the paper to check your work.

1. Informal conversation between friends
  A： What are you doing?
  B： I'm not doing anything.
  A： You are lying!
  B： I was looking at your (Yumi's) second grade pictures.
  A： Don't look!

  A： なにを してるの？
  B： なにも してないよ。
  A： うそ!
  B： ゆみの 小二（しょうに）の ときの しゃしんを みてた。
  A： みないでよ!

2. Polite conversation between two classmates
  A： Won't you go to school with me tomorrow?
  B： Okay. At what time shall we meet?
  A： Let's meet at six o'clock in front of your house.
  B： Is it all right? Thank you.

  A： あした いっしょに がっこうに いきませんか。
  B： いいですよ。 なんじに あいましょうか。
  A： ろくじに あなたの いえの まえで あいましょう。
  B： いいですか。 ありがとう。

3. Polite conversation between a man (A) and a woman (B)

A：I think you're cute. Please marry me.
B：No (I can't).
A：Please!
B：I can't because I am already married.

A：あなたは　かわいいと　おもいます。けっこんしてください。
B：だめです。
A：おねがいします！
B：もう　けっこんしてるから、だめです。

4. Polite conversation between two people who bumped into each other on the street

A：Excuse me. Didn't we meet in high school?
B：Which high school is it?
A：Las Vegas High.
B：I think you are mistaken.

A：すみません。こうこうで　あいませんでしたか。
B：どのこうこうですか。
A：ラスベガスこうこうです。
B：ちがうと　おもいますよ。

6 Reading Comprehension どっかい

Read the sentences below. Use the information to answer the reading comprehension questions later in this lesson.

① あきらくんと　ジョンソンくんは　小がっこうからの　ともだちです。
② 二人は　六ねんまえに　アメリカで　あいました。
③ あきらくんは　なつ休みに　おねえさんの　いえに　きていました。
④ あきらくんの　おねえさんは　アメリカ人と　けっこんしています。
⑤ ジョンソンくんは　おねえさんの　となりに　すんでいました。
⑥ ジョンソンくんの　いえに　ちゃいろいいぬと　とても　かわいいかめが　いました。
⑦ あきらくんは　どうぶつが　大すきだったから、よく　ジョンソンくんの　いえで　あそびました。
⑧ いま、二人は　こうこうせいです。
⑨ ジョンソンくんは　いま、日ほんの　あきらくんの　いえで　一か月ぐらい、ホームステイしています。
⑩ あきらくんの　いえにも　どうぶつが　三びき、います。
⑪ 二ひきの　うさぎと　ぶたが　います。
⑫ 二人の　がっこうの　右よこに　ペットショップが　あります。
⑬ そのペットショップは　おもしろい　どうぶつを　いろいろ　うっています。
⑭ あきらくんは　そこで　アルバイトを　しています。

6 Activities

❏ Reading comprehension questions

Answer the following questions about the reading comprehension from the previous page.

1. あきらくんと ジョンソンくんは いつ、どこで あいましたか。

   _____

2. ジョンソンくんには どんなペットが いましたか。

   _____

3. あきらくんは どうして よく ジョンソンくんの いえで あそびましたか。

   _____

4. ジョンソンくんは どれぐらい にほんに いますか。

   _____

5. あきらくんは ペットショップで アルバイトを しています。どこに ありますか。

   _____

❑ Substitution drill

Compose sentences according to the example.

> **Ex.** みなこさんは <u>にほん</u>に すんでいます。
> → America　　　みなこさんは <u>アメリカ</u>にすんでいます。
> → England　　　みなこさんは <u>イギリス</u>にすんでいます。
> → Australia　　みなこさんは <u>オーストラリア</u>にすんでいます。
> → Where?　　　みなこさんは <u>どこ</u>にすんでいますか。

1. きょう、ともだちと あいます。

→ boyfriend/girlfriend　＿＿＿＿＿＿＿＿＿＿＿＿＿＿＿＿＿＿

→ yesterday　＿＿＿＿＿＿＿＿＿＿＿＿＿＿＿＿＿＿

→ tomorrow　＿＿＿＿＿＿＿＿＿＿＿＿＿＿＿＿＿＿

→ this Sunday　＿＿＿＿＿＿＿＿＿＿＿＿＿＿＿＿＿＿

→ who?　＿＿＿＿＿＿＿＿＿＿＿＿＿＿＿＿＿＿

2. りかちゃんは 中がっこう 三ねんせいです。

→ 6th grade　＿＿＿＿＿＿＿＿＿＿＿＿＿＿＿＿＿＿

→ 8th grade　＿＿＿＿＿＿＿＿＿＿＿＿＿＿＿＿＿＿

→ 10th grade　＿＿＿＿＿＿＿＿＿＿＿＿＿＿＿＿＿＿

→ 1st grade　＿＿＿＿＿＿＿＿＿＿＿＿＿＿＿＿＿＿

→ what grade?　＿＿＿＿＿＿＿＿＿＿＿＿＿＿＿＿＿＿

3. なつ休みに 日ほんで ホームステイを しました。

→ spring break　＿＿＿＿＿＿＿＿＿＿＿＿＿＿＿＿＿＿

→ winter break　＿＿＿＿＿＿＿＿＿＿＿＿＿＿＿＿＿＿

→ in Tokyo　＿＿＿＿＿＿＿＿＿＿＿＿＿＿＿＿＿＿

→ in Osaka　＿＿＿＿＿＿＿＿＿＿＿＿＿＿＿＿＿＿

→ when?　＿＿＿＿＿＿＿＿＿＿＿＿＿＿＿＿＿＿

❑ Particles

Fill in the blanks with appropriate particles.

1. ロサンゼルス _____ にほん _____ ひこうき _____十じかんぐらい かかります。

2. 金よう日 _____ あのレストラン _____ ともだち _____ あいます。

3. きょねん、フランス _____ すんでいました。

4. まい日、六じ _____ がっこう _____ いきます。

5. 日ほんの ビール _____ アメリカの ビール _____ちがいます。

6. たなべさん _____ くるまは あたらしい _____ おもいます。

7. ベッド _____ 上 _____ ざっし _____ あります。

8. いぬ _____ ねこのほう _____ すきです。

9. らいしゅう _____ 月よう日 _____ えいが _____ みましょう。

10. 日ほんご _____ じしょ _____ ほしいです。

❑ Opposite adjectives

Write the opposite words to the following adjectives like the following example.

> おおきい （ big ） ←→ ___ちいさい___ （ small ）

1. おもい （   ） ←→ _____ （   ）

2. うるさい （   ） ←→ _____ （   ）

3. あたらしい （   ） ←→ _____ （   ）

4. あかるい （   ） ←→ _____ （   ）

5. あつい （   ） ←→ _____ （   ）

6. とおい （   ） ←→ _____ （   ）

7. おもしろい （   ） ←→ _____ （   ）

❏ Practice with adjectives

Describe the pictures below.

1

expensive and light cell phone

2

white and small cat

3

cute and heavy piggy bank

4

cheap and blue calculator

5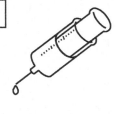

painful and scary shot

COMMENTARY ——————————— It's all about GUTS!

Originally Posted on YesJapan.com
By George Trombley, Jr.

Over the years I have often pondered why some people end up being fluent in Japanese and others just never get it. I have decided that it all boils down to guts and persistence. In the past when a new class began I would form private opinions about who was going to do well and who was going to end up quitting the class. In time I realized that first classes don't give me enough data to say whether one student will fail and another will succeed. It doesn't matter that one student understands the first lessons four times faster than another student. What matters is the student's ambition and guts.

The best students are those who make the most mistakes. Students who don't make mistakes aren't trying hard enough! If you aren't making mistakes, then you aren't using your Japanese enough. It is almost always the students who make the most mistakes that stay with the class and eventually even get jobs in Japan or with Japanese companies. You don't need to be fluent to earn money or benefit from your Japanese skill. Here are a few examples of students that are definitely going to make it to the fluency level:

PAWEL – When Pawel first came to my class he had just started taking classes in college. I didn't have any clue that he would succeed because he was so shy and his face would turn red when you talked to him. But after a few weeks I saw that he was going to become fluent. He won't admit it, but he is now very good and can say the most complicated sentences. His secret is that whenever he has the chance he tries new Japanese phrases. In class he might be considered annoying with the type of crazy questions he asks. In fact, sometimes I have no clue what he is trying to say. But he never gives up. Even while I was writing this article he was using online chat to ask me questions about something Japanese. I wish all of my students had the perseverance of Pawel.

JOHN – John has been learning Japanese in my live classes for about two years. He is currently taking Level 3 for the second time. The impressive thing about John is that he works two jobs totaling sixteen hours a day! Yet he has only missed two classes in two years. Even the week that he got divorced he made the class! HE WILL BE FLUENT!

MICHELLE – Michelle just completed Level 1 in our live classes for the first time. She has restarted Level 1 four times! Each time she gets better and better. I often joke that she has paid more money to us than any other student, and that without her the company would go out of business. I am sure she will be fluent.

MARK – Mark won a free month of classes at YesJapan over the radio and eventually stayed until Level 4. He always did his homework and was constantly renting Japanese videos at the Japanese video store, cramming Japanese into his head. On a visit to Japan he got a job offer from an English school to help teach English. He has been living in Japan for over a year and a half now. How cool is that!?

MIKE – Mike would go to the shopping mall here in Las Vegas and walk up to any Japanese person he saw and strike up a conversation. He did that on the weekends and even got pen pals out of it. Such guts made him the top student in the class.

There are many more exemplary students, and they all have one thing in common: GUTS.

To wrap up: don't be scared. Get out there and speak Japanese. Learning Japanese is a huge project and shouldn't be taken lightly. Many times you will be wrong, and many times you will be embarrassed, but the more embarrassed you are and the more mistakes you make, the closer you will be to fluency.

Kanji Lesson 7

立男女子生

七 New Kanji あたらしい かんじ

Make sure you learn the correct stroke order. Correct stroke order will mean neater symbols when writing fast. Also take time to learn the new words for each kanji, as this will help you memorize the various readings.

立	くんよみ	た				
	おんよみ	リツ、リュウ				
	た・つ **立つ**	たち・ば **立場**	どく・りつ **独立**	し・りつ **私立**	りっ・しゅう **立秋**	やく・だ・つ **役立つ**
5 strokes	to stand	position	independence	private (i.e. school)	the beginning of autumn	to be of use

男	くんよみ	おとこ				
	おんよみ	ダン、ナン				
	おとこ **男**	だん・せい **男性**	ちょう・なん **長男**	じ・なん **次男**	だん・じょ **男女**	おとこ・の・こ **男の子**
7 strokes	boy, man	male	first born son	second born son	boy and girl	a boy

女	くんよみ	おんな、め				
	おんよみ	ジョ、ニョ、ニョウ				
	おんな **女**	おんな・ごころ **女心**	にょう・ぼう **女房**	じょ・せい **女性**	め・がみ **女神**	ちょう・じょ **長女**
3 strokes	girl, woman	woman's mind	speakers wife	female	goddess	first born daughter

子	くんよみ	こ				
	おんよみ	シ、ス				
	こ **子**	こ・ども **子供**	おや・こ **親子**	よう・し **養子**	こ・いぬ **子犬**	せん・す **扇子**
3 strokes	child	child, children	parent and child	adopted child	puppy	folding Japanese fan

生	くんよみ	い、う、は、き、なま					
	おんよみ	セイ、ショウ					
¹ ³ ²→ ⁴→ ⁵	なま **生**	せい・と **生徒**	せん・せい **先生**	は・える **生える**	い・きる **生きる**	う・まれる **生まれる**
5 strokes	raw	pupil, student	teacher	to grow	to live	to be born

---

七　Fun Kanji たのしい　かんじ

❑ Kanji tongue twister

In the next lesson a tough Japanese tongue twister is introduced. But before that, here is one that you can warm up with. It uses the kanji 生(なま), and it goes like this:

生麦、生米、生卵
なまむぎ、なまごめ、なまたまご

The translation is simple: "Raw wheat, raw rice, raw eggs." I never found this hard to say, but it seems to trouble Japanese people. Try saying it fast five times in a row!

七 Kanji Activities

❑ Stroke order

Trace the light gray symbols for practice. Pay attention to stroke order and stroke type.

立	立	立	立	立	立					
男	男	男	男	男	男					
女	女	女	女	女	女					
子	子	子	子	子	子					
生	生	生	生	生	生					

❑ Words you can write

Write the following words in the boxes. This is a great way to practice the new kanji, review thewords, and learn new words at the same time.

おとこ
男
boy, man

男								

おんな
女
girl, woman

女								

た
立つ
to stand

| 立 | つ | | | | | | | | |

おとこ　ひと
男の人
man

| 男 | の | 人 | | | | | | | |

おんな　こ
女の子
girl

| 女 | の | 子 | | | | | | | |

こ
子ども
child, children

| 子 | ど | も | | | | | | | |

こ
子いぬ
puppy

| 子 | い | ぬ | | | | | | | |

せい
せん生
teacher

| せ | ん | 生 | | | | | | | |

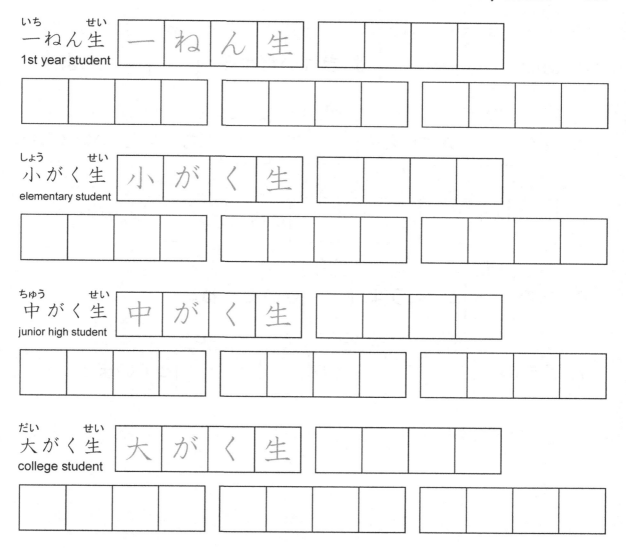

いち　　ねん　せい
一ねん生   一 ねん 生
1st year student

しょう　　　せい
小がく生   小 が く 生
elementary student

ちゅう　　せい
中がく生   中 が く 生
junior high student

だい　　　せい
大がく生   大 が く 生
college student

❑ Fill in the kanji

Fill in the blanks in the following sentences with the appropriate kanji.

　　　　　　ぐち　　　　　　　　　こ　　　　　　　　　ちい
1. やま[　　]さんの　[　　]どもは　[　　]さくて、かわいいです。

　　　　　　　　　　　しょう　　　　　　　ご　　　せい
2. ゆかちゃんは　[　　]がっこう　[　　]ねん[　　]です。

3. あの <ruby>女<rt>おんな</rt></ruby> の <ruby>人<rt>ひと</rt></ruby> は きれいだから、<ruby>目<rt>め</rt></ruby><ruby>立<rt>だ</rt></ruby> ちます。

4. せん <ruby>生<rt>せい</rt></ruby> が つくえの <ruby>上<rt>うえ</rt></ruby> で <ruby>立<rt>た</rt></ruby> たないでと いいました。

5. <ruby>大<rt>だい</rt></ruby> がく <ruby>生<rt>せい</rt></ruby> は <ruby>六<rt>ろく</rt></ruby><ruby>月<rt>がつ</rt></ruby> から なつ <ruby>休<rt>やす</rt></ruby> みです。

6. あの <ruby>中<rt>ちゅう</rt></ruby> がっこうは <ruby>大<rt>おお</rt></ruby> きいですね。

7. えきので <ruby>口<rt>ぐち</rt></ruby> で <ruby>男<rt>おとこ</rt></ruby> の <ruby>人<rt>ひと</rt></ruby> が <ruby>立<rt>た</rt></ruby> っています。

WRITING PRACTICE

Use these sheets as extra writing practice for the kanji you have learned up to this point. Recently you have learned: 耳口手足力、立男女子生

VOCABULARY GROUPS ———————————— set 7

J   more and more body parts

English	Progressive	Kanji +
stomach	い	胃
lungs	はい	肺
muscles	きんにく	筋肉
dimples	えくぼ	笑窪
thumb	おやゆび	親指
index finger	ひとさしゆび	人差し指
middle finger	なかゆび	中指
ring finger	くすりゆび	薬指
pinky (little finger)	こゆび	小指
armpit	わきのした	わきの下
arm	うで	腕
bone	ほね	骨
breasts, chest	むね	胸
front teeth	まえば	前歯
molars	おくば	奥歯
tongue	した	舌
beard	ひげ	髭
pimple	にきび	にきび

Lesson
7
Level ③

Two Chickens
Japanese tongue twister

7 About This Lesson このレッスンについて

Before The Lesson

1. be able to write and read 立男女子生
2. review vocabulary group set 7

Lesson Goals

1. learn four new counters
2. learn how similar sounding words mean totally different things in the tongue twister in this lesson

From The Teachers

1. Memorize the tongue twister in this lesson and the explanation that comes with it. It will help you learn how to explain things in detail.

7 New Words あたらしい ことば

Progressive	Kanji +	English
はや口ことば	早口言葉	tongue twister
にわ	庭	a garden, a yard
うらにわ	裏庭	a back garden, a backyard
にわとり	鶏	a chicken, a hen, a cock
いみ	意味	meaning (of something)
ほとんど	ほとんど	almost all, the majority
かず	数	number
子いぬ	子犬	puppy
子ねこ	子猫	kitten
一ばん	一番	the most, number one

ことば	言葉	speech, language, word, expression
ですから／だから	ですから／だから	therefore, for that reason
あかワイン	赤ワイン	red wine
しろワイン	白ワイン	white wine
ええ	ええ	yes (more formal than はい)

7 New Adjectives あたらしい けいようし

This section lists new adjectives used in the lesson. Remember that な adjectives and い adjectives are used differently.

Adjective	Kanji +	English	Type
ひくい	低い	low, flat	い adjective
みじかい	短い	short in length	い adjective

7 New Verbs あたらしい どうし

Dictionary	Kanji	た-form	English Verb	Verb Type
かう	飼う	かった	to have a pet	regular
みせる	見せる	みせた	to show	いる/える

7 Verb Usage どうしの つかいかた

❑ かう (to have an animal for a pet)

かう conjugates exactly like the verb かう (to buy), which is said in the exact same way, but with a different kanji. The neat thing is that they use the exact same grammar.

> (animal) を かう
> to have (animal) for a pet

Example Sentences

1. いぬを 六ぴき、かっています。
   I am raising six dogs.

2. どんな どうぶつを かっていますか。
   What kind of animals do you have?

3. おばあちゃんは ねこを かってから、げんきに なりました。
   My grandmother got better after she had a cat.

❏ みせる (to show)

The item that is being shown is marked with を. に makes the person to whom it is being shown.

**(item) を みせる
to show (item)**

**(person) に みせる
to show to (person)**

Example Sentences

1. しゃしんを みせて下さい。
   Show me the pictures please.

2. あかいのを みせて下さい。
   Please show me the red one.

3. ともだちに かのじょの しゃしんを みせました。
   I showed a friend my girlfriend's photograph.

7 New Counters あたらしい カウンター

Bird and Rabbit Counter ~わ

1	いちわ	一羽	7	ななわ	七羽
2	にわ	二羽	8	はちわ	八羽
3	さんわ	三羽	9	きゅうわ	九羽
4	よんわ	四羽	10	じゅうわ	十羽
5	ごわ	五羽	11	じゅういちわ	十一羽
6	ろくわ	六羽	12	じゅうにわ	十二羽
How many?			なんわ？		何羽

Position Counter ~ばん

#1	いちばん	一番	#7	ななばん	七番
#2	にばん	二番	#8	はちばん	八番
#3	さんばん	三番	#9	きゅうばん	九番
#4	よんばん	四番	#10	じゅうばん	十番
#5	ごばん	五番	#11	じゅういちばん	十一番
#6	ろくばん	六番	#12	じゅうにばん	十二番
What number?			なんばん？		何番

7 Grammar ぶんぽう

☐ Showing order or rank in numbered items

The ~目(め) counter is not a counter by itself. It must be attached to other counters for it to have meaning. It gives an order to the counter it is attached to (first, second, third, etc.). It can be attached to any Japanese counters.

Examples		
	ひとり目	the **1st** person
	ふたり目	the **2nd** person
	五ひき目	the **5th** small animal
	十一ぴき目	the **11th** small animal
	一ぽん目	**1st** bottle, etc. (long/cylindrical)
	三ぼん目	**3rd** bottle, etc.
	一つ目	**1st** (generic)
	四つ目	**4th**

Example Conversations

1. Polite conversation between friends driving in a car

　　A： あなたの いえは どれですか。
　　B： 三つ目の しろいいえです。

　　A： Which one is your house?
　　B： It's the third white house.

2. Polite conversation between two people at a pet hospital

　　A： いぬを なんびき かっていますか。
　　B： 八ぴきです。わたしは どうぶつが 大すきです。きのう もう一ぴき ねこを かいました。
　　A： ねこは なんびき目ですか。
　　B： 六ぴき目です。

　　A： How many dogs do you have?
　　B： Eight. I really like animals. I bought one more cat yesterday.
　　A： What number cat is it?
　　B： It's the 6th.

---

7 Mini Conversations ミニかいわ J-E

Using a piece of paper cover up the entire English portion of the conversations below. Read the Japanese conversation several times until you understand it. Only then should you move the paper to compare your comprehension to the English translation.

1. Conversation between an English teacher and her student

　　A：このことばの いみが わかりません。
　　B：それは えいごで「happy」ですよ。
　　A：ありがとう。

　　A： I don't understand this word.
　　B： That means "happy" in English.
　　A： Thanks.

2. Conversation between two people in line

　　A： つぎは だれですか。
　　B： わたしです。
　　A： あなたは なんばん目ですか。
　　B： ええっと、四ばん目です。

　　A： Who is next?
　　B： I am.
　　A： What number (in line) are you?
　　B： Umm, I am number four.

3. Informal conversation between a couple
A： あかワインか しろワイン、どっちが おいしいと おもう？
B： ワインを のまないから、わからない。

A： Which do you think tastes good, red wine or white wine?
B： I don't know, because I don't drink wine.

4. Polite conversation between two friends
A： ペットショップで いぬを うっていましたよ。もう、みましたか。
B： ええ、一ばん 小さくて、しろい子いぬを かいました。
A： おとうさんは いいと いいましたか。
B： ええ、かわいいと いってますよ。

A： They are selling dogs at the pet shop. Did you see them already?
B： Yes, I bought the smallest white puppy.
A： Did your dad say it was okay?
B： Yes, he says the dog is cute.

7 Mini Conversations ミニかいわ E-J

Using a piece of paper, cover up the entire Japanese portion of the conversations below. Translate the English conversation to Japanese. Only after you have translated the entire conversation should you move the paper to check your work.

1. Mixed conversation between an American and a Japanese girl
A： Don't you think that the majority of Japanese men have shorter legs than Americans?
B： Yeah and their noses are flat.

A： 日ほんの ほとんどの おとこのひとは アメリカ人より あしが みじかいと おもいませんか。
B： うん、はなも ひくいよ。

2. Informal conversation between two new friends on the phone
A： I really like cats.
B： Really? Well then, since we have 3 cats, why don't you come to our house now?
A： Okay.   I'll go right now.

A： ねこが 大すき。
B： ほんとう？ じゃ、ねこを 三びき かってるから、いまから うちに こない？
A： わかった。いまから いくよ。

3. Polite conversation between two new friends
A: How many siblings do you have?
B: I have five siblings. I am the second (of the siblings)

A: きょうだいは なん人 いますか。
B: 五人 きょうだいです。 ぼくは 二ばん目です。

---

7 Reading Comprehension どっかい

Read the Japanese tongue twister first. Then read the explanation about it below.

Tongue Twister in ひらがな

うらにわ には にわ、にわ には にわ、にわとりが います。

Tongue Twister in かんじ

「裏庭には 二羽、庭には 二羽、鶏 がいます。」

---

7 Reading Comprehension Explanation どっかいの せつめい

Read the sentences below. Use the information to answer the reading comprehension questions later in this lesson.

① これは、日ほんの はや口ことばです。

② 「うらにわ」の いみは いえの うしろの 「にわ」です。

③ このはや口ことばの にわは 二つの いみが あります。

④ 一つ目は いえの まえの 「にわ」です。

⑤ 二つ目は にわとりの かずです。

⑥ むかし、日ほんの ほとんどの いえでは にわとりを かっていました。

⑦ 日ほんの いえの 「にわ」には このとりが いました。

⑧ ですから、このとりの なまえは にわとりに なりました。

7 | Activities

❑ Reading comprehension questions

Answer the following questions about the reading comprehension in this lesson.

1. 「はやくちことば」は えいごで なんですか。

   _____

2. 「うらにわ」の いみは なんですか。

   _____

3. このはやくちことばの 「にわ」は いくつの いみが ありますか。

   _____

4. 一つ目の いみは なんですか。

   _____

5. 二つ目の いみは なんですか。

   _____

6. むかし、日ほんの ほとんどの いえは なにを かっていましたか。

   _____

7. なんで このとりの なまえは 「にわとり」に なりましたか。

   _____

❑ Other tongue twisters

Practice the following Japanese tongue twisters along with the one you have learned in this lesson.

1. なまむぎ なまごめ なまたまご
   (Raw wheat, raw rice, raw eggs)

2. となりの きゃくは よく かきくう きゃくだ。
   (The guest next door eats lots of persimmons.)

3. バス、ガスばくはつ
   (The gas explosion of a bus)

4. たまたま たまごが たまっていたので、たまには たまごを たべようか。
   (Since there are a lot of eggs, shall we eat them for a change?)

❑ Counters

Fill in the blanks with the appropriate counters.

Ex.	ひとつ	ふたつ	(**みっつ**)	よっつ	いつつ

1.	いちわ	にわ	( )	よんわ	ごわ
2.	いちばん	( )	さんばん	よんばん	ごばん
3.	いっぴき	にひき	さんびき	( )	ごひき
4.	ひとり	ふたり	さんにん	( )	ごにん
5.	( )	ふつか	みっか	よっか	いつか
6.	いちじ	にじ	さんじ	( )	ごじ
7.	いちがつ	にがつ	( )	しがつ	ごがつ
8.	( )	にほん	さんぼん	よんほん	ごほん

❑ Short dialogue

Two judges are talking about the dogs that auditioned for an upcoming movie.
Which dog are they going to choose?

しんさいん1： どのいぬが いいと おもいますか。

しんさいん2： そうですね…。わたしは 一ぴき目の いぬが いいと おもいます。

大きさが ちょうど よくて、にんきも ありますから。

しんさいん1： わたしは 三びき目の いぬが スターに なると おもいますよ。

小さくて、かわいいですからね。

しんさいん2： 四ばん目の いぬは どうですか。

しんさいん1： うーん・・・。むかしは にんきが ありましたが、いまの えいがには

ちょっと ふるいですね。

しんさいん2： そうですね。じゃあ、一ばんか 二ばんで きめましょう。

No.1   No.2   No.3   No.4

New Words and Expressions in the dialogue

Progressive	Kanji +	English
ちょうどいい	丁度いい	perfect, just right
にんきがある	人気がある	popular
むかし	昔	a long time ago
きめましょう	決めましょう	let's decide
しんさいいん	審査委員	judge

❑ Short dialogue activities

1. Practice reading the preceding short dialogue in pairs.
2. Look at the birds below. Discuss with your partner which bird should be in your next movie.

No.1

No.2

No.3

No.4

❑ Question and answer

Answer the following questions using the words and patterns in this lesson.

1. ペットを かっていますか。どんな ペットですか。なんびき かっていますか。

   _____

2. 子いぬが ほしいですか。子ねこも ほしいですか。

   _____

3. あかワインか しろワインか、どっちが おいしいと おもいますか。

   _____

4. きょうだいは なん人ですか。あなたは なんばん目ですか。

   _____

5. はやくちことばは むずかしいと おもいますか。

   _____

❏ Translation

Translate the following sentences into Japanese.

1. I am drinking my third beer.

_____

2. I am eating my second hamburger.

_____

3. I am going to buy my third house.

_____

4. I am selling my fourth car.

_____

5. My fifth dog's name is Tarou.

_____

6. Let's eat the second cake!

_____

7. I like the seventh bird from the left.

_____

Kanji Lesson
8

天空気雨山川

八　New Kanji　あたらしい　かんじ

Make sure you learn the correct stroke order. Correct stroke order will mean neater symbols when writing quickly. Also take time to learn the new words for each kanji, as this will help you memorize the various readings.

天	くんよみ	あめ、あま					
	おんよみ	テン					
		<u>てん</u> 天	<u>てん</u>・き 天気	<u>あま</u>・の・がわ 天の川	う・<u>てん</u> 雨天	<u>てん</u>・さい 天才	<u>てん</u>・ごく 天国
4 strokes		heaven	weather	the Milky Way	rainy weather	genius	heaven

空	くんよみ	そら、あ、から、あき					
	おんよみ	クウ					
		<u>そら</u> 空	<u>くう</u>・こう 空港	<u>から</u> 空	<u>あき</u>・や 空家	<u>あ</u>・<u>き</u>・かん 空き缶	あお・<u>ぞら</u> 青空
8 strokes		sky	airport	empty	vacant house	empty can	blue sky

気	くんよみ	none					
	おんよみ	キ、ケ					
		<u>き</u> 気	げん・<u>き</u> 元気	<u>け</u>・はい 気配	<u>き</u>・も・ち 気持ち	くう・<u>き</u> 空気	<u>き</u>・あい 気合
6 strokes		spirit; mood	stamina; vigor; health	indication	feeling, mood	air	fighting spirit

雨	くんよみ	あめ、あま					
	おんよみ	ウ					
		<u>あめ</u> 雨	おお・<u>あめ</u> 大雨	<u>あま</u>・ぐも 雨雲	<u>あま</u>・がえる 雨蛙	<u>う</u>・りょう 雨量	<u>う</u>・てん 雨天
8 strokes		rain	heavy rain	rain clouds	tree frog	amount of rain	rainy weather

	くんよみ	やま					
	おんよみ	サン					
	<u>やま</u> 山	ふ・じ・<u>さん</u> 富士山	<u>さん</u>・みゃく 山脈	<u>さん</u>・そん 山村	<u>やま</u>・のぼ・り 山登り	か・<u>ざん</u> 火山
3 strokes	mountain	Mt. Fuji	mountain range	mountain village	mountain climbing	volcano

	くんよみ	かわ					
	おんよみ	セン					
	<u>かわ</u> 川	か・<u>せん</u> 河川	お・<u>がわ</u> 小川	コロラド・<u>がわ</u> コロラド川	<u>かわ</u>・かみ 川上	<u>かわ</u>・した 川下
3 strokes	river	rivers, river system	brook, stream	Colorado River	upper reaches of a river	downstream

八 Writing Points かくポイント

☐ **The science behind each kanji**

After you get through the basic characters, you will start to see simple kanji being used as parts of other kanji. Look at the various kanji that contain the character for "rain":

あめ	ゆき	かみなり	でん（き）
雨	雪	雷	電
rain	snow	thunder	electricity

八 **Kanji Activities**

❑ **Stroke order**
Trace the light gray symbols for practice. Pay attention to stroke order and stroke type.

天	天	天	天	天	天					
空	空	空	空	空	空					
気	気	気	気	気	気					
雨	雨	雨	雨	雨	雨					
山	山	山	山	山	山					
川	川	川	川	川	川					

❑ **Words you can write**
Write the following words in the boxes. This is a great way to practice the new kanji, review vocabulary and learn new words at the same time.

てんき
天気
weather

天	気								

そら 空 sky	空								

あめ 雨 rain	雨								

やま 山 mountain	山								

かわ 川 river	川								

くうき 空気 air	空	気							

おおあめ 大雨 heavy rain	大	雨							

うてん 雨天 rainy weather	雨	天							

かざん 火山 volcano	火	山							

おがわ 小川 stream, brook	小	川							

てん 天ごく heaven	天	ご	く						

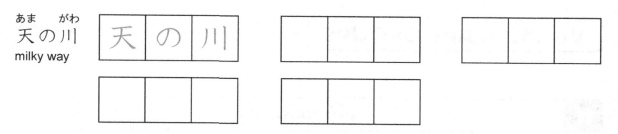

あま　がわ
天 の 川
milky way

❑ Fill in the kanji

Fill in the blanks in the following sentences with the appropriate kanji.

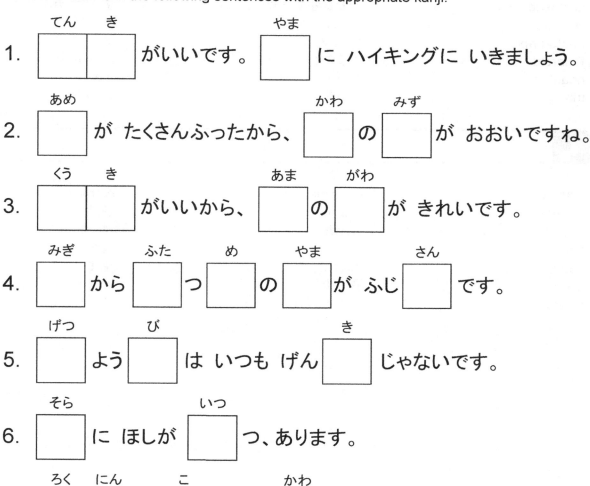

1. てん　き
    □□ がいいです。 やま □ に ハイキングに いきましょう。

2. あめ □ が たくさんふったから、 かわ □ の みず □ が おおいですね。

3. くう　き □□ がいいから、 あま □ の がわ □ が きれいです。

4. みぎ □ から ふた □ つ め □ の やま □ が ふじ さん □ です。

5. げつ □ よう び □ は いつも げん き □ じゃないです。

6. そら □ に ほしが いつ □ つ、あります。

7. ろく　にん □□ の こ □ どもと かわ □ で ピクニックを しました。

VOCABULARY GROUPS ——————————— set 8

K photography

English	Progressive	Kanji +
film	フィルム	フィルム
development	げんぞう	現像
disposable camera	つかいすてカメラ	使い捨てカメラ
film shop	しゃしんや	写真屋
photograph	しゃしん	写真
Polaroid	ポラロイド	ポラロイド
negative	ネガ	ネガ
tripod	さんきゃく	三脚

L bugs

English	Progressive	Kanji +
butterfly	ちょうちょう	喋喋
grasshopper	ばった	ばった
spider	くも	蜘蛛
caterpillar	けむし	毛虫
scorpion	さそり	蠍
ladybug	てんとうむし	てんとう虫

Lesson **8** Level ③

The Music Teacher
starting and beginning

8 | About this Lesson このレッスンについて

Before The Lesson

1. be able to write and read 天空気雨山川
2. know *Additional Vocabulary* word groups K and L (*photography* and *bugs*)

Lesson Goals

1. learn everything is this lesson!

From The Teachers

1. Pay attention to the verbs はじまる and はじめる. Verbs of this pattern are common in Japanese.

8 | New Words あたらしい ことば

Progressive	Kanji +	English
ちち	父	my father
はは	母	my mother
こおり	氷	ice
やっきょく	薬局	pharmacy

8 | New Phrases あたらしい フレーズ

1. いくつ ですか。   A very common way to say, "How old are you?"

This phrase literally means "how many?" but it is much more common than なんさい ですか in everyday conversations.

8   New Verbs あたらしい どうし

Dictionary	Kanji +	た form	English	Type
なる	なる	なった	to become, be	regular
はじまる	始まる	はじまった	to start, to begin	regular
はじめる	始める	はじめた	to originate, start, begin	いる/える
おわる	終わる	おわった	to end, finish	regular

8   Verb Usage どうしの つかいかた

❑ なる (to become, to be)

The particle に is used to mark the thing that the topic is becoming.

> **[*noun*] に なる**
> **to become [*noun*]**

Example Sentences

1. わたしは ことし、二十五さい<u>に</u> なります。   I will be 25 years old this year.

2. もう ふゆ<u>に</u> なりました。   It has already become winter.

3. こおりが 水<u>に</u> なりました。   The ice changed to water.

❑ はじまる (to start, begin)

The thing that is started is marked with the subject particle が, unless using は for stressing purposes.

> **[*something*] が はじまる**
> **[*something*] begins**

Example Sentences

1. あした 八じに がっこう<u>が</u> はじまります。
   School starts at eight o'clock tomorrow.

2. なつ<u>は</u> なん月に はじまりますか。
   What month does summer start?

3. しごとは あさの 六じから はじまります。
   Work starts from six o'clock in the morning.

❑ はじめる (to originate, start, begin)

はじめる is an active verb and はじまる is a passive verb. In other words, はじめる is used when something is actively started by someone. はじまる is used when something starts by itself, without anybody initiating it. With はじめる, the direct object marker を is used to mark the thing being started.

> **[*something*] を はじめる**
> **to start or initiate [*something*]**

Example Sentences

1. せん生は じゅぎょう<u>を</u> 七じに はじめました。
   The teacher started class at seven o'clock.

2. ちちは 二ねんまえに かいしゃを はじめました。
   My father started a company two years ago.

3. パーティーを 八じに はじめましょう。
   Let's start the party at eight o'clock.

❑ おわる (to end, finish)

The subject particle が marks the thing that is ending, unless は is used for emphasis.

> **[*thing*] が おわる**
> **a [*thing*] ends**

Example Sentences

1. がっこうが 十二じに おわりました。
   School ended at twelve o'clock.

2. このクラスは 三月に おわります。
   This class will end in March.

3. しごとが すぐ おわるから、ちょっと まって下さい。
   My work is going to finish soon, so please wait a moment.

8   Grammar ぶんぽう

❑ The difference between はじまる and はじめる

The verb はじまる (to begin, start) and はじめる (to initiate, start, begin) are very similar, but they should not be mixed up. はじまる is used when stating that an event starts or begins passively. はじめる is used when stating that something is originated or was initiated actively. That is, the event is not starting automatically, someone is physically starting the event.

using はじまる

Example Sentences

がっこうが はじまる。	School will start
ハじに はじまる。	It will start at eight o'clock
きのう はじまりました。	It started yesterday
まだ しごとが はじまらない。	My work won't begin yet.
しあいが はじまりません。	The game isn't starting.

using はじめる

Example Sentences

がっこうを はじめる。	(Someone) will start a school
ハじに はじめた。	(Someone) initiated at eight o'clock
きのう はじめました。	(Someone) began yesterday
まだ かいしゃを はじめない。	(Someone) won't start a company yet.

using はじまる and はじめる

Example Q&A

1. もう がっこうが <u>はじまった</u>の？　　　　　　Has school already <u>begun</u>?
   うん、十じから <u>はじまった</u>よ。　　　　　　Yeah, it <u>started</u> from ten.

2. このえいがは なんじに <u>はじまる</u>の？　　　What time will this movie <u>begin</u>?
   三じはんに <u>はじまる</u>。　　　　　　　　　It will <u>begin</u> at three thirty.

3. なんじに しゅくだいを <u>はじめる</u>の？　　　What time will you <u>begin</u> your homework?
   がっこうの あとに <u>はじめる</u>。　　　　　I will <u>start</u> it after school.

4. いつ このかいしゃを <u>はじめた</u>の？　　　When did you <u>start</u> this company?
   こうこうの あと、<u>はじめた</u>。　　　　　I <u>started</u> it after high school.

8 Mini Conversation ミニかいわ J-E

Using a piece of paper to cover up the entire English portion of the conversations below. Read the Japanese conversation several times until you understand it. Only then should you move the paper to compare your translation to the English translation.

1. Polite conversation between two people who just met
   A：どこに すんでいますか。
   B：ニューヨークの きたです。
   A：ニューヨークは きたより みなみの ほうが いいと おもいませんか。
   B：はい おもいます。でも きたの ほうが やすいから すんでいます。

   A：Where do you live?
   B：North of New York.
   A：Don't you think that the south is better that the north?
   B：Yes, I do. But, since the north is cheaper, I live there.

2. Polite conversation between a student and a teacher
   A：せん生、らいしゅうの じゅぎょうで なにを しますか。
   B：テストを します。
   A：ええ！ どんなテストですか。
   B：むずかしいテストです。

   A：Teacher, what are we going to do in next week's class?
   B：We will have (do) a test.
   A：What!? What kind of test is it?
   B：A difficult test.

3. **Conversation between a younger and an older person. Notice that B is polite to A when speaking. We can assume that B is considerably younger than A.**

A： なんさいに なったの？
B： ことし はたちに なりました。
A： まだ こうこう生だと おもったよ。
B： ほんとうですか。

A： How old did have you become?
B： I became (turned) twenty this year.
A： I thought you were still a high school student.
B： Really?

8 Mini Conversation ミニかいわ E-J

Using a piece of paper, cover up the entire Japanese portion of the conversations below. Translate the English conversation to Japanese. Only after you have translated the entire conversation should you move the paper to check your work.

1. Informal conversation between close friends

A： I'll be late. I'll be late. I have no time.
B： Where are you going?
A： My afternoon part time job.
B： About how many minutes will it take from here?
A： 15 minutes by bicycle.

A： おくれる。おくれる。じかんが ないよ。
B： どこに いくの？
A： ごごの アルバイトだよ。
B： ここから なんぷんぐらい かかるの？
A： じてんしゃで 十五ふん。

2. Polite conversation between friends

A： It has already become autumn.
B： The days are still hot. But the nights are cold.
A： Since I like chestnuts, I am going to go to the mountains.
B： That's nice.

A： もう あきに なりましたね。
B： まだ ひるは あついです。でも、よるは さむいです。
A： わたしは くりが 大すきだから、山に いきます。
B： いいですね。

3. Informal conversation between friends

A: What time did the party become?
B: I think it will start around nine. But I don't know yet.
A: It's already late. Around when will you know?
B: I will know after today's afternoon class.

A: パーティーは なんじに なったの？
B: たぶん 九じごろ はじまると おもう。でも まだ わからない。
A: もう おそいね。いつごろ わかるの？
B: きょうの ごごの じゅぎょうの あとで わかるよ。

4. Polite conversation between co-workers who have just met

A: From today I will work here. My best regards.
B: Where did you come from?
A: I came from Kyoto.
B: How old are you?
A: I will be 21 this year.

A: きょうから ここで はたらきます。よろしく おねがいします。
B: どこから きましたか。
A: きょうとから きました。
B: いくつ ですか。
A: ことし 二十一さいに なります。

8 | Reading Comprehension どっかい

Read the sentences below. Use the information to answer the reading comprehension questions later in this lesson.

① さとう あい子さんは 大さかに すんでいます。

② ことし、二十五さいに なりました。

③ あい子さんは おんがくの せん生です。

④ あい子さんの 生とは 十五人です。

⑤ 三さいから 六さいまでの 生とが います。

⑥ がっこうは こうべに あります。

⑦ でんしゃで 二十ぷん ぐらい かかります。

⑧ あさの じゅぎょうは 九じから はじまるから 二じかんまえに おきます。

⑨ じゅぎょうは 十一じに おわります。

⑩ おひるごはんは がっこうの まえの イタリアりょうりの みせで いつも　　　　　たべます。

⑪ この おみせは とても やすいです。

⑫ ごごの じゅぎょうは 一じから はじまります。

⑬ 四じに おわります。

⑭ 一日に 四かい じゅぎょうが あります。

⑮ 五じはんごろ いえに かえります。

⑯ ばんごはんは ほとんど いえで たべます。

⑰ あい子さんの かぞくは おかあさんと おとうさんと いもうとです。

⑱ いもうとは まだ こうこう生です。

⑲ いもうとは 木よう日から 土よう日まで やっきょくで アルバイトを
　　しています。

⑳ おとうさんは サラリーマンです。

㉑ おかあさんも しごとが あります。

㉒ あい子さんは 土よう日と 日よう日に じゅぎょうが ありません。

㉓ 休みの日の あさは 十じまで ねます。

㉔ 日よう日は かぞくの みんなが 休みです。

㉕ 一か月に 一かい、日よう日に いっしょに こうえんで テニスを します。

8 Activities

❑ Reading comprehension questions

Answer the following questions about the reading comprehension in this lesson.

1. さとうあい子さんは どこに すんでいますか。

   _____

2. あい子さんは なんさいですか。

   _____

3. あい子さんの しごとは なんですか。

   _____

4. あい子さんは 生とが なん人いますか。

   _____

5. あい子さんの 生とは なんさいぐらいですか。

   _____

6. あい子さんの がっこうは どこに ありますか。

   _____

7. あさの じゅぎょうは なんじからですか。

   _____

8. おひるごはんは いつも どこで たべますか。

   _____

9. ごごの じゅぎょうは なんじから はじまりますか。

   _____

10. 一日に なんかい じゅぎょうが ありますか。

    _____

11. なんじに いえに かえりますか。

    _____

12. ばんごはんは どこで たべますか。

    _____

13. あい子さんの　かぞくは　なん人ですか。

_____

14. あい子さんの　いもうとさんの　アルバイトは　なんですか。

_____

15. おとうさんの　しごとは　なんですか。

_____

16. あい子さんは　なんよう日に　しごとが　ありませんか。

_____

17. あい子さんの　かぞくは　日よう日に　なにを　しますか。

_____

❑ Substitution drill

Compose sentences according to the example.

> **Ex.** わたしは　ことし、二十八さいに　なります。
>
> → thirty years old　　　わたしは　ことし、<u>三十さい</u>に　なります。
> → last year　　　　　　わたしは　<u>きょねん</u>、三十さいに　なり<u>ました</u>。
> → next year　　　　　　わたしは　<u>らいねん</u>、三十さいに　なり<u>ます</u>。
> → forty years old　　　　わたしは　らいねん、<u>四十さい</u>に　なります。

1. がっこうは　まい日　九じに　はじまります。

→ on Saturdays　　　　　_____

→ this store　　　　　　　_____

→ ten o'clock　　　　　　_____

→ from Monday until Friday_____

2. きょねんから しごとを はじめました。

　→ three years ago　　　_____

　→ seven months ago　　_____

　→ from three o'clock　　_____

　→ started class　　　　_____

3. かいしゃは まい日 五じに おわります。

　→ yesterday　　　　　_____

　→ tomorrow　　　　　_____

　→ I think…　　　　　_____

　→ I heard…　　　　　_____

4. せん月の 八日から コンビニで はたらいています。

　→ since June of last year　_____

　→ at that hotel over there　_____

　→ at this company　　　_____

　→ since the ninth of last month　_____

❑ **Question and answer**

Answer the following questions using the words and patterns in this lesson.

1. いつ にほんごの べんきょうを はじめましたか。

   _____

2. しごと／がっこうは なんじに はじまりますか。

   _____

3. どこで はたらいていますか／どのがっこうに いっていますか。

   _____

4. このべんきょうは なんじに おわると おもいますか。

   _____

5. なん月ごろ、ふゆに なりますか。じゃあ、なん月ごろ、なつに なりますか。

   _____

6. ことし、なんさいに なりますか。

   _____

Kanji Lesson
9

林森石花犬虫町

九 New Kanji あたらしい かんじ

Make sure you learn the correct stroke order. Correct stroke order will mean neater symbols when writing quickly. Take time to learn the new words for each kanji, as this will help you to memorize the different readings.

林	くんよみ	はやし					
	おんよみ	リン					
		<u>はやし</u> **林**	<u>みつ・りん</u> **密林**	<u>さん・りん</u> **山林**	<u>じん・こう・りん</u> **人工林**	<u>りん</u>・ご **林檎**	ばい・<u>りん</u> **梅林**
8 strokes		woods; forest	jungle, thick forest	mountain forest	planted forest (man-made)	apple	plum grove

森	くんよみ	もり			
	おんよみ	シン			
		<u>もり</u> **森**	<u>しん・りん</u> **森林**	あお・<u>もり</u>・けん **青森県**	<u>もり</u>・の・なか **森の中**
12 strokes		forest; woods	forest; woods	Aomori Prefecture	in the forest

石	くんよみ	いし			
	おんよみ	セキ、シャク、コク			
		<u>いし</u> **石**	<u>せき</u>・ざい **石材**	じ・<u>しゃく</u> **磁石**	ほう・<u>せき</u> **宝石**	いっ・<u>せき</u>・に・ちょう **一石二鳥**
5 strokes		stone	stone materials	magnet	jewel stone	two birds with one stone

花	くんよみ	はな				
	おんよみ	カ				
		<u>はな</u> **花**	<u>か</u>・だん **花壇**	くさ・<u>ばな</u> **草花**	<u>はな</u>・び **花火**	ひ・<u>ばな</u> **火花**	い・け・<u>ばな</u> **生け花**
7 strokes		flower	flower bed	flowering plant	fireworks	spark	flower arrangement

犬	くんよみ	いぬ					
	おんよみ	ケン					
		いぬ 犬	けん・し 犬歯	あい・けん 愛犬	の・ら・いぬ 野良犬	いぬ・ご・や 犬小屋	もう・どう・けん 盲導犬
4 strokes		dog	cuspid tooth	pet dog	stray dog	doghouse	seeing-eye dog

虫	くんよみ	むし					
	おんよみ	チュウ					
		むし 虫	むし・ば 虫歯	よう・ちゅう 幼虫	がい・ちゅう 害虫	てん・とう・むし 天道虫	け・むし 毛虫
6 strokes		bug, insect	cavity, bad tooth	larva	harmful bug	ladybug	caterpillar

町	くんよみ	まち				
	おんよみ	チョウ				
		まち 町	まち・はずれ 町外れ	ちょう・かい 町会	した・まち 下町	ちょう・ちょう 町長
7 strokes		town	outskirts of town	town council; town meeting	downtown	head of town

九 Kanji Activities

❑ Stroke order

Trace the light gray symbols for practice. Pay attention to stroke order and stroke type.

花	花	花	花	花	花						
犬	犬	犬	犬	犬	犬						
虫	虫	虫	虫	虫	虫						
町	町	町	町	町	町						

❑ **Words you can write**

Write the following words in the boxes. This is a great way to practice the new kanji, review the vocabulary, and learn new words at the same time.

はやし
林
woods

森
もり
森
forest

いし
石
stone

はな
花
flower

いぬ
犬
dog

犬								

むし
虫
bug, insect

虫								

まち
町
town

町								

さんりん
山林
mountain forest

山	林							

しんりん
森林
woodland

森	林							

はなび
花火
fireworks

花	火							

こいぬ
子犬
puppy

子	犬							

したまち
下町
downtown

下	町							

❏ Fill in the kanji

Fill in the blanks with the appropriate kanji.

1. 　もり　や　はやし　の　なか　は あつくないです。

2. あそこに 　おお　きい 　いし　が 　むっ　つ あります。

3. 　ちい　さい 　むし　が つくえの 　した　に います。

4. 　に　ほんの 　こ　どもは 　はな　び　が 　だい　すきです。

5. この 　まち　に 　に　せん　さん　ねんから すんでいます。

6. 　こ　いぬ　が 　じゅっ　ぴき います。

7. わたしの 　いぬ　は 　め　が あおくて、 　みみ　が グレーです。

VOCABULARY GROUPS ───── set 9

M plants

English	Progressive	Kanji +
potted plants	うえき	植木
bamboo	たけ	竹
palm tree	やしのき	椰子の木
cactus	サボテン	サボテン
tulip	チューリップ	チューリップ
sunflower	ひまわり	向日葵
acorn	どんぐり	団栗
mushroom	きのこ	茸

N shapes

English	Progressive	Kanji +
circle	まる	丸
triangle	さんかく	三角
square	しかく	四角
box	はこ	箱
rectangle	ちょうほうけい	長方形

O clothing

English	Progressive	Kanji +
button	ボタン	ボタン
sandals	サンダル	サンダル
sneakers	スニーカー	スニーカー
high heels	ハイヒール	ハイヒール
one-piece dress	ワンピース	ワンピース
jacket	ジャケット	ジャケット
jeans	ジーパン	ジーパン
shoelace	くつひも	靴紐

Lesson
9
Level ③

My Birthday
wanting to do

9 About this Lesson このレッスンについて

Before The Lesson

1. be able to write and read 林森石花犬虫町
2. review vocabulary group set 9

Lesson Goals

1. learn the "want to" version of verbs

9 New Words あたらしい ことば

Progressive	Kanji +	English
しんゆう	親友	best friend
ざんねん	残念	unfortunate
いつか	いつか	someday
イヤリング	イヤリング	clip-on earrings
ピアス	ピアス	pierced earrings
びょう気	病気	sick
くすり	薬	medicine
中こしゃ	中古車	used car
はやく	早く	quickly, fast, hurry up!
ラップ	ラップ	rap music
いき	息	breath
~い上	以上	over~
~い下	以下	under~
どうして	どうして	why?

9 New Verbs あたらしい どうし

Dictionary	Kanji +	た-form	English Verb	Verb Type
すう	吸う	すった	to smoke, to inhale	regular
すきに なる	すきになる	すきになった	to come to like	regular
きらいに なる	嫌いになる	きらいになった	to come to dislike	regular

9 Verb Usage どうしの つかいかた

❑ すう (to smoke, to inhale)

This verb can also mean "to suck" (as in a vacuum), but it is most commonly understood to mean smoking. The thing being smoked is marked with を.

> **[*something*] を すう**
> **to smoke, inhale [*something*]**

Example Sentences

1. むかしは タバコを すいました。   A long time ago I smoked.

2. タバコを すいますか。   Do you smoke?

3. いきを すいましょう！   Let's inhale!

❑ すきに なる / きらいに なる

This verb is common in Japanese but maybe not in English. It basically means that, although someone might not have liked or disliked something in the past, they have come to like or dislike it. The particle が marks the thing that the person comes to like or dislike.

> **[*something*] が すきに なる**
> **to come to like [*something*]**

> **[*something*] が きらいに なる**
> **to come to dislike [*something*]**

Example Sentences

1. むかしは タバコを すいました。でも、きらいに なりました。
   A long time ago I smoked tobacco. But I don't like it now.

2. なんで、ねこが きらいに なりましたか。
   How come you dislike cats? (What happened to make you come to dislike cats?)

3. ラップが すきに なりました。
   I have come to like rap. (I now like rap.)

   Be careful – when すきになる and きらいになる are in the て-form, then を is used instead of が to mark the item.

4. わたしを きらいに ならないで下さい。
   Don't come to dislike me.

---

9 Culture Clip カルチャー・クリップ

In America, when we say earrings, it can mean clip-on or pierced earrings. In Japan, when they say イヤリング, they mean clip-on earrings. Pierced earrings are referred to as ピアス.

---

9 Grammar ぶんぽう

❑ What is なの?

When you ask something using a noun or a な-adjective informally, you can replace ですか with なの. And with a verb you can replace ですか with a simple の.

> **[*noun* / *な-adjective*] + なの?**
> **Is it [*noun* / *な-adjective*] ?**

> **[*informal verb* / い *adjective*] + の?**
> **Is it [い-*adjective*] / Does it [*verb*]?**

Example Sentences

1. このいろが すきなの？	Do you like this color?
2. きょうは 月よう日なの？	Is today Monday?
3. おすしが きらいなの？	Do you dislike sushi?
4. いま、オーストラリアは あついの？	Is Australia hot now?
5. どうして べんきょうしないの？	How come you don't study?
6. もう うちに かえるの？	You are going home already?

❑ Over and under an amount

This is an easy grammar point using い 上 (~ or above) and い 下 (~ or below.) When you want to say a certain amount and above, or a certain amount and below, い上 or い下 is added after the amount. This works with any kind of quantity.

$$[amount] + \text{い上 or い下}$$

over or under and including   [amount]

Examples	千ドルい上	1000 dollars or greater
	百人い下	100 people or less
	二つい上	two things or more

❑ I want to… The たい verb form

To make the "want to" form of a verb, たい is added to the い form of the verb. For regular verbs the following pattern is used:

Regular Verbs

$$[\text{い-}form\ verb] + \text{たい}$$

I want to [verb]

いる／える Verbs

$$[\text{う-}form\ verb\ minus\ \text{る}] + \text{たい}$$

I want to [verb]

Examples

たべ<u>たい</u>	want to eat
いき<u>たい</u>	want to go
かえり<u>たい</u>	want to return
のみ<u>たい</u>	want to drink
あい<u>たい</u>	want to meet
し<u>たい</u>	want to do
はじめ<u>たい</u>	want to start
なり<u>たい</u>	want to become

Example Sentences

Notice that the particles for the verbs in the たい form do not change in the sentence. However, the object marker を is often replaced with が.

1. パイロットに なりたいです。	I want to be a pilot.
2. ピザ<u>を</u> たべたいです。	I want to eat pizza.
3. 水<u>が</u> のみたいです。	I want to drink water.
4. つめたいビール<u>を</u> のみたいです。	I want to drink a cold beer.
5. ヨーロッパに いきたいです。	I want to go to Europe.

❑ Wanted to…, don't want to…, didn't want to…

The たい form is conjugated into other tenses just like い-adjectives are. Here are all of the たい forms:

present/future positive **want to ~**	たい
present/future negative **don't want to ~**	たくない
past positive **wanted to ~**	たかった
past negative **didn't want to ~**	たくなかった

present/future negative **don't want to ~**

Examples

たべたくない	don't want to eat
いきたくない	don't want to go
かえりたくない	don't want to return
のみたくない	don't want to drink
あいたくない	don't want to meet
したくない	don't want to do
はじめたくない	don't want to start
なりたくない	don't want to become
はたらきたくない	don't want to work

past positive **wanted to ~**

Examples

たべたかった	wanted to eat
いきたかった	wanted to go
かえりたかった	wanted to return
のみたかった	wanted to drink
あいたかった	wanted to meet
したかった	wanted to do
はじめたかった	wanted to start
なりたかった	wanted to become

past negative **didn't want to ~**

Examples

たべたくなかった	didn't want to eat
いきたくなかった	didn't want to go
かえりたくなかった	didn't want to return
のみたくなかった	didn't want to drink
あいたくなかった	didn't want to meet
したくなかった	didn't want to do
はじめたくなかった	didn't want to start
なりたくなかった	didn't want to become

❏ **The formality of the たい verb forms**

The たい forms by themselves are informal. To make them polite, です is added after the verb.

┌─────────────────── **polite forms of たい** ───────────────────┐

Example Sentences

イタリアりょうりが たべたい<u>です</u>。   I want to eat Italian food.
ホットドッグが たべたかった<u>です</u>。   I wanted to eat hotdogs.
いまは あんまり たべたくない<u>です</u>。   I don't want to eat much now.
なにも たべたくなかった<u>です</u>。   I didn't want to eat anything.

└──┘

9 **Mini Conversation ミニかいわ J-E**

Using a piece of paper, cover up the entire English portion of the conversations below. Read the Japanese conversation several times until you understand it. Only then should you move the paper to compare your translation to the English translation.

1. Polite conversation between friends
A: いっしょに いたいけど、あした アメリカに かえります。
B: なんで かえりますか。
A: かえりたくないけど、おかあさんが びょう気だからです。
B: いつか わたしも アメリカに いきたいです。

A: I want to be with you, but tomorrow I am returning to America.
B: Why are you going back?
A: I do not want to go back, but my mother is sick.
B: Someday, I also want to go to America.

2. Informal conversation between friends
A: あたらしいくるまを かいたいけど、お金が ないよ。
B: いくらなの？
A: ぜんぶ たかい。一まん五千ドルい上だよ。
B: なんで やすくて、いい中こしゃを かわないの？
A: 中こしゃは あんまり いいと おもわない。かいたくないよ。

A: I want to buy a new car, but I don't have any money.
B: How much is it?
A: They are all expensive. They are over $15,000.
B: Why don't you buy a cheap and nice used car?
A: I don't think used cars are good. I don't want to buy one.

3. Polite conversation at a Japanese Inn

A: あした あさごはんに なにが たべたいですか。
B: たまごが たべたいです。あと ハムも おねがいします。
A: わかりました。六じに おきて下さい。

A: What do you want to eat for breakfast tomorrow morning?
B: I want to eat eggs. And also ham, please.
A: Okay. Please wake up at six.

9 Mini Conversation ミニかいわ E-J

Using a piece of paper, cover up the entire Japanese portion of the conversations below. Translate the English conversation to Japanese. Only after you have translated the entire conversation should you move the paper to check your work.

1. Informal conversation between a boyfriend and a girlfriend

A: I want to take a trip with you someday.
B: Sure. Where do you want to go?
A: I want to go to Europe the most.
B: Europe is far! I don't want to go. Where is the second place (you want to go)?
A: I want to go to Canada.
B: I also wanted to go to Canada since a long time ago.

A: いつか いっしょに りょこうしたいね。
B: そうね。どこに いきたいの？
A: ヨーロッパに 一ばん いきたい。
B: ヨーロッパは とおいよ。 いきたくないよ。二ばん目は どこ？
A: カナダに いきたい。
B: ぼくも むかしから カナダに いきたかった。

2. Informal conversation between friends

A: Your face sure is red.
B: I know. I took some medicine, but it didn't work.
A: Are you working tomorrow?
B: Yes, but I don't want to go.

A: かおが あかいね。
B: そう．．．。くすりを のんだけど、だめ。
A: あしたは、しごと？
B: うん、でも、いきたくないよ。

3. Conversation between a mother and a child

A: Did you take some medicine?
B: Not yet.
A: Take it right away, please.
B: I don't want to take it because it is bitter.

A: くすりを のんだの？
B: まだ。
A: はやく のんでよ。
B: にがいから のみたくないよ。

4. Informal conversation between friends

A: どこに いきたいの？
B: にしこうえんに いきたい。
A: にしこうえんは もう ないよ。
B: ええ、うそ。ざんねんだね。

A: Where do you want to go?
B: I want to go to East park.
A: There is no more East park.
B: Oh, man. That sure is unfortunate.

5. Conversation between co-workers.
A's status is higher in the company, so A is informal and B is polite.

A: きのう なぜ 二じの パーティーに こなかったの？
B: いきたかったけど、しごとが 五じまで ありました。
A: ざんねんだったね。 とても たのしかったよ。

A: How come you didn't come to the two o'clock party yesterday?
B: I wanted to go, but I had work until five o'clock.
A: That's unfortunate. It was really fun.

9 │ Reading Comprehension どっかい

Read the sentences below. Use the information to answer the reading comprehension questions later in this lesson.

① あしたは わたしの たんじょう日です。

② 二十一さいに なります。

③ たんじょう日パーティーは おばあさんの いえで 二じから はじまります。

④ たぶん、三十人ぐらい くると おもいます。

⑤ わたしの しんゆうの たか子さんは しごとが 五じに おわるから、パーティーに こないと いいました。

⑥ ざんねんです。

⑦ パーティーの あと、トム・クルーズの あたらしい えいがが みたいです。

⑧ わたしは トム・クルーズの 大ファンです。

⑨ パーティーの あと

⑩ パーティーは とても たのしかったです。

⑪ たか子さんは こなかったけど、あしたの 四じに かのじょと かいものを します。

⑫ たか子さんは けしょうひんが かいたいと いいました。

⑬ わたしは なにも かいたくないです。

⑭ でも、たか子さんに たんじょう日の プレゼントを みせたいです。

9 | Activities

❑ Reading comprehension questions

Answer the following questions about the reading comprehension in this lesson.

1. <u>わしゃ</u>の たんじょう日は いつですか。

_____

2. <u>わしゃ</u>は あした なんさいに なりますか。

_____

3. たんじょう日パーティーは どこで しますか。

_____

4. たんじょう日パーティーは なんじから はじまりますか。

_____

5. <u>わしゃ</u>の しんゆうの なまえは なんですか。

_____

6. たか子さんは あした パーティーに きますか。

_____

7. なんで ですか。

_____

8. <u>わしゃ</u>は パーティーのあと、なにが したいですか。

_____

9. <u>わしゃ</u>は パーティーの つぎの 日に だれと いっしょに かいものを しますか。

_____

10. たかこさんは なにが ほしいですか。

_____

11. <u>わしゃ</u>は なにが かいたいですか。

_____

❑ Verb conjugation review

Fill in the blanks on the chart with the correct verb conjugations.

	English	Dictionary Form	ない-form	たい-form
1	to do your best	がんばる	がんばらない	がんばりたい
2	to work			
3	to shop			
4	to pay			
5	to answer			
6	to meet			
7	to play; hang out			
8	to live			
9	to show			
10	to smoke			
11	to raise an animal			
12	to begin (active)			

❑ **Substitution drill**
Compose sentences according to the example.

> **Ex.** きょう、しごとを　したくないです。
>
> → don't want to study   きょう、べんきょうしたくないです。
> → yesterday   きのう、べんきょうしたくなかったです。
> → didn't want to eat   きのう、たべたくなかったです。
> → today   きょう、たべたくないです。

1. タバコが　きらいに　なりました。

→ come to like   _____

→ Japanese homework   _____

→ Japanese food   _____

→ dislike   _____

2. このコンピューターは　ニ千ドル　い上です。

→ $1,500 or less   _____

→ $10,000 or more   _____

→ $30,000 or less   _____

→ $3,000 or more   _____

3. そのシャツが　きらいなの

→ Do you disike rap music?   _____

→ Do you like that store?   _____

→ Is Saturday tomorrow?   _____

→ Is today the fifth?   _____

4. 水が のみたいです。

→ eat an apple   _____

→ buy pierced earrings _____

→ study Spanish   _____

→ become a teacher   _____

→ go to the concert   _____

❑ Translation

Translate the following sentences with the correct -たい verb form.

1. I want to work at this company.

    _____

2. I wanted to eat sukiyaki in Japan.

    _____

3. I don't want to hear rap music.

    _____

4. I didn't want to take (drink) medicine yesterday.

    _____

5. I want to watch a movie this Saturday.

    _____

6. I wanted to work part-time at a Japanese restaurant.

    _____

7. I didn't want to have (buy) a dog.

    _____

❑ **Short dialogue**

Mr. Tanaka and Mr. Yamada are talking about smoking.

たなかさん：　やまださん、また たばこを すっていますね。

やまださん：　はい。さいきん、くせに なっています。

たなかさん：　それは きょう、なんぼん目ですか。

やまださん：　たぶん、十五ほん目です。わたしは いつも 二十ぽんいじょう、すいますよ。

たなかさん：　そうですか。わたしは ぜんぜん、すいません。

やまださん：　どうしてですか。

たなかさん：　がんに なると きいたから、たばこが きらいに なりました。

やまださん：　そうですか…。じゃあ、十ぽん いかなら、大じょうぶだとおもいますか。

たなかさん：　だめですよ！ たばこは やめましょう！

New Words and Expressions in the dialogue

Progressive	Kanji +	English
さいきん	最近	recently
くせ	癖	habit
がん	癌	cancer
なら	なら	if…
やめる	止める	to quit

❑ Question and answer

Answer the following questions using the words and patterns in this lesson.

1. こんしゅうの 日よう日に なにが したいですか。

   _____

2. こんや、日ほんごを べんきょうしたいですか。

   _____

3. ばんごはんは なにが たべたいですか。

   _____

4. 日ほんで なにが したいですか。

   _____

5. たばこを よく すいますか。 なんぼんい上、すいますか。

   _____

6. どんなえいがが すきに なりましたか。

   _____

7. 一日に なんじかんいじょう、日ほんごを べんきょうしますか。

   _____

Kanji Lesson 10

村田夕赤青白見

✚ New Kanji あたらしい かんじ

Make sure you learn the correct stroke order. Correct stroke order will mean neater symbols when writing quickly. Also, take time to learn the new words for each kanji, as this will help you to memorize the different readings.

村 7 strokes	くんよみ	むら				
	おんよみ	ソン				
	<u>むら</u> 村	<u>そん</u>・ちょう 村長	のう・<u>そん</u> 農村	ぎょ・<u>そん</u> 漁村	<u>むら</u>・びと 村人	さん・<u>そん</u> 山村
	village	village chief	farming village	fishing village	villager	mountain village

田 5 strokes	くんよみ	た			
	おんよみ	デン			
	<u>た</u>・んぼ 田んぼ	ゆ・<u>でん</u> 油田	<u>でん</u>・ち 田地	あき・<u>た</u>・けん 秋田県	すい・<u>でん</u> 水田
	rice paddy, field	oil field	farmland	Akita Prefecture	rice paddy filled with water

夕 3 strokes	くんよみ	ゆう			
	おんよみ	セキ			
	<u>ゆう</u>・がた 夕方	<u>ゆう</u>・べ 夕べ	<u>ゆう</u>・ひ 夕日	いっ・ちょう・いっ・<u>せき</u> 一朝一夕	<u>ゆう</u>・しょく 夕食
	evening	last night	setting sun	in a brief space of time, in a day	dinner

赤 7 strokes	くんよみ	あか			
	おんよみ	セキ、シャク			
	<u>あか</u> 赤	<u>あか</u>・ちゃん 赤ちゃん	<u>せき</u>・じゅう・じ 赤十字	<u>せき</u>・どう 赤道	<u>あか</u>・じ 赤字	<u>あか</u>・しお 赤潮
	red	baby	the Red Cross	the equator	in the red, in debt	red tide

青 1 2 3 4 5 6 7 8	くんよみ	あお				
	おんよみ	セイ、ショウ				
	<u>あお</u> **青**	<u>せい</u>・ねん **青年**	<u>あお</u>・ば **青葉**	<u>あお</u>・しん・ごう **青信号**	<u>あお</u>・ぞら **青空**	<u>せい</u>・しゅん **青春**
8 strokes	blue	young man	green leaves	green light	blue sky	youth, adolescent

白 1 2 3 4 5	くんよみ	しろ				
	おんよみ	ハク、ビャク				
	<u>はく</u>・じん **白人**	<u>しろ</u> **白**	<u>しら</u>・<u>じら</u>・しい **白々しい**	こく・<u>はく</u> **告白**	おも・<u>しろ</u>・い **面白い**	ひょう・<u>はく</u>・ざい **漂白剤**
5 strokes	caucasian	white	feigned, plastic	confession	interesting	bleach, bleaching agent

見 1 2 3 4 5 6 7	くんよみ	み				
	おんよみ	ケン				
	<u>み</u>・る **見る**	<u>み</u>・せる **見せる**	い・<u>けん</u> **意見**	がい・<u>けん</u> **外見**	<u>けん</u>・がく **見学**	<u>み</u>・ほん **見本**
7 strokes	to look	to show	opinion	outward appearance	study by observation	sample

✛ Kanji Activities

❑ Stroke order

Trace the light gray symbols for practice. Pay attention to stroke order and stroke type.

村	村	村	村	村	村				
田	田	田	田	田	田				
夕	夕	夕	夕	夕	夕				
赤	赤	赤	赤	赤	赤				
青	青	青	青	青	青				
白	白	白	白	白	白				
見	見	見	見	見	見				

❏ Words you can write

Write the following words in the boxes. This is a great way to practice the new kanji, review the words, and learn new words at the same time.

むら
村
village

| 村 | | | | | | | |

あか
赤
red

| 赤 | | | | | | | |

あお
青
blue

| 青 | | | | | | | |

しろ
白
white

| 白 | | | | | | | |

さんそん
山村
mountain village

| 山 | 村 | | | | | | | | |

すいでん
水田
flooded paddy

| 水 | 田 | | | | | | | | |

ゆう
夕べ
evening

| 夕 | べ | | | | | | | | |

ゆうひ
夕日
setting sun

| 夕 | 日 | | | | | | | | |

はくじん
白人
caucasion

| 白 | 人 | | | | | | | | |

み
見る
to see

見 | る | | | | | | |

た
田んぼ
rice paddy

田 | ん | ぼ

み
見せる
to show

見 | せ | る

❑ Fill in the kanji

Fill in the blanks in the following sentences with the appropriate kanji.

1. その 〔むら〕 に 〔ひと〕 が 〔よん〕〔ひゃく〕〔にん〕 います。

2. 〔に〕 ほんには 〔すい〕〔でん〕 が たくさん あります。

3. 〔やま〕 の 〔うえ〕 の 〔あか〕 い 〔ゆう〕〔ひ〕 が きれいですね。

4. 〔あお〕 い 〔そら〕 に 〔しろ〕 いくもが 〔なな〕 つ あります。

5. あの 〔はく〕〔じん〕 の 〔おんな〕 の 〔こ〕 は だれですか。

6. 〔ど〕 よう 〔び〕 は 〔やす〕 みです。えいがが 〔み〕 たいです。

7. 〔た〕 んぼのよこに 〔しろ〕 と 〔あか〕 の 〔はな〕 が あります。

WRITING PRACTICE

Use these sheets as extra writing practice for the kanji you have learned up to this point.
Recently you have learned: 林森石花犬虫町、村田夕赤青白見

VOCABULARY GROUPS ─── set 10

P · in the tool shed

English	Progressive	Kanji +
paint	ペンキ	ペンキ
nail	くぎ	釘
screw	ねじ	ねじ
saw	のこぎり	鋸
hammer	ハンマー	ハンマー
screwdriver	ドライバー	ドライバー
flathead screwdriver	マイナス ドライバー	マイナス ドライバー
Phillips screwdriver	プラス ドライバー	プラス ドライバー
bucket	バケツ	バケツ
car battery	バッテリー	バッテリー
battery	でんち	電池
flashlight	かいちゅうでんとう	懐中電灯
ladder	はしご	はしご

Q · in the classroom

English	Progressive	Kanji +
vocabulary, words	たんご	単語
noun	めいし	名詞
adjective	けいようし	形容詞
verb	どうし	動詞
grammar	ぶんぽう	文法
test	テスト / しけん	テスト / 試験

Lesson
10
Level ③

Yumiko's Cavity

using とき

10 ## About This Lesson このレッスンについて

Before The Lesson

1. be able to write and read 村田夕赤青白見
2. review vocabulary group set 10

Lesson Goals

1. learn to use とき when saying phrases such as "when I …"

10 ## New Words あたらしいことば

Japanese	Kanji +	English
虫ば	虫歯	cavity
たくさん	沢山	a lot, many
はいしゃ（さん）	歯医者	dentist
パイロット	—	pilot
はじめて	初めて	first time
大じょうぶ	大丈夫	all right, safe
そのとき	その時	that time
すぐ	すぐ	right away, immediately
ポップコーン	—	popcorn
けさ	今朝	this morning
だけ	—	only
しんしゃ	新車	a new car
女の子	女の子	a girl (usually a little girl)

10 ## New Adjectives あたらしいけいようし

Adjective	Kanji +	English	Type
わかい	若い	young	い-adjective

10 Word Usage ことばの つかいかた

❏ たくさん (a lot, many)

たくさん can be used with a verb to say something like たくさん たべました (I ate a lot) or たくさん CD が かいたいです (I want to buy a lot of CDs). It is usually placed directly in front of the verb and it can be used with any verb tense.

Example Sentences
1. けさ テレビを たくさん みました。
   I watched a lot of TV this morning.

2. 日ほんで おすしが たくさん たべたいです。
   In Japan I want to eat a lot of sushi.

3. メアリーさんは けしょうひんを たくさん かいました。
   Mary bought a lot of make-up.

たくさん can also be made into an adjective by adding の.

Examples
たくさんの いぬ	many dogs
たくさんの くるま	many cars
たくさんの さかな	many fish
たくさんの 生と	many students

❏ はじめて (the first time)

はじめて can be placed directly in front of a verb to say things like はじめて たべました (It is the first time that I ate it). It can be placed almost anywhere in a statement to say that it is the first time that something is done. It can also be used alone to say はじめてです (It's the first time). はじめて can also be made into an adjective by adding の to it.

Example Sentences
1. きょねんの なつに はじめて 日ほんに いきました。
   I went to Japan for the first time last summer.

2. あさって はじめての しんしゃを かいます。
   I will buy my first new car the day after tomorrow.

3. わたしの 八さいの むす子が きのう はじめて 女の子に でんわを しました。
   My 8-year-old son called a girl for the first time yesterday.

❏ だけ (only)

だけ is used just like the English "only" except that it is placed after the word.

Examples

一つ <u>だけ</u>	only one	中ごく <u>だけ</u>	only China
わたし <u>だけ</u>	only me	きょう <u>だけ</u>	only today

Example Sentences

1. きょうは おちゃだけ のみます。
   I am only going to drink tea today.

2. わたしの やすみは にちようびだけです。
   My only day off is Sunday.

3. いっかげつに いっかいだけ、テニスを します。
   I only play tennis once a month.

---

10   Grammar ぶんぽう

❏ Using とき to say "when"

とき can be used in several ways to describe a situation. It can come after verbs and adjectives, and can be linked to other words using the の particle. When used with verbs, the verb tense doesn't matter, but the verb must be in the dictionary form. If you are talking about a specific time, then the time marker に is used after とき.

---

informal verb form + とき

when [*subject*] + verb

とき with verbs

Examples	わたしが いく<u>とき</u>	when I go
	わたしが たべる<u>とき</u>	when I eat
	あなたが のまない<u>とき</u>	when you don't drink
	あなたが こない<u>とき</u>	when you don't come
	田中さんを みた<u>とき</u>	when I saw Tanaka
	手がみが きた<u>とき</u>	when the letter came

Example Sentences

1. 日ほんに いった<u>とき</u>、なんさいでしたか。
   How old were you when you went to Japan?

2. わたしは かいものを する<u>とき</u>、いつも ともだちと いっしょです。
   When I shop, I am always with friends.

3. あなたが いえに いない<u>とき</u>、 わたしは さびしいです。
   When you are not at home, I am sad.

When saying sentences like, "When my father returns home, we will eat," the Japanese sentence must be おとうさんが かえったとき、たべます. Notice that the verb "to return" is in the past tense. The reason for this is you can only eat after your father has returned home. If the sentence was おとうさんが かえるとき、たべます, then it would mean, "At the point when my father leaves to come home, we will eat". Look at the next set of sentences. One of them will use the present tense form and one will not.

Example Sentences
1. <u>きた</u>とき、 いいます。
   I will tell you when you <u>come</u>.

2. えいがを <u>見る</u>とき、ポップコーンを たべます。
   We will eat popcorn when we <u>watch</u> the movie.

3. うちに <u>かえった</u>とき、でんわを しますね。
   I will call you when I <u>have returned</u> home.

❑ Using とき with nouns and い adjectives

You can also use とき to say a phrase like, "When I was a child," こどものとき. Notice that there are no verbs in this phrase. It can also be used with な and い adjectives.

[*noun*] + の + とき

when something/someone is [*noun*]

[い adjective] + とき

when something/someone is [い-adjective]

とき with nouns and い adjectives

Examples

十六さいの とき   when I was sixteen years old
こうこう生の とき   when I was in high school
びょう気の とき   when I am sick

わたしが 小さかったとき   when I was small
あつい<u>とき</u>   when it is hot
おとうとが うるさい<u>とき</u>   when my little brother is loud

Example Sentences

1. そとが あつい<u>とき</u>、うちに いたいです。
   I want to stay home when it is hot outside.

2. いそがしくない<u>とき</u>、あいましょう。
   Let's meet <u>when</u> we are not busy.

3. あたまが いたい<u>とき</u>、なにも したくないです。
   I don't want to do anything <u>when</u> I have a headache.

❏ Using とき with な adjectives

When you use とき with な adjectives you must have the な before the とき.

な adjective + な とき
when something / someone is [な *adjective*]

とき with な adjectives

Examples

そとが しずかなとき
when it is quiet outside

いえが きれいなとき
when the house is clean

10 Mini Conversations ミニかいわ J-E

Using a piece of paper, cover up the entire English portion of the conversations below. Read the Japanese conversation several times until you understand it. Only then should you move the paper to compare your translation to the English translation.

1. Polite conversation between two friends at work
A： けさ、なにも たべませんでした。
B： なんで ですか。
A： あさ、まだ ねむいとき、なにも たべたくないからです。
B： わたしは まいあさ あさごはんを たべますよ。

A： I didn't eat anything this morning.
B： Why?
A： In the morning, when I am still sleepy, I don't want to eat anything.
B： I eat breakfast every morning.

2. Polite conversation between two friends
A： いつから 日ほんごの べんきょうを していますか。
B： こうこうの ときからです。
A： なんねんに なりますか。
B： 三ねんに なります。

A： Since when have you been studying Japanese?
B： From when I was in high school.
A： How many years has it been?
B： It has been three years.

3. Polite conversation between two business people
A： かいしゃを はじめたとき、スタッフが 二人だけでした。
B： いまは なん人 いますか。
A： 三十一人に なりました。
B： すごいですね。

A： When I started the company, there were only two staff members.
B： How many are there now?
A： There are now 31.
B： That's amazing.

4. Polite conversation between two friends

A： 小さいとき、なにに なりたかったですか。
B： パイロットに なりたかったです。あなたは？
A： わたしは ほんやさんに なりたかったです。

A： What did you want to be when you were little?
B： I wanted to be a pilot. What about you?
A： I wanted to be a bookshop keeper.

10 Mini Conversations ミニかいわ E-J

Using a piece of paper, cover up the entire Japanese portion of the conversations below. Translate the English conversation to Japanese. Only after you have translated the entire conversation should you move the paper to check your work.

1. Casual conversation between a boy and a girl

A： When are you going to America?
B： I am leaving next month on the 21st.
A： I will go to the airport with you when you go.
B： Really? Good (I am happy).
A： Are you going by taxi?
B： No, I am going by bus.
A： Okay.

A： いつ アメリカに いくの？
B： らい月の 二十一日に いく。
A： くうこうに いくとき、いっしょに いくよ。
B： ほんとう？ うれしいな。
A： タクシーで いくの？
B： ううん。バスで。
A： わかった。

2. Polite conversation between friends

A： Do you like your little brother?
B： I don't like him when he is bothersome, but I like him when he is not bothersome.
A： I see.
B： But I like him the most when he is not here.

A： おとうとが すきですか。
B： うるさいときは きらいです。でも、うるさくないときは すきです。
A： そうですか。
B： でも、いないときが 一ばん すきです。

3. Polite conversation between friends
A： When I want to see a movie, I never have any money.
B： What do you do then?
A： I watch TV.

A： いつも えいがを みたいとき、お金が ありません。
B： そのとき、なにを しますか。
A： テレビを みます。

4. Polite conversation between friends
A： How old were you when you came to Canada?
B： I think I was seven years old.
A： That sure is young.

A： カナダに きたとき、なんさいでしたか。
B： 七さいだったと おもいます。
A： わかいですね。

10 Reading Comprehension どっかい

Read the sentences below. Use the information to answer the reading comprehension questions later in this lesson.

① ゆみ子さんは 小さいとき、虫ばが たくさん ありました。
② はいしゃが 大きらいだったから、あんまり はいしゃに いきませんでした。
③ 小がっこう 五ねんせいのとき、はじめて となりの 町の はいしゃさんに いきました。
④ そこに とても やさしい アシスタントの おねえさんが いました。
⑤ そのおねえさんは いつも 「大じょうぶよ」と いいました。
⑥ ゆみ子さんは そのときから はいしゃが すこし すきに なりました。
⑦ いま ゆみ子さんは はいしゃさんで はたらいています。

10 Activities

☐ Reading comprehension questions
Answer the following questions about the reading comprehension in this lesson.

1. ゆみ子さんは 小さいとき 虫ばが ありましたか。

   _____

2. ゆみ子さんは はいしゃが すきでしたか。

   _____

3. ゆみ子さんは いつ はじめて はいしゃさんに いきましたか。

   _____

4. どこの はいしゃさんに いきましたか。

   _____

5. そこに どんな アシスタントが いましたか。

   _____

6. そのアシスタントは いつも ゆみ子さんに なんと いいましたか。

   _____

7. ゆみ子さんは なんで はいしゃが すきに なりましたか。

   _____

8. ゆみ子さんは いま、どこで はたらいていますか。

   _____

☐ Substitution drill
Compose sentences according to the example.

Ex. けさ、テレビを たくさん 見ました。

→ a little	けさ、テレビを <u>すこし</u> 見ました。
→ only five minutes	けさ、テレビを <u>五ふんだけ</u> 見ました。
→ only ten minutes	けさ、テレビを <u>十ぷんだけ</u> 見ました。
→ didn't	けさ、テレビを <u>見ませんでした</u>。

1. 虫ばが 一ぽんだけ あります。

   → only two dogs   _____

   → only three girls   _____

   → only $10.00 in cash   _____

   → lots of cash   _____

2. きょねん、二かい 日ほんに いきました。

   → four times   _____

   → for the first time   _____

   → bought a new car   _____

   → skied   _____

3. はたちに なったとき、パーティーを しました。

   → when I was in Japan   _____

   → when my child turned one year old   _____

   → when my best friend came back from Japan   _____

   → when I went to Las Vegas   _____

4. さびしいとき、でんわしてください。

   → when you have time   _____

   → when you are not busy   _____

   → when you are bored   _____

   → when you are not having fun   _____

❏ Translation

Circle the correct verb form before とき and translate the sentences into English.

Ex. 日ほんに いく／いった とき、おすしを たくさん たべたいです。
    When I go to Japan, I want to eat a lot of sushi.

1. しゅくだいを する／した とき、このかんじが わかりませんでした。

   _____

2. おとうさんが かえる／かえった とき、いっしょに ごはんを たべましょう。

   _____

3. かんじの れんしゅうを する／した とき、いつも ねむいです。

   _____

4. ギャンブルを する／した とき、お金が たくさん ほしいです。

   _____

❏ Question and answer

Answer the following questions using the words and patterns in this lesson.

1. おなかが いたいとき、どうしますか。

   _____

2. さびしいとき、なにを しますか。

   _____

3. しごと／がっこうが いそがしいとき、日ほんごを べんきょうしますか。

   _____

4. しゅくだいが ないとき、うれしいですか。

   _____

5. どんな テレビばんぐみ (program)を 見ているとき、たのしいですか。

   _____

6. えいがを 見るとき、ポップコーンを たべますか。

   _____

7. べんきょうするとき、おんがくを ききますか。

_____

8. 小さいとき、なにに なりたかったですか。

_____

9. 小さいとき、どんなスポーツを しましたか。

_____

❑ **Useful expressions**

Fill in the blanks and complete the sentences below.

1. よる、ねるとき、「   」と いいます。

2. あさ、人にあったとき、「   」と いいます。

3. ひる、人にあったとき、「   」と いいます。

4. よる、人にあったとき、「   」と いいます。

5. ごはんを たべるとき、「   」と いいます。

6. ごはんが おわったとき、「   」と いいます。

7. うちに かえったとき、「   」と いいます。

8. わたしが うちを でるとき、「   」と いいます。
         (to leave)

9. かぞくが うちに かえったとき 「   」と いいます。

Kanji Lesson 11

出入先早本文

11 New Kanji あたらしい かんじ

Make sure you learn the correct stroke order. Correct stroke order will mean neater symbols when writing fast. Also, take time to learn the new words for each kanji, as this will help you memorize the various readings.

出	くんよみ	で(る)、だ(す)					
	おんよみ	シュツ、スイ					
	で・る	だ・す	しゅっ・ぱつ	で・ぐち	いえ・で	すい・とう	
	出る	出す	出発	出口	家出	出納	
5 strokes	to come out, to leave	to put out, to send	departure	exit	leaving home, running away	receipts; expenditures	

入	くんよみ	い(る)、はい(る)					
	おんよみ	ニュウ					
	はい・る	い・れる	い・り・ぐち	にゅう・いん	い・れ・もの	にゅう・がく	
	入る	入れる	入り口	入院	入れ物	入学	
2 strokes	to enter; to join	to put in	entrance	hospitalization	container	entry into school	

先	くんよみ	さき				
	おんよみ	セン				
	さき	ゆび・さき	さき・ばらい	せん・せい	せん・げつ	
	先	指先	先払い	先生	先月	
6 strokes	tip; future; first priority	finger tip	advance payment	teacher	last month	

早	くんよみ	はや					
	おんよみ	ソウ、サッ					
	はや・い	はや・おくり	はや・くち	さっ・そく	そう・き	はや・おき	
	早い	早送り	早口	早速	早期	早起き	
6 strokes	early; fast	fast forward	fast talking	right away	early stages	early rising	

本	くんよみ	もと				
	おんよみ	ホン				
	ほん **本**	に・ほん **日本**	ほん・しゅう **本州**	え・ほん **絵本**	さん・ぼん **三本**	やま・もと **山本**
5 strokes	book; main	Japan	main island of Japan	picture book	three cylindrical objects	Yamamoto (common surname)

文	くんよみ	ふみ				
	おんよみ	ブン、モン、も				
	ぶん **文**	ぶん・ぽう **文法**	ぶん・がく **文学**	も・じ **文字**	ぶん・か **文化**	もん・く **文句**
3 strokes	sentence	grammar	literature	letter (of alphabet)	culture	phrase, complaint

11 Kanji Activities

❑ Stroke order

Trace the light gray symbols for practice. Pay attention to stroke order and stroke type.

出	出	出	出	出	出				
入	入	入	入	入	入				
先	先	先	先	先	先				
早	早	早	早	早	早				

本 本 本 本 本 本

文 文 文 文 文 文

❑ Words you can write

Write the following words in the boxes. This is a great way to practice the new kanji, review the vocabulary, and learn new words at the same time.

ほん
本
book

本

ぶん
文
sentence

文

で
出る
to exit, leave

出 る

だ
出す
to put out

出 す

で ぐ ち
出口
exit

出 口

はい
入る
to enter

入 る

せんせい
先生
teacher

先 生

せんげつ
先 月
last month
先 月

はや
早 い
early
早 い

に ほん
日 本
Japan
日 本

い
入 れる
to put inside
入 れ る

い　ぐち
入 り口
entrance
入 り 口

❑ **Fill in the kanji**

Fill in the blanks in the following sentences with the appropriate kanji.

1. せん せい 　□□　は　はや くち □□　ことばを　いいました。

2. ゆみ　こ□　ちゃんは　し がつ □□　に　ちゅう□　がく　せい□　になります。

3. せん□　しゅうの　もく□　よう　び□　に　しゅくだいを　だ□　しました。

4. に ほん □□　ごの　ぶん□　は　むずかしいですね。

5. で ぐち □□　は　あのエスカレーターの　みぎ□　に　あります。

6. まい　にち□　、　はち□　じに　いえを　で□　ます。

7. はや□　く、　だい□　がくに　いきたいです。

VOCABULARY GROUPS — set 11

R   bodily functions

We don't intend any offense by the next set of words – you never know when such vocabulary might come in handy.

English	Progressive	Kanji +
hiccups	しゃっくり	しゃっくり
fart	おなら	おなら
burp	げっぷ	げっぷ
sneeze	くしゃみ	くしゃみ
urine	おしっこ (everyday way)	おしっこ
feces	うんこ (everyday way)	うんこ
booger	はなくそ	鼻くそ
snot	はなみず	鼻水
slobber	よだれ	涎
snoring	いびき	いびき
yawn	あくび	欠伸

Lesson
11
Level ③

Scott in Tokyo
な adjectives

11 About This Lesson このレッスンについて

Before The Lesson

1. be able to write and read 出入先早本文
2. review vocabulary group set 11

Lesson Goals

1. learn a ton of な adjectives

11 New Words あたらしいことば

Progressive	Kanji +	English
つうきん	通勤	commuting to work
てんきん	転勤	a transfer (job)
二人べや	二人部屋	a room for two
ふどうさん	不動産	real estate
ふどうさんやさん	不動産屋さん	real estate agent / office
ところ	所	place
しんじゅくえき	新宿駅	Shinjuku station (train)
マンション	マンション	large apartment, apartment house
ワンルーム・マンション	ワンルーム・マンション	one room apartment
じゃあ	じゃあ	long version of じゃ (well, then)
シドニー	シドニー	Sydney (Australia)
せんそう	戦争	a war
からだ	体	body

11 New Adjectives あたらしい けいようし

Adjective	Kanji +	English	Type
ふくざつ	複雑	complicated, complex; difficult	な adjective
かんたん	簡単	easy	な adjective
しんせつ	親切	kind, warm-hearted, friendly	な adjective
だいじ	大事	important	な adjective
いや	嫌	unpleasant, disagreeable	な adjective
ながい	長い	long	い adjective
かっこいい	かっこいい	cool, stylish	い adjective

11 New Verbs あたらしい どうし

Dictionary	Kanji	た form	English Verb	Verb Type
てんきんになる	転勤になる	てんきんになった	to be transferred	regular (なる)
さがす	探す	さがした	to look for, search for	Regular
やる	やる	やった	to do, play	Regular
はなせる	話せる	話せた	to be able to speak	いる/える

11 Verb Usage どうしの つかいかた

☐ **てんきんに なる (to be transferred)**
The person being transferred is marked with が, and は is used for emphasis.

> **[*person*] が てんきんに なる**
>
> **[*person*] will be transferred**

Example Sentences

1. スコットさんが 大さかに てんきんに なりました。
   Scott was transferred to Osaka.

2. ぼくは らい月、とうきょうに てんきんに なります。
   I will be transferred to Tokyo next month.

❑ **さがす (to look for, search for)**

The object particle を marks the object being searched for.

> **[*item*] を さがす**
>
> **to look for [*item*]**

Example Sentences

1. なにを さがして いますか。
   What are you looking for?

2. あした やすくて、かっこいい くるまを さがします。
   Tomorrow I am going to look for a cheap, cool car.

❑ **やる (to do, to play)**

やる is similar to する, but its meaning can be rougher (potentially carrying the same implications of "do it" in English), but it doesn't necessarily make the statement rude. やる is often used in informal conversations and writings. You will have to experience the conversations and watch lots of Japanese TV to know when and when not to use やる.

> **[*thing*] を やる**
>
> **to do [*thing*]**

Example Sentences

1. しゅくだいを やって ください。
   Please do you homework.

2. きょうは なにも やりたくないです。
   I don't want to do anything today.

3. 土よう日に ともだちと サッカーを やります。
   I am going to play soccer with my friends on Saturday.

❑ **はなせる (to be able to speak)**

This verb is actually the "can do" form of the verb はなす (to speak). The "can do" and "can't do" form of verbs will be discussed further in Lesson 13. This verb form is also commonly referred to as the "potential" verb form.

> **[*language*] が はなせる**
>
> **to be able to speak [*language*]**

Example Sentences

1.   日ほんごが はなせますか。
     Can you speak Japanese?

2.   フランスごが はなせません。
     I cannot speak French.

3.   たかはしさんは ちゅうごくごと かんこくごが はなせると おもいます。
     I think Mr. Takahashi can speak Chinese and Korean.

11 Grammar ぶんぽう

❑ Using な-adjectives

な-adjectives are placed in front of any noun to modify it. の can never be used in place of the な. な adjectives can not directly modify (describe) a word without な. It is important to understand that すき and きらい are also な-adjectives.

> **[な-*adjective*] + な + [*word*]**

Example Sentences

1.   わたしの すき<u>な</u> たべものは ピザです。
     My favorite food is pizza.

2.   まつもとさんは とても しんせつ<u>な</u>人です。
     Matsumoto is a very kind person.

3.   コンビニで べんり<u>な</u> ものを たくさん うっています。
     They sell many convenient things at the convenience store.

4.   林さんは いや<u>な</u> 人です。
     Hayashi is a disagreeable person.

❑ な adjectives and the "one" pronoun

In Level One of Japanese From Zero! you learned how to say the "one" pronoun in Japanese by using the particle の. For example, a "hot one" is あついの, and a "green one" would be みどりの. When using the "one" pronoun with な adjectives, the な must not be removed. For example, if you wanted "a convenient one" it would be べんりなのが ほしいです。

Example Conversation

A： どんなはなが ほしいですか。　　　What kind of flowers do you want?
B： きれいなのが ほしいです。　　　　I want pretty ones.

❑ **The very useful でしょう**

By this level you have probably heard でしょう used many times. It can mean: "right?"
"probably," "(I) think," "(I) hope," "(I) guess," "don't you agree?" and "I thought you'd say
that!" Of course this all depends on the context of the sentence. でしょう always comes at
the end of the sentence or stands alone. When used with verbs, the verb must be in its
informal form.

Example Sentences

1. あした とうきょうに いく<u>でしょう</u>。
   When the sentence is said with rising intonation at the end it means:
   You are going to Tokyo tomorrow, right?

   When the sentence is said with a flat intonation it means:
   They will probably go to Tokyo tomorrow.

   By changing the intonation of the sentence you can change the meaning.

2. 日ほんごを べんきょうしている<u>でしょう</u>。
   You are studying Japanese right? / He is probably studying Japanese.

11　Mini Conversations ミニかいわ J-E

1. Informal conversation between new friends
A： すきな たべものは なに？
B： ハンバーガーが 大すき。
A： じゃあ、きらいな たべものは？
B： あんまり ないよ。

A： What is your favorite food?
B： I really like hamburgers.
A： Then, what foods do you dislike?
B： There isn't much.

2. Informal conversation between two guys

A： あの人は　だれ？
B： ぼくの　おねえちゃんだよ。
A： きれいな　ひとだね。
B： そう？
A： かのじょを　さがしてます。よろしく　おねがいします。

A： Who is that person?
B： It is my older sister.
A： She sure is a pretty person.
B： Really?
A： I am looking for a girlfriend. Your help is appreciated.

3. Polite conversation between two people on an airplane

A： どこに　すんでいますか。
B： シドニーに　すんでいます。
A： シドニーは　どんな　ところですか。
B： しずかな　ところです。でも、べんりじゃないです。

A： Where do you live?
B： I live in Sydney.
A： What kind of place is Sydney?
B： It is a quiet place, but it is not convenient.

4. Semi-polite conversation between a teacher and a student

A： 先生、このしゅくだいは　むずかしいよ。もっと　かんたんな　しゅくだいを　下さい。
B： だめだよ。もう　三年生でしょう。
A： でも、むずかしいよ。
B： あしたまでに　やって下さい。

A： Teacher, this homework is difficult. I want easier homework.
B： No. You are already a third-grader right?
A： But it is difficult!
B： Please do it by tomorrow.

11 | Mini Conversations ミニかいわ E-J

Using a piece of paper, cover up the entire Japanese portion of the conversations below. Translate the English conversation to Japanese. Only after you have translated the entire conversation should you move the paper to check your work.

1. Informal conversation between co-workers
A: I hate men!
B: Why?
A: Because they are complicated.
B: What kind of boyfriend is good?
A: A warm-hearted man.

A: 男の人が 大きらい！
B: なんで？
A: ふくざつだから！
B: どんな かれしが いいの？
A: しんせつな 男の人。

2. Polite conversation between co-workers
A: Why are you going to Nagasaki?
B: Because I have been transferred.
B: When are you going?
A: Next week on Thursday.

A: なんで、ながさきに いきますか。
B: てんきんに なったからです。
B: いつ、いきますか。
A: らいしゅうの 木よう日です。

3. Polite conversation between new high school graduates
A: What kind of work do you want to do?
B: I want to do easy work.
A: There probably isn't any in this town.

A: どんな しごとが したいですか。
B: かんたんな しごとが したいです。
A: この町には ないでしょう。

11 Reading Comprehension どっかい

Read the sentences below. Use the information to answer the reading comprehension questions later in this lesson.

① スコットさんは 二しゅうかんまえに とうきょうに てんきんに なりました。

② いま、かいしゃの りょうに います。

③ スコットさんの かいしゃでは アメリカの くつを うっています。

④ りょうの へやは 二人べやだから、かれは しょくばに ちかいアパートを さがしています。

⑤ きょうは ふどうさんやさんに いきました。

⑥ ふどうさんやさんは しんせつな人でした。

⑦ スコットさんは 日ほんごを アメリカの がっこうで べんきょうしたから、 日ほんごが はなせます。

11 | Main Conversation メインかいわ

ふどうさんやさん:	いらっしゃいませ。へやを さがしていますか。
スコットさん:	はい、アパートを さがしています。
ふどうさんやさん:	どんな アパートが いいですか。
スコットさん:	つうきんと かいものに べんりな ところが いいです。
ふどうさんやさん:	しょくばは どこですか。
スコットさん:	しんじゅくえきに ちかいです。
ふどうさんやさん:	ええっと…二つ ありますね。　一つ目の アパートは あたらしくて、しんじゅくえきから でんしゃで 十五ふん、かかります。そして、二つ目の ワンルーム・マンションは ふるくて、バスで 二十五ふん、かかります。一つ目のは 二つ目のより すこし たかいです。でも、とても しずかな ところですよ。
スコットさん:	じゃあ、そのアパートが みたいです。
ふどうさんやさん:	わかりました。いまから いきましょう。

11 Activities

❏ Reading comprehension questions

Answer the following questions about the reading comprehension in this lesson.

1. 「てんきん」は　えいごで　なんですか。

_____

2. スコットさんは　いつ、とうきょうに　てんきんに　なりましたか。

_____

3. いま、どこに　すんでいますか。

_____

4. スコットさんの　かいしゃは　どんな　かいしゃですか。

_____

5. スコットさんは　ルームメイトが　いますか。

_____

6. スコットさんは　りょうに　いたいですか。

_____

7. なんでですか。

_____

8. じゃあ、どこに　すみたいですか。

_____

9. スコットさんは　きょう、どこに　いきましたか。

_____

10. ふどうさんやさんは　どんな人でしたか。

_____

11. スコットさんは　日ほんごが　はなせますか。

_____

12. なんで、日ほんごが　はなせますか。

_____

❑ **Substitution drill**
Compose sentences according to the example.

> **Ex. ゆうごはんの あと、しゅくだいを やります。**
> → want to do　　　　　 ゆうごはんの あと、しゅくだいを やりたいです。
> → don't want to do　　 ゆうごはんの あと、しゅくだいを やりたくないです。
> → please do　　　　　 ゆうごはんの あと、しゅくだいを やってください。
> → please don't do　　 ゆうごはんの あと、しゅくだいを やらないでください。

1. **田中さんは しずかな人です。**

   → kind　　　　　　　_____

   → complicated　　　 _____

   → unpleasant　　　 _____

   → pretty　　　　　　 _____

2. **日本ごが はなせます。**

   → French　　　　　 _____

   → can't speak　　　 _____

   → Spanish　　　　　_____

   → Chinese　　　　　_____

3. **いいマンションを さがしています。**

   → big refrigerator　　 _____

   → convenient dictionary _____

   → easy Japanese book _____

   → quiet place　　　　 _____

❑ Translation

Fill in the blanks and translate the resulting sentences into Japanese.

1. My favorite restaurant is _____

   Translation: _____

2. My least favorite food is _____

   Translation: _____

3. My favorite movie is _____

   Translation: _____

4. My least favorite actor（はいゆう）is_____

   Translation: _____

❑ Question and Answer

Answer the following questions using the words and patterns in this lesson.

1. すきな たべものは なんですか。

   _____

2. きらいな テレビ ばんぐみ（program）は なんですか。

   _____

3. すきな ところは どんな ところですか。

   _____

4. どんな アパート／いえを さがしていますか。

   _____

5. どんな かのじょ／かれを さがしていますか。

   _____

6. なにごが はなせますか。

   _____

7. 日本ごは むずかしいでしょう？

8. 日本ごの　しゅくだいは　たいへんでしょう？

❑ **Short dialogue**

Mr. Murata is not happy that he has been transferred to New York.

> 出口さん：　　村田さん、げん気が　ありませんね。どうしましたか。
>
> 村田さん：　　じつは、ニューヨークに　てんきんに　なりました。
>
> 出口さん：　　すごいですね。いつ、しゅっぱつですか。
>
> 村田さん：　　らい月の十日です。でも、いきたくないです。
>
> 出口さん：　　どうしてですか。
>
> 村田さん：　　わたしは　えいごが　はなせませんから。
>
> 出口さん：　　ぜんぜん、はなせませんか。
>
> 村田さん：　　あいさつだけは　だいじょうぶです。ニューヨークで　えいごの
>
> 　　　　　　　先生を　さがします。
>
> 出口さん：　　がんばってください。

New words and expressions in the dialogue

Progressive	Kanji +	English
じつは	実は	actually
しゅっぱつ	出発	departure
あいさつ	挨拶	greetings

WRITING PRACTICE

Use these sheets as extra writing practice for the kanji you have learned up to this point.
Recently you have learned: 村田夕赤青白見、出入先早本文

Kanji Lesson 12

名字学校正年王

12 New Kanji あたらしい かんじ

Make sure you learn the correct stroke order. Correct stroke order will mean neater symbols when writing quickly. Also, take time to learn the new words for each kanji, as this will help you to memorize the different readings.

名

くんよみ	な				
おんよみ	メイ、ミョウ				
な・まえ **名前**	ゆう・めい **有名**	めい・じん **名人**	みょう・じ **名字**	あだ・な **あだ名**	めい・ぶつ **名物**
6 strokes	name	famous	master, expert	last name	nickname	specialty, famous product

字

くんよみ	あざ				
おんよみ	じ				
じ **字**	かん・じ **漢字**	じ・かく **字画**	おお・あざ **大字**	こ・も・じ **小文字**	しゅう・じ **習字**
6 strokes	letter, character	Kanji, Chinese character	character stroke	larger section (of village)	lower case letter	calligraphy

学

くんよみ	まな(ぶ)				
おんよみ	ガク				
まな・ぶ **学ぶ**	がっ・こう **学校**	だい・がく **大学**	がく・せい **学生**	がく・ねん **学年**	すう・がく **数学**
8 strokes	to learn	school	college	student	year in school	mathematics

校

くんよみ	none				
おんよみ	コウ				
がっ・こう **学校**	よび・こう **予備校**	こう・こう **高校**	こう・もん **校門**	こう・ちょう **校長**	しょう・こう **将校**
10 strokes	school	prep school	high school	gate; entrance to school	school principal	commissioned officer

正 5 strokes	くんよみ	ただ（しい）、まさ					
	おんよみ	セイ、ショウ					
		<u>ただ</u>・しい **正しい**	<u>まさ</u>・ゆめ **正夢**	<u>せい</u>・かい **正解**	<u>しょう</u>・じき **正直**	<u>しょう</u>・がつ **正月**	<u>てい</u>・<u>せい</u> **訂正**
		correct	dreams that come true	correct answer	honest	New Years	correction, revision

年 6 strokes	くんよみ	とし					
	おんよみ	ネン					
		<u>とし</u> **年**	<u>ねん</u>・れい **年齢**	<u>とし</u>・より **年寄り**	<u>とし</u>・ご **年子**	いち・<u>ねん</u> **一年**	すう・<u>ねん</u> **数年**
		year, age	age	old person	second child within a year	1 year	several years

王 4 strokes	くんよみ	none				
	おんよみ	オウ				
		<u>おう</u>・さま **王様**	<u>おう</u>・じ **王子**	<u>おう</u>・じょ **王女**	じょ・<u>おう</u> **女王**	めい・<u>おう</u>・せい **冥王星**
		king	prince	princess	queen	planet Pluto

12 Kanji Activities

❑ Stroke order

Trace the light gray symbols for practice. Pay attention to stroke order and stroke type.

名　名　名　名　名　名

字　字　字　字　字　字

学　学　学　学　学　学

校	校	校	校	校	校				
正	正	正	正	正	正				
年	年	年	年	年	年				
王	王	王	王	王	王				

❏ Words you can write

Write the following words in the boxes. This is a great way to practice the new kanji, review the vocabulary, and learn new words at the same time.

じ
字
character

字								

おう
王
king

王								

みょうじ
名字
last name

名	字							

な
名まえ
name

名	ま	え						

もじ
文字
letter
| 文 | 字 |

がっこう
学校
school
| 学 | 校 |

がくせい
学生
student
| 学 | 生 |

がくねん
学年
grade, year
| 学 | 年 |

ごねん
五年
5 years
| 五 | 年 |

しょうがっこう
小学校
elementary school
| 小 | 学 | 校 |

ただ
正しい
correct
| 正 | し | い |

しょうがつ
お正月
New Year's
| お | 正 | 月 |

❏ **Fill in the kanji**
  Fill in the blanks in the following sentences with the appropriate kanji.

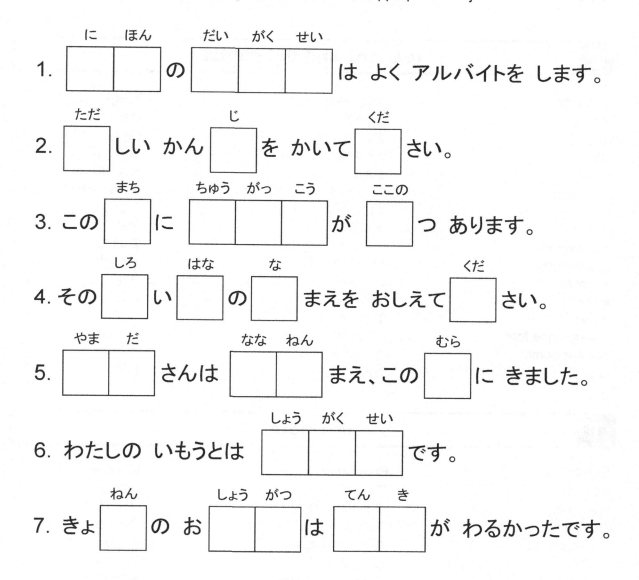

1. [に][ほん] の [だい][がく][せい] は よく アルバイトを します。

2. [ただ] しい かん [じ] を かいて [くだ] さい。

3. この [まち] に [ちゅう][がっ][こう] が [ここの] つ あります。

4. その [しろ] い [はな] の [な] まえを おしえて [くだ] さい。

5. [やま][だ] さんは [なな][ねん] まえ、この [むら] に きました。

6. わたしの いもうとは [しょう][がく][せい] です。

7. きょ [ねん] の お [しょう][がつ] は [てん][き] が わるかったです。

VOCABULARY GROUPS — set 12

S — weapons and the military

English	Progressive	Kanji +
rocket	ロケット	ロケット
bomb	ばくだん	爆弾
rifle	ライフル	ライフル
pistol	ピストル	ピストル
army knife	アーミーナイフ	アーミーナイフ
canteen	すいとう	水筒
war	せんそう	戦争
war aircraft	せんとうき	戦闘機
submarine	せんすいかん	潜水艦
air force	くうぐん	空軍
army	りくぐん	陸軍
navy	かいぐん	海軍
self-defense force	じえいたい	自衛隊
nuclear bomb	げんしばくだん	原子爆弾
tank	せんしゃ	戦車

T — in a hotel

English	Progressive	Kanji +
front desk	フロント	フロント
checkout	チェックアウト	チェックアウト
check-in	チェックイン	チェックイン
room service	ルームサービス	ルームサービス
buffet	ビュッフェ	ビュッフェ
vending machine	じどうはんばいき	自動販売機

Lesson
12
Level ③

Atsuko's Letter
one action after another

12 About This Lesson このレッスンについて

Before The Lesson

1. be able to write and read 名字学校正年王
2. review vocabulary group set 12

Lesson Goals

1. learn to say actions successively

From The Teachers

1. The grammar in this lesson is pretty powerful and it leads to even more powerful grammar. Make sure you fully understand how to do successive actions in Japanese.

12 New Words あたらしい ことば

Progressive	Kanji +	English
がいこく	外国	a foreign country
え	絵	a drawing or painting
うら	裏	the back
ドレス	ドレス	a dress
また	又	again
天のうへい下	天皇陛下	emperor
ランニング	ランニング	running
ダイエット	ダイエット	diet
お玉じゃくし	お玉じゃくし	tadpole

12 Culture Clip カルチャークリップ

Notice the date on the top of Atsuko's letter at the end of this lesson. The year is listed as H17. It could have also been written as 平成（へいせい）15 年. The traditional Japanese way of counting years is based how many years the emperor has reigned.   Each emperor's reign is assigned an era name.   As of 2005, the emperor of Japan is あきひと.   His era is the Heisei (へいせい) Era.   He has reigned for 19 years, so the year in Japan (2008) is H20 (Heisei 20 year).

It is considered rude to call the emperor by his name. The royal family does not even have a last name.   They simply refer to the emperor as "Emperor" (てんのう へいか).   Only after his death will the emperor be referred to as the Heisei Emperor.

Name of Emperor	Name of Period		Meaning of Era	Period of Rule
あきひと	へいせい	平成	everlasting peace	1989-present
ひろひと	しょうわ	昭和	shining peace	1926-1989
よしひと	たいしょう	大正	big justice	1912-1926
むつひと	めいじ	明治	wishing for a bright era	1868-1912

12 New Verbs あたらしい どうし

Dictionary	Kanji	た-form	English Verb	Verb Type
できる	出来る	できた	to be able to do, can do, make	いる/える
かわる	変わる	かわった	to change, turn into	regular

12 Verb Usage どうしの つかいかた

❑ **できる (to be able to do, can do, make)**
　　Use が to mark the thing that can be done. は can also be used for emphasis.

> **[*thing*] + が できる**
> **[*thing*] can be done**

Example Sentences

1. 森さんは コンピューターが できます。
   Mr. Mori can do computers.

2. 日本ごが できますか。
   Can you speak Japanese?
   (This phrase is pretty common. It is another way of asking if someone can speak Japanese.)

3. ともだちが たくさん できました。
   I made many friends.

❏ **かわる (to change, turn into)**

Use が to mark the thing that is changing. は can also be used for emphasis. The thing that it is being changed into is marked by に.

> **[thing 1] が [thing 2] に かわる**
>
> **[thing 1] changes into [thing 2]**

Example Sentences

1. あきが ふゆに かわります。
   Fall will change into winter.

2. おたまじゃくしが かえるに かわります。
   Tadpoles turn into frogs.

3. けっこんしたから、さびしいお正月が いいお正月に かわりました。
   Because I got married, sad New Year holidays have changed into good New Year holidays.

12 **Grammar ぶんぽう**

❏ **One action after another**

Look at the next set of sentences to see how から (after; since) and the て verb form are used together to say things like, "After I eat lunch, I am going home," or, "I will call you after I eat." The tense of the て form is determined by the tense of the second sentence.

> **[First action using て form verb] から、[second action]**
>
> **After I [first action] I will [second action]**

Example Sentences

1. 日本に <u>いってから</u>、パリに いきます。
   <u>After I go to Japan</u>, I will go to Paris.

2. ハンバーガーを <u>たべてから</u>、テニスを します。
   <u>After I eat a hamburger</u>, I will play tennis.

3. 学校に <u>いってから</u>、 サッカーを します。
   <u>After I go to school</u>, I play soccer.

4. いえに <u>かえってから</u>、 でんわします。
   I will call you <u>after I get home</u>.

❏ Adverbs

For those of you who have forgotten what an adverb is (or didn't ever really know), it is basically just an adjective for verbs. For example, "quick" is an adjective in the phrase "quick lunch," but an adverb in the phrase "quickly eat lunch." You can make any い adjective into an adverb by dropping the final い and then adding a く in its place. The verb always comes after the adverb.

[い *adjective*] drop い add く

Example Sentences

1. <ruby>早<rt>はや</rt></ruby>く きてください。
   Please come <u>quickly</u>.

2. きのうは <u>おそく</u> ねました。
   Yesterday I went to bed <u>late</u>.

3. 六さいの むすめは <u>かわいく</u> 犬の えを かきました。
   My six-year-old daughter drew a picture of dogs <u>cutely</u>.

12 | Q&A しつもんとこたえ

1. どんなスポーツが できますか。
   What kind of sports can you play?

   サッカーが できます。
   I can play soccer.

   やきゅうと テニスが できます。
   I can play baseball and tennis.

2. あきに はっぱの いろは なにいろに かわりますか。
   In the fall what color do the leaves change to?

   赤と オレンジと きいろに かわります。
   They change to red, orange and yellow.

12 | Mini Conversations ミニかいわ J-E

Using a piece of paper cover up the entire English portion of the conversations below. Read the Japanese conversation several times until you understand it. Only then should you move the paper to compare your translation to the English translation.

1. **Polite conversation between a boy and a girl who is interested in him**
   A: 日よう日に えきの まえで あって下さい。
   B: 日よう日は アルバイトを してから、ともだちと やきゅうを するから だめです。
   A: やきゅうは なんじまでですか。やきゅうの あとで あってください。
   B: そのあとも ちょっと・・・
   A: そうですか。ざんねんです。

   A: Please meet me at the station on Sunday.
   B: As for Sunday, I am going to play baseball with my friends after my part-time job, so it's no good. (I can't).
   A: Until what time is baseball? Please see me after baseball.
   B: After that, it is a little…
   A: I see. It is too bad.

2. Informal conversation between two school friends

A: いつも あさ なにを するの？
B: しゅくだいを してから、学校に いく。
A: ええ！ あさ しゅくだいを するの？
B: よる はやく ねるから。あさの ほうが いいよ。

A: What do you always do in the morning?
B: After I do my homework, I go to school.
A: What!? You do your homework in the morning?
B: Since I go to bed early at night, morning is better.

3. Polite conversation between two housewives

A: いつも このじかんに なにを しますか。
B: そうじを してから、テレビを みます。
A: まい日 そうじを しますか。
B: はい、そうじが すきですから。ときどき、しゅ人も します。

A: What do you always do at this time?
B: I watch TV after cleaning.
A: Do you clean everyday?
B: Yes, because I like cleaning. Sometimes my husband does it too.

4. Mixed conversation between friends

A: きょうの おひるやすみに なにを しますか。
B: ひるごはんを たべてから、ランニングを する。
A: わたしは おちゃを のんでから、ほんを よみます。
B: おちゃだけ？ ひるごはんは たべないの？
A: はい、いま ダイエットを しています。

A: What are you going to do at lunch break?
B: After eating lunch, I am going to go running.
A: I am going to read a book after I drink some green tea.
B: Just tea? Aren't you going to eat lunch?
A: No. I am on a diet now.

12 Reading Comprehension どっかい

Read the sentences below. Use the information to answer the reading comprehension questions later in this lesson.

H18年10月27日

たけちゃんへ

①お手がみ ありがとう。②がいこくは たのしいですか。
③わたしは 三年生に ないました。
④クラスも かわりました。そして、あたらしい ともだちも
できました。⑤わたしは 三年生に なってから、学校が
すきに なりました。

⑥たけちゃんと さちこちゃんは げん気ですか。⑦わたしと
ゆう子は げん気です。⑧てがみの うらに ドレスの えを
かきました。⑨ 見てください。

⑩また お手がみ くださいね。

あつ子より

(This reading comprehension is based on an actual letter from a Japanese girl who was eight years old at the time she wrote the letter. Only small portions of the letter have been changed in order to fit the grammar introduced.)

12 Activities

❑ **Reading comprehension questions**
Answer the following questions about the reading comprehension in this lesson.

1. この手がみは だれが だれに かきましたか。

   _____

2. あつ子ちゃんは いま なん年生ですか。

   _____

3. あつ子ちゃんの クラスは まえと おなじですか。

   _____

4. 三年生に なってから、あたらしいともだちが できましたか。

   _____

5. 「さち子ちゃん」は だれだと おもいますか。

   _____

6. 「ゆう子ちゃん」は だれだと おもいますか。

   _____

7. この手がみの うらに なにが ありますか。

   _____

8. ドレスのえは だれが かきましたか。

   _____

9. あつ子ちゃんは いつ、この手がみを かきましたか。

   _____

❑ **Substitution drill**

Compose sentences according to the example.

> **Ex.** ゆうべ、はやく いえに かえりました。
>   → went to bed   ゆうべ、はやく ねました。
>   → tonight   こんや、はやく ねます。
>   → late   こんや、おそく ねます。
>   → last night   ゆうべ、おそく ねました。

1. **学校に いってから、べんきょうします。**

    → after I watch TV   _____

    → after I return home   _____

    → after I write a letter _____

    → after I eat lunch   _____

2. **雨が ゆきに かわりました。**

    → water to ice   _____

    → Shouwa to Heisei   _____

    → spring to summer   _____

    → green to yellow   _____

3. **コンピューターが できます。**

    → baseball   _____

    → cooking   _____

    → Spanish language   _____

    → piano   _____

❑ **Question and answer**

Answer the following questions using the words and patterns in this lesson.

1. どんな スポーツが できますか。

   _____

2. どんな がっき (musical instrument) が できますか。

   _____

3. いつも 夕ごはんを たべてから、なにを しますか。

   _____

4. あした、しごと／学校が おわってから、 なにが したいですか。

   _____

5. 今しゅうの 土よう日は あさ おきてから、なにを しますか。

   _____

❑ **Short dialogue**

A couple is planning their honeymoon.

ひろし:　　ゆきこ、ハネムーンは どこに いきたい？

ゆきこ:　　そうだなあ・・・。イタリアは どう？

ひろし:　　いいね。けっこんしきを してから、すぐ いきたい？

ゆきこ:　　ううん。ひとばん、やすんでから、いきたい。

ひろし:　　わかった。イタリアだけに いく？

ゆきこ:　　フランスと ドイツにも いきたい。

ひろし:　　じゃあ、あした しごとが おわってから、りょこうがいしゃに いくよ。
　　　　　　そして、ヨーロッパの パッケージツアーについて、きくね。

ゆきこ:　　わたしも いっしょに いきたい。

ひろし:　　じゃあ、りょこうがいしゃに いってから、いつもの レストランで
　　　　　　ばんごはんを たべよう。

New words and expressions in the dialogue

Progressive	Kanji +	English
ハネムーン	ハネムーン	honeymoon
けっこんしき	結婚式	wedding ceremony
ひとばん	一晩	one night
やすむ	休む	to rest, to have a break
りょこうがいしゃ	旅行会社	travel company
パッケージツアー	パッケージツアー	package tour
きく	聞く	to ask
～について	～について	about ~, regarding ~
たべよう	食べよう	let's eat! (informal "let's do" verb form)

WRITING PRACTICE

Use these sheets as extra writing practice for the kanji you have learned up to this point.
Recently you have learned: 出入先早本文、名字学校正年王

Kanji Lesson
13

音糸車貝玉草竹

13 New Kanji あたらしい かんじ

Make sure you learn the correct stroke order. Correct stroke order will mean neater symbols when writing quickly. Also take time to learn the new words for each kanji, as this will help you to memorize the different readings.

音	くんよみ	おと、ね				
	おんよみ	オン、イン				
	<u>おと</u> 音	<u>おん</u>・<u>がく</u> 音楽	ほん・<u>ね</u> 本音	はつ・<u>おん</u> 発音	あし・<u>おと</u> 足音	<u>おん</u>・<u>ち</u> 音痴
9 strokes	sound	music	true feelings	pronunciation	footsteps (sound)	tone deaf

糸	くんよみ	いと				
	おんよみ	シ				
	<u>いと</u> 糸	け・<u>いと</u> 毛糸	はり・と・<u>いと</u> 針と糸	<u>いと</u>・くず 糸くず	めん・<u>し</u> 綿糸	<u>いと</u>・でんわ 糸電話
6 strokes	thread, string	knitting yarn	needle and thread	fluff; piece of thread	cotton thread	string phone (kids' toy)

車	くんよみ	くるま				
	おんよみ	シャ				
	<u>くるま</u> 車	は・<u>ぐるま</u> 歯車	でん・<u>しゃ</u> 電車	<u>しゃ</u>・こ 車庫	じ・どう・<u>しゃ</u> 自動車	<u>しゃ</u>・りん 車輪
7 strokes	car; wheel	gear	train	bicycle	automobile	wheel

貝	くんよみ	かい			
	おんよみ	None			
	<u>かい</u> 貝	<u>かい</u>・<u>がら</u> 貝殻	ほら・<u>がい</u> ほら貝	まき・<u>がい</u> 巻貝	<u>かい</u>・<u>るい</u> 貝類
7 strokes	shell	outer shell	trumpet shell	spiral shell	shellfish

	くんよみ	たま				
玉 1 2 3 4 5	おんよみ	ギョク				
	たま 玉	みず・たま 水玉	お・たま・じゃくし お玉じゃくし	ひゃく・えん・だま 百円玉	たま・ねぎ 玉ねぎ	
5 strokes	ball, sphere	polka dots	tadpole	100 yen coin	onion	

	くんよみ	くさ				
草 1 2 3 4 5 6 7 8 9	おんよみ	そう				
	くさ 草	そう・げん 草原	ざっ・そう 雑草	ぞう・り 草履	し・ぐさ 仕草	くさ・ばな 草花
9 strokes	grass	grasslands; savannah	weed	Japanese footwear	gesture, behavior	poisonous plant

	くんよみ	たけ				
竹 1 4 2 5 3 6	おんよみ	チク				
	たけ 竹	たけ・の・こ 竹の子	ちく・りん 竹林	ばく・ちく 爆竹	たけ・うま 竹馬	たけ・やぶ 竹やぶ
6 strokes	bamboo	bamboo shoots	bamboo (woods)	firecracker	stilts	bamboo grove

13 Writing Point: What are kanji radicals?

You may have already noticed that some kanji are made up of similar strokes, or even several kanji put together. These are called *radicals*, and if you have a good understanding of a radical's meaning, you can have a pretty good guess at what a particular kanji might mean, even if you have never seen it before. Let's take a look at some of these radicals in action.

The kanji for person 人 squeezes up to become the にんべん radical: 亻 . Put this together with the kanji for "tree" 木 and you get 休 which means "rest."   A person next to a tree is resting.   If you take the same tree kanji and add the kanji for stand 立 and look 見 you get a person standing on a tree watching you, or 親 which means "parent."

Here are some other common radicals and the kanji that included them:

さんずい means water. Kanji with this radical are water-related.

海 ocean 池 pond 汽 steam

辶　しんにょう has to do with going and coming.

遠　道　近
far　street　near

艹　くさかんむり means grass, and is found in many kanji.

草　花　茶
grass　flower　tea

13　Kanji Activities

❑ **Stroke order**
Trace the light gray symbols for practice. Pay attention to stroke order and stroke type.

音	音	音	音	音	音				
糸	糸	糸	糸	糸	糸				
車	車	車	車	車	車				
貝	貝	貝	貝	貝	貝				
玉	玉	玉	玉	玉	玉				

草 草草草草草

竹 竹竹竹竹竹

❑ Words you can write

Write the following words in the boxes. This is a great way to practice the new kanji, review the vocabulary, and learn new words at the same time.

おと
音
sound

音

いと
糸
thread

糸

くるま
車
car

車

かい
貝
shell

貝

たま
玉
ball

玉

くさ
草
grass

草

たけ
竹
bamboo

竹

みずたま
水玉
polka dots

| 水 | 玉 |

くさばな
草花
flowering
grass

| 草 | 花 |

おん
音 がく
music

| 音 | が | く |

でん車
しゃ
train

| でん | ん | 車 |

ひゃくえんだま
百円玉
100 yen coin

| 百 | 円 | 玉 |

❑ **Fill in the kanji**
Fill in the blanks in the following sentences with the appropriate kanji.

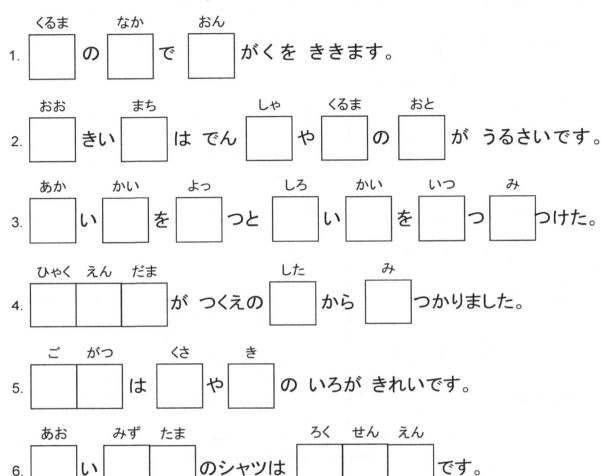

1. くるま□ の なか□ で おん□ がくを ききます。

2. おお□ きい まち□ は でん しゃ□ や くるま□ の おと□ が うるさいです。

3. あか□ い かい□ を よっ□ つと しろ□ い かい□ を いつ□ つ み□ つけた。

4. ひゃく えん だま□□□ が つくえの した□ から み□ つかりました。

5. ご がつ□□ は くさ□ や き□ の いろが きれいです。

6. あお□ い みず たま□□ のシャツは ろく せん えん□□□ です。

7. ちく りん□□ で たけ□ の こ□ を さがしました。

Lesson
13
Level ③

Amelia's Interview
the potential verb form

13 About this Lesson このレッスンについて

Before The Lesson

1. be able to write and read 音糸車貝玉草竹
2. review all of the vocabulary groups

Lesson Goals

1. learn to make the potential form of verbs to say phrases such as "I can do" and "I can't do."

13 New Words あたらしい ことば

Progressive	Kanji +	English
めんせつ	面接	an interview
めんせつかん	面接官	an interviewer
ひしょ	秘書	a secretary
日じょう	日常	normal, everyday, ordinary
プログラミング	プログラミング	programming
しそ	しそ	Japanese basil
がまん	我慢	patience; endurance; self-control
うみ	海	the ocean, the beach
かい水よく	海水浴	ocean bathing
一人で	一人で	by yourself, alone
さいふ	財布	wallet

13 New Adjectives あたらしい けいようし

Adjective	Kanji +	English	Type
あぶない	危ない	dangerous	い adjective

13 New Verbs あたらしい どうし

Dictionary	Kanji	た form	English Verb	Verb Type
およぐ	泳ぐ	およいだ	to swim	regular
なくす	なくす	なくした	to lose	regular
みつける	見つける	みつけた	to find (active)	いる/える
みつかる	見つかる	みつかった	to be found (passive)	regular
がまんする	我慢する	がまんした	to have patience; endure	する

13 Verb Usage どうしの つかいかた

☐ **およぐ (to swim)**
   で marks the location where the swimming takes place.

> **[*place*] で およぐ**
> **to swim at [*place*]**

Example Sentences

1. 金よう日に ともだちと プールで およぎました。
   I was at the pool with friends on Friday.

2. こんど 日本に いくとき、日本かいで およぎたいです。
   When I go to Japan next time, I want to swim in the Japan Sea.

3. きょうは さむいから およぎたくないです。
   Because it is cold today I don't want to swim.

4. あぶないから、一人で およがないで下さい。
   It is dangerous, so please don't swim alone.

❑ なくす (to lose)

The object particle を marks the object that is lost.

> ### [*item*] を なくす
> ### to lose [*item*]

Example Sentences

1. 先しゅうの 木よう日に さいふを なくしました。
   I lost my wallet last Thursday.

2. ぼくは よく 車の かぎを なくします。
   I often lose my car keys.

❑ みつける (to find)

見つける is an active verb, which means that when someone says it, it means "I will find it," or "they will find it." Active verbs always imply that they were done by someone and didn't just happen on their own. Active verbs generally use the particle を to mark the object the verb acts on.

> ### [*thing*] を みつける
> ### to find [*thing*]

Example Sentences

1. とうきょうで やすいアパートを 見つけました。
   I found a cheap apartment in Tokyo.

2. いいレストランを 見つけましたか。
   Did you find a good restaurant?

3. ペットショップで とても かわいい子犬を 見つけた。
   I found a very cute puppy at the pet shop.

❑ みつかる (to be found)

見つかる is a passive verb. 見つかる states that something has been found, and does not imply who found the item. Passive verbs generally use the particle が to mark the object used with the verb. If you are not directly saying that some particular person has found the lost item, then 見つかる should be used to say simply, "it was found"

> **[something] が みつかる**
>
> **[something] is found**

Example Sentences

1. さいふが 見つかりましたか。
   Was your wallet found?

2. 山に いったけど、おてあらいが 見つからなかった。
   We went to the mountains, but the bathroom was not found.

❑ がまんする (to have patience; endure, bear with)

In Japan, this verb is very cultural in that supposedly Japanese are known for their ability to hold back their emotions in public. (No comment on this, just an observation.) The thing that is being endured is marked with を, but normally this verb is used alone.

> **[something] を がまんする**
>
> **to endure [something]**

Example Sentences

1. ひるごはんを がまんしました。
   I endured lunch. (This means that the person didn't eat lunch.)

2. ここは さむいけど、がまんしてください。
   This place is cold, but please be patient.

13 Grammar ぶんぽう

❑ Changing regular verbs into the potential verb form

There is a pattern used to make a verb into the potential verb form. The "can-do" / "able-to-do" verb form is made by changing the last syllable of the dictionary form of the verb, which is always the う-form, to the え-form, and then adding る.

> ### the え form of a verb + る

Look at the following regular verbs and see how this formula is applied to them.

Dictionary Form	Potential Form Positive	Potential Form Past	Potential Form Negative
いく to go	いける can go	いけた could go	いけない can't go
のむ to drink	のめる can drink	のめた could drink	のめない can't drink
うる to sell	うれる can sell	うれた could sell	うれない can't sell
かう to buy	かえる can buy	かえた could buy	かえない can't buy

❑ Changing いる/える verbs into the potential verb form

Not all verbs fit into the pattern from above. If it is a いる/える verb, you need to drop the last る and then add られる. In other words, the る on the end of each dictionary form is replaced with られる.

> ### (いる/える verb) drop る + られる

Look at the following いる/える verbs and see how this formula is applied to them.

Dictionary From	Potential Form Positive	Potential Form Past	Potential Form Negative
たべる to eat	たべられる can eat	たべられた could eat	たべられない can't eat

みる to see	みられる can see	みられた could see	みられない can't see
おきる to wake up	おきられる can wake up	おきられた could wake up	おきられない can't wake up
ねる to sleep	ねられる can sleep	ねられた could sleep	ねられない can't sleep

Since the following いる/える verbs are actually いる/える exception verbs and follow the regular verb style of conjugation, they are conjugated as follows:

Dictionary From	Potential Form Positive	Potential Form Past	Potential Form Negative
かえる to return	かえれる can return	かえれた could return	かえれない can't return
きる to cut	きれる can cut	きれた could cut	きれない can't cut

Other exception verbs:

しる (to know)	はいる (to enter)	いる (to need)
すべる (to slide)	へる (to decrease)	ねる (to knead)
ける (to kick)	かじる (to bite)	まじる (to be mixed)
しゃべる (to talk)	せびる (to extort)	あせる (to be in a hurry)
はしる (to run)	ちる (to scatter)	てる (to shine)

❏ Particle switch

When using the potential verb form, the particle が is used instead of the object marker を.

Example Sentences

1. わたしは おすし<u>が</u> たべられないです。
   I cannot eat sushi.

2. いまは 車<u>が</u> かえません。
   I cannot buy a car now.

3. きのうは かぜだったから、ビール<u>が</u> のめなかった。
   I had a cold yesterday, so I couldn't drink beer.

4. とうきょうは たかいから、いえ<u>が</u> かえないよ。
   Tokyo is expensive, so I cannot buy a house there.

13 | Mini Conversation ミニかいわ J-E

Using a piece of paper cover up the entire English portion of the conversations below.   Read the Japanese conversation several times until you understand it.   Only then should you move the paper to compare your translation to the English translation.

1. Polite conversation between a newcomer to Japan and a Japanese person
A： これは たべられますか。
B： はい、たべられますよ。とても おいしいですよ。
A： なんですか。
B： しそです。

A： Can you eat this?
B： Yes I can eat it. It is very delicious.
A： What is it?
B： It's Japanese basil.

2. Polite conversation between a person from the country and his Tokyo friend
A： とうきょうで へやを さがしています。
B： どんな へやですか。
A： やちんが 五まん円までの へやです。
B： とうきょうでは さがせないですよ。
A： ええ、なんでですか。
B： とうきょうは 日本で 一ばん やちんが たかいです。

A： I am looking for a room in Tokyo.
B： What kind of room is it?
A： A room in which the rent is up to ¥50,000
B： You won't be able to find one in Tokyo.
A： What!? Why?
B： Because Tokyo has the most expensive rent in Japan.

3. Casual conversation between newlyweds
A： この ホテルの プールは 大きいね。
B： うん、それに 二十四じかん およげるよ。
A： すごいね。いまから およがない？

A： This hotel's pool is big.
B： Yes, and you can also swim 24 hours.
A： That is great. Why don't we swim now?

4. Informal conversation between old friends

A： いま しごとを してない。
B： なんで してないの？
A： 足が いたいから、はたらけない。

A： I am not working now.
B： Why aren't you working?
A： Since my foot hurts, I cannot work.

13 Mini Conversation ミニかいわ E-J

Using a piece of paper, cover up the entire Japanese portion of the conversations below. Translate the English conversation to Japanese. Only after you have translated the entire conversation should you move the paper to check your work.

1. Informal conversation between two school friends

A： Can you swim?
B： Yes, I can swim.
A： Won't you go to the pool with me tomorrow?
B： That sounds good. How shall we go?
A： Let's go by bicycle.
B： It's far to the pool! You can't go by bicycle!
A： Well then let's go by bus.

A： およげるの？
B： うん、およげるよ。
A： あした わたしと プールに いかない？
B： いいよ。なにで いく？
A： じてん車で いこう（いきましょう）。
B： プールまで とおいよ。じてん車では いけないよ。
A： じゃ、バスで いこう。

2. Polite conversation between friends

A： What languages can you speak?
B： I can speak French and English.
A： That is amazing.   What other language do you want to speak?
B： I want to speak Chinese.

A： なにごが はなせますか。
B： フランスごと えいごが はなせます。
A： すごいですね。あと なにごを はなしたいですか。
B： 中ごくごを はなしたいですね。

13 Reading Comprehension どっかい

Read the sentences below. Use the information to answer the reading comprehension questions later in this lesson.

① アミリアさんは あたらしい しごとを さがしています。
② かの女は いま スーパーで はたらいています。
③ 三年はんまえに 日本に いってから、日本ごの べんきょうを はじめました。
④ 日本ごが はなせるから、日本の かいしゃで はたらきたいと おもっています。
⑤ あした コンピューターがいしゃで めんせつが あります。

13 The Interview めんせつ

めんせつかん： アミリアさんですね。

アミリアさん： はい、アミリアと もうします。よろしく おねがいします。

めんせつかん： よろしく おねがいします。なぜ ここで はたらきたいですか。

アミリアさん： 日本に はじめて いったとき、わたしは 日本が とても すきに なりました。それに わたしは コンピューターが できます。こちらは アメリカで 一ばん 大きい日本のコンピューターがいしゃですから、はたらきたいと おもいました。

めんせつかん： そうですか。ひしょの しごとが ありますが、なにごが はなせますか。

アミリアさん： えいごと スペインごと 日本ごが できます。

めんせつかん： 日本ごは どれぐらい できますか。

アミリアさん： 日じょうかいわが はなせます。

めんせつかん： あと、日本ごで 手がみが かけますか。

アミリアさん： すこし、かけます。ひらがなと カタカナが かけますが、かん字は まだ べんきょうしています。

めんせつかん： どこで コンピューターを べんきょうしましたか。

アミリアさん： 大学で コンピューター・プログラミングを べんきょうしました。

めんせつかん： それは いいですね。らい月 一日に また ここに こられますか。
アミリアさん： はい。もちろんです。

めんせつかん：　じゃあ、八じはんに きて下さい。二かい目のめんせつを します。

アミリアさん：　　はい、わかりました。ありがとうございます。

13 Activities

❑ Reading comprehension questions
Answer the following questions about the reading comprehension in this lesson.

1. アミリアさんは いま なにを さがしていますか。

   _____

2. かの女は いま どこで はたらいていますか。

   _____

3. かの女は いつ 日本に いきましたか。

   _____

4. かの女は どんなかいしゃで はたらきたいと おもっていますか。

   _____

5. なぜですか。

   _____

6. かの女は どのかいしゃで めんせつを していますか。

   _____

7. なぜ、そのかいしゃで めんせつを したいと おもいましたか。

   _____

8. アメリアさんは なにごが はなせますか。

   _____

9. かの女は 日本ごが どれぐらい はなせますか。

   _____

10. かん字が かけますか。

   _____

11. コンピューターが できますか。

_____

12. アメリアさんは コンピューターがいしゃで しごとが みつかりましたか。

_____

❑ Substitution drill
Compose sentences according to the example.

> **Ex. まいあさ、はやく おきられます。**
> → can't get up   まいあさ、はやく おきられません。
> → can eat breakfast   まいあさ、はやく あさごはんが たべられます。
> → can't eat breakfast   まいあさ、はやく あさごはんが たべられません。
> → can go to work   まいあさ、はやく しごとに いけます。

1. 先しゅうの 金よう日に 車の かぎを なくしました。

→ wallet _____

→ last Wednesday _____

→ cell phone _____

→ the day before yesterday _____

2. とうきょうで やすいアパートを 見つけました。

→ cute dress at this store _____

→ cool T-shirt at Disneyland _____

→ sea shells at the beach _____

→ nice ring at the department store _____

3. わたしの さいふが 見つかりました。

→ Keiko's puppy   _____

→ Mr. Tanaka's keys   _____

→ good Japanese dictionary   _____

→ inexpensive Japanese restaurant _____

4. ことしの なつ、日本に いけます。

→ can buy a new house   _____

→ can return home   _____

→ can sell my old car   _____

→ can see my best friend   _____

❑ Question and answer

Answer the following questions using the words and patterns in this lesson.

1. ときどき、プールで およぎますか。

    _____

2. おすしが たべられますか。どんな おすしが すきですか。

    _____

3. あなたの町で、日本の テレビばんぐみ（TV programs）が 見られますか。

    _____

4. いくつぐらい かん字が かけますか。

    _____

5.　日本の　しんぶんが　よめますか。

❑ Short dialogue

Ken lost his house key at school and he was waiting outside until his mother came back home.

おかあさん：　けんちゃん、そとで　なに　してるの？かぎが　あるでしょう？

けんちゃん：　ううん。きょう、学校の　プールで　およいでるときに　なくした…。

おかあさん：　ええっ！なくしたの？

けんちゃん：　うん。さがしたけど、見つけられなかった・・・。

おかあさん：　じゃあ、どうするの？

けんちゃん：　もう　一ぽん、かぎが　ある？

おかあさん：　もう　ないよ。　あした、学校の　わすれものセンターに　いって。

けんちゃん：　うん。そこで　ないときは　あたらしいのを　つくって。

おかあさん：　わかった。でも、もう　なくさないでね。

New words and expressions in the dialogue

Progressive	Kanji +	English
わすれもの	忘れ物	forgotten items
つくる	作る	to make

❑ **Particles**

Fill in the blanks with appropriate particles.

1. きょう、五じ＿＿＿＿＿ いえ＿＿＿＿＿ かえれます。

2. 先しゅう＿＿＿＿ 土よう日＿＿＿＿＿、うみ＿＿＿＿＿ ゆびわ＿＿＿＿＿ なくした。

3. 山田さんは 三月＿＿＿＿＿ 大さか＿＿＿＿＿ てんきん＿＿＿＿＿ なります。

4. きのう、車＿＿＿＿＿ かぎ＿＿＿＿＿ 学校＿＿＿＿＿ なくしました。

5. きょねん、シドニー＿＿＿＿＿ ホームステイ＿＿＿＿＿ しました。

6. 先生＿＿＿＿＿ 「もっと かん字を べんきょうして下さい」＿＿＿＿＿ いいました。

7. らいねん、とうきょう＿＿＿＿＿ いきます。そして、えいご＿＿＿＿＿ せんせい

＿＿＿＿＿ なります。

8. ロサンゼルス＿＿＿＿＿ 日本＿＿＿＿＿ おみせ＿＿＿＿＿＿ たくさん、あります。

9. お金がない＿＿＿＿＿＿、あたらしいコンピューター＿＿＿＿＿＿ かえないです。

The
APPENDICES

APPENDIX A ——————— Vocabulary Groups

A   geography

Asia	アジア	アジア
Europe	ヨーロッパ	ヨーロッパ
Oceania	オセアニア	オセアニア
Middle East	ちゅうとう	中東
Africa	アフリカ	アフリカ
North Pole	ほっきょく	北極
South Pole	なんきょく	南極
equator	せきどう	赤道
Atlantic Ocean	たいせいよう	大西洋
Pacific Ocean	たいへいよう	太平洋
Japan Sea	にほんかい	日本海
national border	こっきょう	国境
United Nations	こくれん	国連

B   at the house

electricity	でんき	電気
wall	かべ	壁
emergency exit	ひじょうぐち	非常口
door	ドア	ドア
curtains	カーテン	カーテン
carpet	カーペット	カーペット
roof	やね	屋根
floor	ゆか	床
ceiling	てんじょう	天井
rooftop	おくじょう	屋上
basement	ちかしつ	地下室
shower	シャワー	シャワー
electric outlet	コンセント	コンセント
hanger	ハンガー	ハンガー
iron	アイロン	アイロン
radio	ラジオ	ラジオ
washing machine	せんたくき	洗濯機

C   kitchen and bath

brush	ブラシ	ブラシ
safety pin	あんぜんピン	安全ピン
toilet paper	トイレットペーパー	トイレットペーパー
flower vase	かびん	花瓶
pots and pans	なべ	鍋
kitchen knife	ほうちょう	包丁
frying pan	フライパン	フライパン
cutting board	まないた	まな板
kettle	やかん	やかん
candle	ろうそく	蝋燭

D   Christmas words

Christmas tree	クリスマスツリー	クリスマスツリー
Santa Claus	サンタクロース	サンタクロース
reindeer	トナカイ	トナカイ
fireplace	だんろ	暖炉
snowman	ゆきだるま	雪だるま
bell	ベル / すず	ベル / 鈴
Merry Christmas	メリークリスマス	メリークリスマス

E   scary words

grave	（お）はか	墓
bat	こうもり	こうもり
devil	あくま	悪魔
skeleton	がいこつ	骸骨
ghost	おばけ	お化け
blood	ち	血

F   marriage words

wedding ring	けっこんゆびわ	結婚指輪
bouquet	ブーケ	ブーケ
wedding cake	ウエディング・ケーキ	ウエディング・ケーキ
wedding dress	ウエディング・ドレス	ウエディング・ドレス

divorce	りこん	離婚
lawyer	べんごし	弁護士
heart	ハート	ハート
wine	ワイン	ワイン
red wine	あかワイン	あかワイン
rose wine	ロゼワイン	ロゼワイン
white wine	しろワイン	しろワイン
champagne	シャンパン	シャンパン

G   around town

parking lot	ちゅうしゃじょう	駐車場
taxi stand	タクシーのりば	乗り場
elevator	エレベーター	エレベーター
escalator	エスカレーター	エスカレーター
bus stop	バスてい	バス停
library	としょかん	図書館
railroad crossing	ふみきり	踏み切り
sidewalk	ほどう	歩道

H   around the office

calculator	けいさんき	計算機
tape (cellophane)	セロテープ	セロテープ
two-sided tape	りょうめんテープ	両面テープ
stapler	ホッチキス	ホッチキス
file cabinet	ファイル	ファイル　キャビネット
paper clip	（ペーパー）クリップ	（ペーパー）クリップ
folder	フォルダー	フォルダー
ballpoint pen	ボールペン	ボールペン
ink	インク	インク
correction fluid	しゅうせいえき	修正液
hole puncher	パンチ	パンチ
pencil sharpener	えんぴつけずり	鉛筆削り
appointment book	システムてちょう	システム手帳
laptop computer	ラップトップ	ラップトップ
safe (to secure valuables)	きんこ	金庫
piggy bank	ちょきんばこ	貯金箱
tip (for services)	チップ	チップ

I around the hospital

handicap	ハンディキャップ	ハンディキャップ
a cold	かぜ	風邪
headache	ずつう	頭痛
injury	けが	怪我
thermometer (for body)	たいおんけい	体温計
x-ray	レントゲン	レントゲン
surgery	しゅじゅつ	手術
shot	ちゅうしゃ	注射
cough	せき	咳
tears	なみだ	涙
bandage, dressing	ほうたい	包帯
balloon	ふうせん	風船
dentures (false teeth)	いれば	入歯
hives, rash	じんましん	蕁麻疹
vitamins	ビタミン	ビタミン
wheelchair	くるまいす	車椅子

J more and more body parts

stomach	い	胃
lungs	はい	肺
muscles	きんにく	筋肉
dimples	えくぼ	笑窪
thumb	おやゆび	親指
index finger	ひとさしゆび	人差し指
middle finger	なかゆび	中指
ring finger	くすりゆび	薬指
pinky (little finger)	こゆび	小指
armpit	わきのした	わきの下
arm	うで	腕
bone	ほね	骨
breasts, chest	むね	胸
front teeth	まえば	前歯
molars	おくば	奥歯
tongue	した	舌
beard	ひげ	髭
pimple	にきび	にきび

K   photography

film	フィルム	フィルム
development	げんぞう	現像
disposable camera	つかいすてカメラ	使い捨てカメラ
film shop	しゃしんや	写真屋
photograph	しゃしん	写真
Polaroid	ポラロイド	ポラロイド
negative	ネガ	ネガ
tripod	さんきゃく	三脚

L   bugs

butterfly	ちょうちょう	喋喋
grasshopper	ばった	ばった
spider	くも	蜘蛛
caterpillar	けむし	毛虫
scorpion	さそり	蠍
ladybug	てんとうむし	てんとう虫

M   plants

potted plants	うえき	植木
bamboo	たけ	竹
palm tree	やしのき	椰子の木
cactus	サボテン	サボテン
tulip	チューリップ	チューリップ
sunflower	ひまわり	向日葵
acorn	どんぐり	団栗
mushroom	きのこ	茸

N   shapes

circle	まる	丸
triangle	さんかく	三角
square	しかく	四角
box	はこ	箱
rectangle	ちょうほうけい	長方形

O clothing

button	ボタン	ボタン
sandals	サンダル	サンダル
sneakers	スニーカー	スニーカー
high heels	ハイヒール	ハイヒール
one-piece dress	ワンピース	ワンピース
jacket	ジャケット	ジャケット
jeans	ジーパン	ジーパン
shoelace	くつひも	靴紐

P in the tool shed

paint	ペンキ	ペンキ
nail	くぎ	釘
screw	ねじ	ねじ
saw	のこぎり	鋸
hammer	ハンマー	ハンマー
screwdriver	ドライバー	ドライバー
flathead screwdriver	マイナス ドライバー	マイナス ドライバー
Phillips screwdriver	プラス ドライバー	プラス ドライバー
bucket	バケツ	バケツ
car battery	バッテリー	バッテリー
battery	でんち	電池
flashlight	かいちゅうでんとう	懐中電灯
ladder	はしご	はしご

Q in the classroom

vocabulary, words	たんご	単語
noun	めいし	名詞
adjective	けいようし	形容詞
verb	どうし	動詞
grammar	ぶんぽう	文法
test	テスト / しけん	テスト / 試験

R — bodily functions

We don't intend any offense by the next set of words – you never know when such vocabulary might come in handy.

hiccups	しゃっくり	しゃっくり
fart	おなら	おなら
burp	げっぷ	げっぷ
sneeze	くしゃみ	くしゃみ
urine	おしっこ (everyday way)	おしっこ
feces	うんこ (everyday way)	うんこ
booger	はなくそ	鼻くそ
snot	はなみず	鼻水
slobber	よだれ	涎
snoring	いびき	いびき
yawn	あくび	欠伸

S — weapons and the military

rocket	ロケット	ロケット
bomb	ばくだん	爆弾
rifle	ライフル	ライフル
pistol	ピストル	ピストル
army knife	アーミーナイフ	アーミーナイフ
canteen	すいとう	水筒
war	せんそう	戦争
war aircraft	せんとうき	戦闘機
submarine	せんすいかん	潜水艦
air force	くうぐん	空軍
army	りくぐん	陸軍
navy	かいぐん	海軍
self-defense force	じえいたい	自衛隊
nuclear bomb	げんしばくだん	原子爆弾
tank	せんしゃ	戦車

T — in a hotel

front desk	フロント	フロント
checkout	チェックアウト	チェックアウト
check-in	チェックイン	チェックイン

room service	ルームサービス	ルームサービス
buffet	ビュッフェ	ビュッフェ
vending machine	じどうはんばいき	自動販売機

APPENDIX B ──────────────── **Answer Key**

❑ **Lesson 1**

Fill in the kanji

1. あした 六じ四じゅう五ふんに おきます。
   Tomorrow I will get up at 6:45.

2. かみが 三まいと えんぴつが 二ほん、あります。
   There are three sheets of paper and two pencils.

3. 二がつ三かの 四じに いきます。
   I will go on the third of February at four o'clock.

4. おとうさんは 六じゅう一さいです。
   My dad is 61 years old.

5. まいにち、ビールを 一ぽん、のみます。
   Everyday, I drink one bottle of beer.

6. にほんに ともだちが 五にん、います。
   I have five friends in Japan. (There are five friends in Japan.)

7. 二じ四じゅっぷんごろ、きます。
   I will come around 2:40.

Reading comprehension translation

① My girlfriend is a 26-year-old nurse.
② She is Japanese.
③ Her name is Masumi.
④ Masumi will be coming to America on December 5th for the first time.
⑤ She will be staying at my house until December 13th.
⑥ She will return to Japan on the morning of the 13th.
⑦ She works everyday until seven in the evening.
⑧ She often calls me after work.
⑨ I call her every Monday night.
⑩ We always talk about two hours.
⑪ But, the last time was about four hours, so I don't have any more money.
⑫ My phone bill for the last month was $459 in total.

Mother	Hello? This is Takahara.
Chris	Hello, this is Chris. Is Masumi there?
Mother	Yes, please wait a moment.

Masumi	Hello?
Chris	Hello, this is Chris.
Masumi	Oh, Chris! What time is it in America now?
Chris	It is five o'clock in the morning. How about Japan?
Masumi	It is nine o'clock in the evening. What are you going to do today?
Chris	I am going to work at seven thirty. When are you coming to America?
Masumi	I am going (there) on December fifth. It is a 3:45 flight.
Chris	I am happy. Come here soon. I am lonely because I am alone.

Masumi   Me too. Oh, sorry. We are going to have dinner now, so I will call you later.
Chris   Ok. Well, talk to you later. Bye.
Masumi   Do you best on your work. Bye.

Reading comprehension questions

1.   What is the speaker's girlfriend's name?
　　　ますみさんです。

2.   When is Masumi coming to America?
　　　じゅう二がつ五かに アメリカに きます。

3.   Does Masumi stay at a hotel in America?
　　　いいえ、ますみさんは ホテルに とまりません。 かれの いえに とまります。

4.   When is she going back to Japan?
　　　じゅう三にちの あさに にほんに かえります。

5.   What is her job?
　　　かんごふです。

6.   Until what time does she work?
　　　よるの しちじまでです。

7.   When does she call the narrator?
　　　よく しごとの あと、でんわをします。

8.   When does the speaker call Masumi?
　　　まいしゅう、げつようびの よるに、ますみさんに でんわを します。

9.   About how many hours does the speaker normally talk to Masumi on the phone?
　　　二じかんぐらいです。

10. Why doesn't the speaker have any money?
　　　このあいだ 四じかん でんわで はなしたから、でんわだいが とてもたかかったです。

Substitution drill

1.   きのう 二じかん べんきょうしました。
　　　きのう 二じかん テレビを みました。
　　　きのう 二じかん ほんを よみました。
　　　きのう 三じかんぐらい ほんを よみました。

2.   四じから しごとを します。
　　　いまから しごとを します。
　　　いまから おんがくを ききます。
　　　いまから ねます。

3.   一ねんまえに けっこんしました。
　　　六かげつまえに けっこんしました。
　　　六かげつまえに アメリカに きました。
　　　六かげつまえに にほんに いきました。

4.   なんにち（かん） とうきょうに いましたか。
　　　なんしゅうかん とうきょうに いましたか。
　　　なんかげつ とうきょうに いましたか。

Question and answer (sample answers)

1. よく ボーイフレンドと でんわで はなします。
   よく おかあさんと でんわで はなします。

2. いつも 一じかんぐらい はなします。
   いつも 三じゅっぷんぐらい はなします。

3. 二ねんまえに ここ [or the name of the city you live in now] に きました。
   四かげつまえに ここに きました。

4. まいにち しごとは くじから 五じまでです。
   まいにち がっこうは しちじから 四じまでです。

5. まいにち はちじかん、はたらきます。
   まいにち 五じかん、べんきょうします。

6. はい、ときどき にほんごで はなします。
   いいえ、にほんごで はなしません。

7. はい、ときどき ともだちの いえに とまります。
   いいえ、とまりません。

❏ Lesson 2

Fill in the kanji

1. にほんに 十四ねんはん、いました。
   I was in Japan for fourteen and half years.

2. 二十ねんまえに アメリカに きました。
   I came to America twenty years ago.

4. 五がつ八かの 七じに きてください。
   Please come at seven o'clock on May 8th.

4. おばあさんは 八十三さいです。
   My grandma is 83 years old.

5. このシャツは 九千八百えんです。
   This shirt is 9,800 yen.

6. ひとが 七にんと ねこが 六ぴき います。
   There are seven people and six cats.

7. チケットを 二千九百まい かいます。
   I will buy 2,900 tickets.

Writing Review – Katakana countries

1. アメリカ	2. イギリス	3. フランス	4. イタリア
5. ベルギー	6. ベトナム	7. スイス	8. ロシア
9. ブラジル	10. スペイン	11. カナダ	12. メキシコ
13. スコットランド	14. オーストラリア	15. ニュージーランド	

Reading comprehension translation

Dear. Mr. Mikami,
① Hello. It's been a while.
② How is everyone?
③ Everyone here is fine.
④ Today, Las Vegas is very hot.
⑤ It was very hot yesterday, too.
⑥ It's our first time in Las Vegas.
⑦ We came here from Japan three days ago.
⑧ It took eleven hours to Las Vegas by plane.
⑨ My mom is shopping everyday.
⑩ The night before last, I bought a cute mini skirt and shoes at the shopping mall with my older sister.
⑪ They were very cheap.
⑫ My dad loves gambling.
⑬ I don't like it because I don't have so much money.
⑭ We are going back to Japan tomorrow.
⑮ Well, please take care of yourself.
From Mariko Kudo

Reading comprehension questions

1. Where is Mariko now?
   まりこさんは いま ラスベガスに います。

2. Is it cold in Las Vegas today?
   いいえ、ラスベガスは きょう とても あついです。

3. Was it cold yesterday?
   いいえ、きのうも とても あつかったです。

4. How long does it take from Japan to Las Vegas by plane?
   十一じかん、かかります。

5. What did Mariko buy the day before yesterday?
   かわいいミニスカートと くつを かいました。

6. Where did she buy them?
   ショッピングモールで かいました。

7. With whom did she go to the shopping mall?
   おねえさんと いっしょに いきました。

8. Does her dad like gambling?
   はい、だいすきです。

9. Does Mariko dislike gambling?
   はい、きらいです。

10. Why does she dislike gambling?
    おかねが あまりないから、すきじゃないです。

11. When is she going back to Japan?
    あした、にほんに かえります。

Substitution drill

1. スプーンで　たべます。
   フォークで　たべます。
   てで　たべます。
   フォークと　ナイフで　たべます。

2. 一ねんに　二かい　にほんに　いきます。
   一ねんに　二かい　アメリカに　かえります。
   二ねんに　一かい　アメリカに　かえります。
   よく　アメリカに　かえります。

3. にほんごの　クラスに　バスで　きました。
   にほんごの　クラスに　くるまで　きました。
   にほんごの　クラスに　でんしゃで　きました。
   にほんごの　クラスに　あるいて　きました。

4. クレジットカードで　でんわだいを　はらいました。
   げんきんで　でんわだいを　はらいました。
   げんきんで　でんきだいを　はらいました。
   げんきんで　ホテルだいを　はらいました。

Question and answer (sample answers)

1. いいえ、てで　たべます。
   いいえ、フォークで　たべます。

2. てで　たべます。
   おはしで　たべます。

3. はい、くるまで　いきます。
   いいえ、くるまで　いきません。バスで　いきます。

4. スーパーに　くるまで　いきます。
   スーパーに　じでんしゃで　いきます。

5. 一ねんに　二かいぐらい、りょこうします。
   一ねんに　五かいぐらい、りょこうします。

6. 一にちに　二じかんぐらい、べんきょうします。
   一にちに　三十ぷんぐらい、べんきょうします。

7. くるまで　二十ぷんぐらい、かかります。
   くるまで　一じかんぐらいです。

8. にほんごの　ほんは　三十ドルでした。
   にほんごの　ほんは　三千五百えんでした。

Practice (sample answers)

1. いっしゅうかんに　にかい、ほんを　よみます。　　I read a book twice a week.
2. いちねんに　いっかい、てがみを　かきます。　　　I write a letter once a year.
3. いちにちに　はちじかん、ねます。　　　　　　　　I sleep eight hours a day.

❑ **Lesson 3**

Fill in the kanji

1. お[金]が [五千三百]えん、あります。
   There is five thousand three hundred yen.

2. [六月七日]に [日]ほんに いきます。
   I will leave for Japan on June 7th.

3. [火]よう[日]は [四]じから しごとです。
   On Tuesdays, my work is from four o'clock.

4. あそこに [木]が [二十]ぽん、あります。
   There are twenty trees over there.

5. [水]を [四]つと メニューを おねがいします。
   Please give me four waters and a menu.

6. らいしゅうの [月]よう[日]は [十日]です。
   Next Monday is the 10th.

Reading comprehension translation

① My name is Yoshie.
② My mom's name is Shizuka.
③ The meaning of "shizuka" in English is "quiet".
④ But my mom is very loud.
⑤ She is loud from morning till night.

⑥ Listen everyone.
⑦ For example, this is our conversation in the morning:

Mom:	Wake up, Yoshie! It's already eight o'clock.
Yoshie:	Huh? Is it eight already? I'll be late for work!
Mom:	Eat breakfast, okay?
Yoshie:	I don't have time, so I'll go now. I'll eat this apple in the car.
Mom:	No, no, please drink milk too!
Yoshie:	Okay, okay. I'm leaving.
Mom:	See you later.

Reading comprehension questions

1. What is Yoshie's mom's name?
   よしえさんの おかあさんの なまえは、「しずか」です。

2. What does "shizuka" mean in English?
   「しずか」の いみは "quiet" です。

3. Is Yoshie's mom quiet?
   いいえ、よしえさんの おかあさんは しずかじゃないです。 とても うるさいです。

4. What time did Yoshie wake up?
   八じに おきました。

5. What kind of breakfast did Yoshie eat?
    りんごを　たべました。

6. Where did she eat her breakfast?
    くるまの　なかで　たべました。

7. What did she drink?
    ミルクを　のみました。
8. What does *ittekimasu* mean in English?
    「いってきます」は　えいごで　"I am leaving (and come back)"　です。

9. What does *itterasshai* mean in English?
    「いってらっしゃい」は　えいごで　"Go and come back safely"　です。

Substitution drill

1. 日ほんに　かえってください／もどってください。
    日ほんに　きてください。
    アメリカに　きてください。
    アメリカに　こないでください。

2. そこで　かいもの(を)してください。
    そこで　たべてください。
    あそこで　たべてください。
    あそこで　たべないでください。

3. 日ほんごを　よんでください。
    日ほんごを　かいてください。
    日ほんごを　きいてください。
    日ほんごを　きかないでください。

4. この CD を　かってください。
    このじしょを　かってください。
    そのざっしを　かってください。
    そのざっしを　かわないでください。

Practice (sample answers)

1. あんまり　ビールを　のまないでください。
2. 水を　のんでください。
3. あんまり　たべないでください。
4. おきてください。
5. がっこうに　おくれないでください。
6. インターネットで　あんまり　かいものを　しないでください。

Translation

1. 日ほんごで　しつもんしてください。
2. あのレストランに　いかないでください。
3. このゆびわを　かってください。

4. わたしの　くるまを　うらないでください。
5. 五じに　わたしの　いえに　きてください。
6. 水よう日に　クラスに　こないでください。

7. この日ほんごの しんぶんを よんでください。
8. もう ねてください。

❏ Lesson 4

Fill in the kanji

1. 木の下に ひとが 十にん います。
   There are ten people under the tree.

2. 十一月三日は 休みです。
   November 3rd is a holiday.

3. 土よう日は 十二じに ひるごはんを たべる。
   On Saturdays, I eat lunch at 12:00 o'clock.

4. テーブルの 上に かみが 四十まい、あります。
   There are forty sheets of paper on the table.

5. 左に いすが 六つ、あります。
   There are six chairs on my left.

6. 上下左右を よく みて下さい。
   Please look every direction carefully.

7. らいしゅうの 金よう日に 休まないで下さい。
   Please don't take a day off on Friday of next week.

Reading comprehension translation

① I am going to Ken Mikami's concert with my friend today.
② I love Ken Mikami's songs.
③ I want all of his CDs.
④ Because Ken Mikami has lots of fans, I bought tickets three months ago.
⑤ The ticket was 5,800 yen.
⑥ My friend said it is expensive, but I don't think it is expensive.
⑦ The concert starts at nine o'clock.
⑧ We will wait in front of the concert hall starting at eight.
⑨ It takes an hour from my friend's house to the concert hall.
⑩ My friend said she will stay home until six fifty.
⑪ I am going by my friend's car.

Reading comprehension questions

1. Where will the speaker go today?
   三上けんの コンサートに いきます。

2. Why is she going to Ken Mikami's concert?
   三上けんの うたが だいすきだからです。

3. When did she buy the tickets?
   三か月まえに かいました。

4. How much was the ticket?
   五千八百えんでした。

5. Who said, "The ticket is expensive"?
   わしゃの ともだちが「チケットはたかい」と いいました。

6. Did the speaker think the ticket was expensive?
   いいえ、おもいませんでした。

7. What time does the concert begin?
   九じからです。

8. What does the speaker do between eight and nine o'clock?
   かいじょうの まえで まちます。

9. How long does it take from the friend's house to the hall?
   くるまで 一じかん、かかります。

10. Until what time does the friend stay home?
    六じ五十ぷんまで います。

Substitution drill

1. あさって、コンピューターを うると おもいます。
   あさって、このほんを よむと おもいます。
   あさって、ごご十二じまで ねると おもいます。
   あさって、えいがを みないと おもいます。
   あさって、がっこうに いかないと おもいます。

2. まりこさんが ちゅうごくに いくと ききました。
   まりこさんが ビールを たくさん のんだと ききました。
   まりこさんが あたらしい くるまを かったと ききました。
   まりこさんが そのみせで かいものすると ききました。
   まりこさんが ほんを かいたと ききました。

3. なにも かいません。
   なにも たべません。
   なにも しませんでした。
   なにも よみませんでした。
   なにも ききませんでした。

Translation (sample answers)

1. I think my Japanese class is difficult.
   日ほんごの クラスは むずかしいと おもいます。

2. I think Mt. Fuji is pretty.
   ふじさんは きれいだと おもいます。

3. I think sushi is not delicious.
   おすしは おいしくないと おもいます。

4. I think I will go to the park this Saturday.
   こんしゅうの 土よう日に こうえんに いくと おもいます。

5. I think I won't study Japanese this Sunday.
   こんしゅうの 日よう日に 日ほんごを べんきょうしないと おもいます。

6. I think my mom likes my boyfriend.
   ははは わたしの かれが すきだと おもいます。

7. I heard my teacher dislikes fish.
   せんせいは さかなが きらいだと ききました。

8. I heard there are lots of hot springs in Japan.
   日ほんに たくさん おんせんが あると ききました。

❏ Lesson 5

Fill in the kanji

1. あした、大がくで 三つ クラスが あります。
   I have three classes at college tomorrow.

2. へやの中に 小さいテーブルが 二つ あります。
   There are two small tables in a room.

3. 大きいりんごは 六百円です。
   A big apple is six hundred yen.

4. あのおんなの人は 三十さいだと ききました。
   I heard that lady over there is thirty years old.

5. いつも ウインクは 右目で します。
   I always wink with my right eye.

6. このクラスに 人が 二十五人 います。
   There are twenty five people in this class.

7. いまは しごと中だから、五じに あいましょう。
   I am in the middle of work right now, let's meet at five o'clock.

Reading comprehension translation

① On the 20th of next month, Mr. Sato will take a trip with his family.
② He (dad) asked everyone in his family, "where would you like (to go)?".
③ Mom answered, "A hot spring would be good. Let's all eat something delicious."
④ Older sister said, "Disneyland is better than a hot spring.
⑤ Younger brother, Jun, thinks Disneyland would be better too.
⑥ Dad said to the kids, "Since mom is always cleaning, cooking, and doing laundry, (going to) a hot spring would be better than Disneyland."
⑦ In the end, we went to a hot spring resort.
⑧ In Japanese hot springs, there are men's baths and women's baths.
⑨ There is also "mixed bathing" (men and women)
⑩ Japanese people love hot springs.
⑪ The meals at hot springs are Japanese-style.
⑫ The kids thought the hot spring resort was better than the a hotel.

Reading comprehension questions

1. When will Mr. Sato's family take a trip?
   らい月の　二十日に　りょこうします。

2. What did the mom say would be good?
   おかあさんは「おんせんが　いいよ」と　いいました。

3. What did the older sister say would be good?
   おねえさんは「おんせんより　ディズニーランドのほうがいい」と　いいました。

4. Why did the dad say that a hot spring is good?
   おかあさんが　いつも　いえの　そうじと　りょうりと　せんたくを　しているからです。

5. Where did everyone go after all?
   おんせんに　いきました。

6. Which one did the kids like, a hotel or a hot spring?
   ホテルより　おんせんのほうが　よかったと　おもいました。

Practice 1

1. ねています。
2. べんきょうしています。
3. ピザを　たべています。
4. スープを　のんでいます。
5. おきゃくさんを　まっています。
6. ほんを　かっています。

Practice 2 (sample answers)

1. ケーキより　アイスクリームのほうが　すきです。
2. エスカレーターより　エレベーターのほうが　はやいです。
3. ピアスより　ゆびわのほうが　たかいです。
4. りんごより　ぶどうのほうが　あまいです。

Substitution drill

1. 日ほんごを　べんきょうしています。
   ラジオを　きいています。
   ワインを　のんでいます。
   ワインを　のんでいません。

2. てがみを　かいています。
   りょこうしています。
   でんわを　しています。
   でんわを　していません。

3. さしみより　すしのほうが　すきです。
   チョコレートより　アイスクリームのほうが　すきです。
   そうじより　せんたくのほうが　すきです。
   ジュースより　水のほうが　すきです。

Question and answer (sample answers)

1. はい、みています。
   いいえ、みていません。

2. はい、たべています。
   いいえ、たべていません。

3. はい、しています。
   いいえ、していません。

4. わたしのへやは、あかるいです。
   くらいです。

5. はい、コーラより ジュースのほうが すきです。
   りょうほう すきです。

6. はい、おんせんより ホテルのほうが いいです。
   いいえ、ホテルのほうが いいです。

7. そうじのほうが たのしいです。
   せんたくのほうが たのしいです。

8. ディズニーランドのほうが おもしろいです。
   マジックマウンテンのほうが おもしろいです。

9. カタカナのほうが むずかしいです。
   りょうほう、むずかしいです。

10. えいがのほうが すきです。
    ピクニックのほうが すきです。えいがは きらいです。

11. にほんりょうりのほうを よく たべます。
    中かりょうりを よく たべます。

❑ Lesson 6

Fill in the kanji

1. わたしの 手と 足は 大きいです。
   My hands and feet are big.

2. あのいり口のまえに 人が 四人 います。
   There are four people in front of that entrance over there.

3. から手の クラスは 水よう日です。
   The karate class is on Wednesdays.

4. 右足が いたいです。 力が ありません。
   My right leg hurts. It doesn't have any strength.

5. わたしのいぬは 耳が 小さいです。
   My dog has small ears.

6. 左のメロンは 三千円です。
   The melon to your left is three thousand yen.

7. とうきょうの 人口は 千二百まん人 ぐらいです。
   The population of Tokyo is about twelve million.

Reading comprehension translation

① Akira and Johnson are friend's since elementary school.
② The two of them met six years ago in America.
③ Akira was visiting his older sister's home on summer vacation.
④ Akira's older sister is married to an American.
⑤ Johnson lived next to his sister's house.
⑥ There was a brown dog and a very cute turtle at Johnson's house.
⑦ Since Akira really liked animals, he often played at Jonson's house.
⑧ Both of them are high school students now.
⑨ Johnson is currently homestaying at Akira's house in Japan for about one month.
⑩ There are also three animals at Akira's house.
⑪ They are two rabbits and a pig.
⑫ There is a petshop next to their school.
⑬ That petshop sells various interesting animals.
⑭ Akira works there part time.

Reading comprehension questions

1. Where did they meet?
   アメリカで あいました。

2. What kind of pets did Johnson have?
   ちゃいろいいぬと とてもかわいいかめが いました。

3. Why did Akira often play in Johnson's house?
   あきらくんは、どうぶつが 大すきだったからです。

4. How long has Johnson been staying in Japan?
   一か月ぐらい、います。

5. Akira has been working part time at a pet shop. Where is it?
   がっこうの 右よこに あります。

Substitution drill

1. きょう、かれ／かのじょと あいます。
   きのう、かれ／かのじょと あいました。
   あした、かれ／かのじょと あいます。
   こんしゅうの 日よう日に かれ／かのじょと あいます。
   こんしゅうの 日よう日に だれと あいますか。

2. りかちゃんは 小がっこう 六ねんせいです。
   りかちゃんは 中がっこう 二ねんせいです。
   りかちゃんは こうこう 一ねんせいです。
   りかちゃんは 小がっこう 一ねんせいです。
   りかちゃんは なんねんせいですか。

3. はる休みに 日ほんで ホームステイを しました。
   ふゆ休みに 日ほんで ホームステイを しました。
   ふゆ休みに とうきょうで ホームステイを しました。
   ふゆ休みに 大さかで ホームステイを しました。
   いつ、大さかで ホームステイを しましたか。

Particles

1. ロサンゼルス<u>から</u> 日ほん<u>まで</u> ひこうき<u>で</u> 十じかんぐらい かかります。

2. 金ようび<u>に</u> あのレストラン<u>で</u> ともだち<u>に／と</u> あいます。

3. きょねん、フランス<u>に</u> すんでいました。

4. まい日、六じ<u>に</u> がっこう<u>に</u> いきます。

5. 日ほんの ビール<u>は</u> アメリカの ビール<u>と</u> ちがいます。

6. たなべさん<u>の</u> くるまは あたらしい<u>と</u> おもいます。
7. ベッド<u>の</u> 上<u>に</u> ざっし<u>が</u> あります。

8. いぬ<u>より</u> ねこのほう<u>が</u> すきです。

9. らいしゅう<u>の</u> 月よう日<u>に</u> えいが<u>を</u> みましょう。

10. 日ほんご<u>の</u> じしょ<u>が</u> ほしいです。

Adjectives

1. (heavy)	かるい	(light)	
2. (loud)	おとなしい	(quiet)	
3. (new)	ふるい	(old)	
4. (bright)	くらい	(dark)	
5. (hot)	さむい	(cold)	
6. (far)	ちかい	(near)	
7. (interesting)	つまらない	(boring)	

Practice
1. たかくて、かるい けいたいでんわ
2. しろくて、小さい ねこ
3. かわいくて、おもい ちょきんばこ
4. やすくて、あおい けいさんき
5. いたくて、こわい ちゅうしゃ

❏ Lesson 7

Fill in the kanji

1. やま口さんの 子どもは 小さくて、かわいいです。
   Mr. Yamaguchi's kids are small and cute.

2. ゆかちゃんは 小がっこう 五ねん生 です。
   Yuka is in fifth grade.

3. あの女の人は きれいだから 目立ちます。
   That lady over there is pretty, so she stands out.
4. せん生が つくえの上で 立たないでと いいました。
   A teacher said, "Don't stand on your desk".

5. 大がく生は 六月から なつ休みです。
   College students have summer vacation starting in June.

6. あの田がっこうは 大きいですね。
    That middle school over there is big, isn't it?

7. えきので口で 男の人が 立っています。
    There is a man standing at the exit of the station.

Reading comprehension translation

（Tongue Twister）
In the backyard there are two, in the front yard there are two, there are chickens.

① This is a Japanese tongue twister.
② The *uraniwa* means "backyard".
③ The *niwa* in this tongue twister has two meanings.
④ The first one is a "front yard".
⑤ The second one is the number of chickens.
⑥ A long time ago, the majority of Japanese homes raised chickens.
⑦ In the yard (*niwa*) of Japanese houses, there were these birds (*tori*).
⑧ Therefore, the name of these birds became "*niwatori*".

Reading comprehension questions

1. How do you call *hayakuchi kotoba* in English?
    はやくちことばは えいごで tongue twister です。

2. What is the meaning of *uraniwa*?
    うらにわの いみは backyard です。

3. How many meanings does the *niwa* in this tongue twister have?
    二つ、あります。

4. What does the first *niwa* mean?
    一つ目の いみは いえの まえの にわです。

5. What does the second *niwa* mean?
    二つ目の いみは にわとりの かずです。

6. What did most Japanese homes raise a long time ago?
    むかし、にほんの ほとんどの いえでは にわとりを かっていました。

7. Why did the name of this bird become *niwatori*?
    にわで かっていたから、にわとりに なりました。

Counters
1. さんわ   (three birds or rabbits)
2. にばん   (number two)
3. よんひき   (four small animals)
4. よにん   (four people)
5. ついたち   (first of the month)
6. よじ   (four o'clock)
7. さんがつ   (March)
8. いっぽん   (one long object)

Short dialogue translation

Judge 1: Which dog do you think is good?
Judge 2: Let's see… I think the first dog is good, since the size is just right and he is also popular.
Judge 1: I think the third dog is going to become a star because he is small and cute.
Judge 1: How about the fourth dog?
Judge 2: Umm…he was popular a long time ago, but he is a little too old for current movies.
Judge 1: I see. Well then, let's decide between the first and the second one.

Question and answer (sample answers)

1. はい、かっています。いぬを 二ひき、かっています。
    いいえ、かっていません。

2. はい、子いぬが ほしいです。でも、子ねこは ほしくないです。
    はい、子いぬが ほしいです。子ねこも ほしいです。

3. あかワインのほうが おいしいと おもいます。
    どっちも すきじゃないです。

4. きょうだいは 三人です。わたしは 二ばん目です。
    きょうだいは いません。

5. はい、むずかしいと おもいます。
    いいえ、むずかしくないです。

Translation
1. 三ぼん目の ビールを のんでいます。
2. 二つ目（二こ目）の ハンバーガーを たべています。
3. 三つ目の いえを かいます。
4. 四だい目の くるまを うります。
5. わたしの 五ひき目の いぬの なまえは たろうです。
6. 二こ目（二つ目）の ケーキを たべましょう。
7. 左から 七ばん目（七わ目）の とりが すきです。

❑ Lesson 8

Fill in the kanji

1. 天気が いいです。山に ハイキングに いきましょう。
    The weather is good. Let's go hiking in the mountains.

2. 雨が たくさん ふったから、川の水が おおいですね。
    Because it rained a lot, there is a lot of water in the river.

3. 空気が いいから、天の川が きれいです。
    Because the air is clean, the Milky Way is pretty.

4. 右から 二つ目の 山が ふじ山です。
    The second one from the right is Mt. Fuji.

5. 月よう日は いつも げん気じゃないです。
    I am always not in high spirits on Mondays.

6. 空に ほしが 五つ、あります。
    There are five stars in the sky.

7. 六人の 子どもと 川で ピクニックを しました。
   I went on a picnic by the river with six kids.

Reading comprehension translation

1. Aiko Sato lives in Osaka.
2. This year, she became twenty-five years old.
3. Aiko is a music teacher.
4. Aiko has fifteen students.
4. She has students from three years old to six years old.

6. Her school is in Kobe.
7. It takes about twenty minutes by train.
8. Morning classes start from nine o'clock, so she gets up two hours before that.
9. Those classes end at eleven.
10. She always eats her lunch at an Italian restaurant in front of school.

11. This restaurant is very cheap.
12. Afternoon classes start at one.
13. They end at four.
14. There are four classes in a day.
15. She returns to her home around five thirty.

16. Mostly she eats dinner at home.
17. Aiko's family is mother, father and younger sister.
18. Her younger sister is still a high school student.
19. Her younger sister has a part time job at a pharmacy from Thursday to Saturday.
20. Her father is a salary man.

21. Her mother has a job too.
22. Aiko doesn't have classes on Saturday and Sunday.
23. She sleeps until ten in the morning on her days off.
24. Every family member has a day off on Sunday.
25. Once a month, they play tennis at a park on Sunday.

Reading comprehension questions

1. Where does Aiko Sato live?
   大さかに すんでいます。

2. How old is Aiko?
   ことし 二十五さいに なりました。

3. What is Aiko's job?
   おんがくの せん生です。
4. How many students does Aiko have?
   十五人、います。

5. About how old are her students?
   三さいから 六さいまでです。

6. Where is Aiko's school?
   こうべに あります。

7. What time does her morning class start?
   九じから はじまります。

8. Where does she always eat lunch?
    がっこうの まえの イタリアりょうりの みせで たべます。

9. What time does her afternoon class start?
    一じから はじまります。

10. How many classes a day does she have?
    一日に 四かい、あります。

11. What time does she go home?
    五じはんごろ、かえります。

12. Where does she eat dinner?
    ほとんど いえで たべます。

13. How many people are there in Aiko's family?
    四人です。

14. What kind of part-time job does Aiko's sister have?
    やっきょくで アルバイトを しています。

15. What does her father do?
    サラリーマンです。

16. What day of the week are her days off?
    土よう日と 日よう日に しごとが ありません。

17. What does Aiko's family do on Sunday?
    一か月に 一かい、日よう日に こうえんで テニスを します。

Substitution drill

1. がっこうは 土よう日の 九じに はじまります。
    このみせは 土よう日の 九じに はじまります。
    このみせは 土よう日の 十じに はじまります。
    このみせは 月よう日から 金よう日まで 十じに はじまります。

2. 三ねんまえ、しごとを はじめました。
    七か月まえ、しごとを はじめました。
    三じから、しごとを はじめました。
    三じから、じゅぎょうを はじめました。

3. かいしゃは きのう 五じに おわりました。
    かいしゃは あした 五じに おわります。
    かいしゃは あした 五じに おわると おもいます。
    かいしゃは あした 五じに おわると ききました。

4. きょねんの 六月から コンビニで はたらいています。
    きょねんの 六月から あのホテルで はたらいています。
    きょねんの 六月から このかいしゃで はたらいています。
    せん月の 九日から このかいしゃで はたらいています。

Question and answer (sample answers)

1. きょ年、はじめました。
    六か月まえに、はじめました。

2. しごとは 九じに はじまります。
   がっこうは 八じはんに はじまります。

3. ソニー (Sony) で はたらいています。
   カリフォルニア大がく (University of California) に いっています。

4. このべんきょうは 九じごろ、おわると おもいます。
   このべんきょうは きょう、おわらないと おもいます。

5. 十二月ごろ、ふゆに なります。
   六月ごろ、なつに なります。

6. ことし、はたちに なります。
   ことし、三十二さいに なります。

❑ **Lesson 9**

Fill in the kanji

1. 森や 林の 中は あつくないです。
   It isn't hot in the forests and woods.

2. あそこに 大きい石が 六つ あります。
   There are six big stones over there.

3. 小さい虫が つくえの下に います。
   There is a small bug under the desk.

4. 日ほんの 子どもは 花火が 大すきです。
   Japanese kids love fire works.

5. この町に 二千三ねんから すんでいます。
   I have lived in this town since 2003.

6. 子犬が 十ぴき います。
   There are ten puppies.

7. わたしの犬は 目が あおくて、耳が グレーです。
   My dog has blue eyes and gray ears.

Reading comprehension translation

① Tomorrow is my birthday.
② I will be twenty one years old.
③ My birthday party starts from two at my grandmother's house.
④ I think thirty people will probably come.
⑤ My best friend Takako said she won't come to the party because her work ends at five.
⑥ That's too bad.
⑦ I would like to watch Tom Cruise's new movie after the party.
⑧ I am a big fan of Tom Cruise.
⑨ After the party
⑩ The party was very fun.
⑪ Takako didn't come, but I am going to go shopping with her tomorrow at four.
⑫ Takako said she wants to buy some cosmetics.
⑬ I don't want to buy anything.
⑭ But I want to show my birthday gifts to Takako.

Reading comprehension questions

1. When is the speaker's birthday?
   あしたです。

2. How old will she be tomorrow?
   二十一さいに なります。

3. Where will they have her birthday party?
   おばあさんの いえで します。

4. What time does the birthday party begin?
   二じから はじまります。

5. What is the name of the speaker's best friend?
   たか子さんです。

6. Will Takako come to the party tomorrow?
   いいえ、きません。

7. Why is that?
   たか子さんは しごとが 五じに おわるからです。

8. What do you think the speaker will do after the party?
   トム・クルーズの あたらしいえいがが 見たいです。

9. On the day after the party, with whom will the speaker go shopping?
   たか子さんと いっしょに かいものを します。

10. What does Takako want?
    けしょうひんが ほしいです。

11. What does the speaker want to buy?
    なにも かいたくないです。

Verb conjugation review

	English	Dictionary Form	ない form	たい form
1	to do your best	がんばる	がんばらない	がんばりたい
2	to work	はたらく	はたらかない	はたらきたい
3	to shop	かいものをする	かいものをしない	かいものをしたい
4	to pay	はらう	はらわない	はらいたい
5	to answer	こたえる	こたえない	こたえたい

6	to meet	あう	あわない	あいたい
7	to play	あそぶ	あそばない	あそびたい
8	to live	すむ	すまない	すみたい
9	to show	みせる	みせない	みせたい
10	to smoke	すう	すわない	すいたい
11	to raise an animal	かう	かわない	かいたい
12	to begin (active)	はじめる	はじめない	はじめたい

Substitution drill

1. タバコが すきに なりました。
   日ほんごの しゅくだいが すきに なりました。
   日ほんりょうりが すきに なりました。
   日ほんりょうりが きらいに なりました。

2. このコンピューターは 千五百ドルい下です。
   このコンピューターは 一まんドルい上です。
   このコンピューターは 三まんドルい下です。
   このコンピューターは 三千ドルい上です。

3. ラップが きらいなの？
   あのみせが すきなの？
   あしたは 土よう日なの？
   きょうは 五日なの？

4. りんごが たべたいです。
   ピアスが かいたいです。
   スペインごが べんきょうしたいです。
   せん生に なりたいです。
   コンサートに いきたいです。

Translation

1. このかいしゃで はたらきたいです。

2. 日ほんで すきやきが たべたいです。

3. ラップを ききたくないです。

4. きのう、くすりを のみたくなかったです。

5. こんしゅうの 土よう日に えいがを みたいです。

6. 日ほんりょうりの レストランで アルバイトが したかったです。

7. いぬを かいたくなかったです。

Short dialogue translation

Tanaka   Mr. Yamada, you are smoking cigarettes again, aren't you?
Yamada   Yes. It is becoming my habit lately.
Tanaka   How many cigarettes have you smoked today?
Yamada   Maybe this is the fifteenth one. I always smoke more than twenty cigarettes (a day).
Tanaka   I see. I don't smoke at all.
Yamada   Why?
Tanaka   Since I heard that you are going to get cancer (if you smoke),
            I came to dislike cigarettes.
Yamada   I see…well then, do you think I will be okay if I smoke less than ten cigarettes?
Tanaka   No good! Let's stop smoking!

Question and answer (sample answers)

1. こんしゅうの 日よう日に えいがが みたいです。
   こんしゅうの 日よう日に いえで ねたいです。

2. いいえ、べんきょうしたくないです。
   はい、べんきょうしたいです。

3. ばんごはんは すきやきが たべたいです。
   ばんごはんは ハンバーガーと ポテトが たべたいです。

4. かんこうが したいです。
   おすしが たべたいです。

5. いいえ、ぜんぜん すいません。
   はい、すいます。十ぽんいじょう、すいます。

6. ロマンチック・コメディーが すきに なりました。
   アクションえんがが すきに なりました。

7. 五じかんいじょう、べんきょうします。
   一じかんいじょう、べんきょうします。

❑ Lesson 10

Fill in the kanji

1. その村に 人が 四百人 います。
   There are four hundred people in that village.

2. 日ほんには 水田が たくさん あります。
   There are many rice paddies in Japan.

3. 山の上の 赤い夕日が きれいですね。
   The red sunset over the mountain is beautiful, isn't it?

4. 青い空に 白いくもが 七つ あります。
   There are seven white clouds in the blue sky.

5. あの白人の 女の子は だれですか。
   Who is that Caucasian girl?

6. 土よう日は 休みです。えいがが 見たいです。
   Saturday is my day off. I want to see a movie.

7. 田んぼのよこに 白と 赤の 花が あります。
   There are white and red flowers by the rice paddy.

Reading comprehension translation

① Yumiko had a lot of cavities when she was little.
② She hated dentists, so she didn't go to the dentist so much.
③ When she was in the fifth grade, she went to a dentist's office in a town next to hers for the first time.
④ There was a very kind female assistant in the office.
⑤ The lady always said, "It's okay".
⑥ Yumiko began to like dentists from then.
⑦ Now she is working for a dentist.

Reading comprehension questions

1. Did Yumiko have cavities when she was little?
   はい、たくさん 虫ばが ありました。

2. Did Yumiko like dentists?
   いいえ、大きらいでした。

3. When did she go to a dentist's office for the first time?
   小がっこう五ねん生のとき、はじめて はいしゃさんに いきました。

4. Where was the dentist that she went?
   となりの 町の はいしゃさんに いきました。

5. What kind of assistant was there?
   とても やさしい アシスタントの おねえさんが いました。

6. What did the assistant always say to Yumiko?
   いつも 「大じょうぶよ」と いいました。

7. Why did Yumiko become to like dentists?
   アシスタントの おねえさんが やさしかったからです。

8. Where does she work now?
   いま、はいしゃで はたらいています。

Substitution drill

1. 犬が 二ひきだけ います。
   女の子が 三人だけ います。
   げん金が 十ドルだけ あります。
   げん金が たくさん あります。

2. きょねん、四かい 日ほんに いきました。
   きょねん、はじめて 日ほんに いきました。
   きょねん、はじめて くるまを かいました。
   きょねん、はじめて スキーを しました。

3. 日ほんに いたとき、パーティーを しました。
   子どもが 一さいに なったとき、パーティーを しました。
   しんゆうが 日ほんから もどったとき、パーティーを しました。
   ラスベガスに いったとき、パーティーを しました。

4. じかんが あるとき、でんわしてください。
   いそがしくないとき、でんわしてください。
   つまらないとき、でんわしてください。
   たのしくないとき、でんわしてください。

Translation

1. しゅくだいを した とき、このかんじが わかりませんでした。
   When I did the homework, I didn't understand/know this kanji.

2. おとうさんが かえった とき、一しょに ごはんを たべましょう。
   When dad comes back, let's have a meal together.

3. かんじの れんしゅうを する とき、いつも ねむいです。
   When I practice kanji, I am always sleepy.

4. ギャンブルを する とき、お金が たくさん ほしいです。
   When I gamble, I want lots of money.

Question and answer (sample answers)

1. くすりを のみます。
   やすみます。

2. ともだちに でんわします。
   おんがくを ききます。

3. 日ほんごを べんきょうしません。
   がっこうが いそがしいときも、日ほんごを べんきょうします。

4. はい、とても うれしいです。
   いいえ、うれしくないです。たくさん しゅくだいが ほしいです。

5. コメディーを 見ているとき、たのしいです。
   テレビは 見ません。すきじゃないです。

6. はい、いつも ポップコーンを たべます。
   いいえ、ポップコーンは たべません。ソーダを のみます。

7. はい、いつも おんがくを ききます。
   いいえ、おんがくは ききません。でも、ときどき テレビを 見ます。

8. はいしゃさんに なりたかったです。
   パイロットに なりたかったです。

9. よく サッカーと バスケットボールを しました。
   スキーと スケートを しました。ときどき テニスも しました。

Useful Expressions

1. おやすみなさい
2. おはようございます
3. こんにちは
4. こんばんは
5. いただきます
6. ごちそうさまでした
7. ただいま
8. いってきます
9. おかえりなさい

❑ Lesson 11

Fill in the kanji

1. 先生が 早口ことばを いいました。
   My teacher said a tongue twister.

2. ゆみ子ちゃんは 四月に 中がく生に なります。
   Yumiko will become a middle school student in April.

3. 先しゅうの 木よう日に しゅくだいを 出しました。
   I turned my homework in last Thursday.

4. 日本ごの 文は むずかしいですね。
   Japanese sentences are hard.

5. 出口は、あのエスカレーターの 右に あります。
   An exit is on the right side of that escalator over there.

6. まい回、八じに いえを 出ます。
   I leave home at eight o'clock every day.

7. 早く、大がくに いきたいです。
   I want to go to college soon.

Reading comprehension translation

① Scott got transferred to Tokyo two weeks ago.
② He is in his company's dorm now.
③ His company sells American shoes.
④ His dorm room is a two-person room, so he is looking for an apartment that's close to his work.
⑤ Today, he went to a realtor's office.
⑥ The realtor was a nice person.
⑦ Scott studied Japanese in school in America, so he can speak Japanese.

Main Conversation Translation

Realtor:	Welcome. Are you looking for a room?
Scott:	Yes, I am looking for an apartment.
Realtor:	What kind of apartment is good?
Scott:	A convenient place for shopping and commuting to work would be good.
Realtor:	Where is your place of work?
Scott:	It is close to Shinjuku station.
Realtor:	Well… there are two. The first apartment is new and it takes 15 minutes from Shinjuku station by train. And the second one-room apartment is old and it takes 25 minutes by bus. The first one is a little more expensive than the second one. But it is a very quiet place.
Scott:	Well then, I want to see the apartment.
Realtor:	Okay. Let's go now.

Reading comprehension questions

1. How do you say *tenkin* in English?
    「てんきん」は えいごで job transfer です。

2. When did Scott get transferred to Tokyo?
    二しゅうかんまえに、てんきんに なりました。

3. Where does he live now?
    いま、かいしゃの りょうに すんでいます。

4. What kind of company is Scott's company?
    スコットさんの かいしゃは アメリカの くつを うっています。

5. Does Scott have a roommate?
    はい、います。

6. Does Scott want to stay in his dorm?
    いいえ、いたくないです。

7. Why?
    りょうの へやは 二人べやだからです。

8. Then where does he want to live?
    しょくばに ちかい アパートに すみたいです。

9. Where did he go today?
    ふどうさんやに いきました。

10. What kind of person was the realtor?
    しんせつな人でした。

11. Can Scott speak Japanese?
    はい、はなせます。

12. Why can he speak Japanese?
    アメリカの がっこうで 日本ごを べんきょうしたからです。

Substitution drill

1. 田中さんは しんせつな人です。
    田中さんは ふくざつな人です。
    田中さんは いやな人です。
    田中さんは きれいな人です。

2. フランスごが はなせます。
    フランスごが はなせません。
    スペインごが はなせません。
    中ごくごが はなせません。

3. 大きい れいぞうこを さがしています。
    べんりな じしょを さがしています。
    かんたんな 日本ごの 本を さがしています。
    しずかな ところを さがしています。

❏ Lesson 12

Fill in the kanji

1. 日本の 大学生は よく アルバイトを します。
   Japanese college students often work part-time.

2. 正しいかん字を かいて下さい。
   Please write correct kanji.

3. この町に 中学校が 九つ あります。
   There are nine middle schools in this town.

4. その白い花の 名まえを おしえて下さい。
   Please tell me the name of that white flower.

5. 山田さんは 七年まえ、この村に きました。
   Mr. Yamada came to this village seven years ago.

6. わたしの いもうとは 小学生です。
   My younger sister is an elementary school student.

7. きょ年のお正月は 天気が わるかったです。
   The weather was bad on New Year's Day last year.

Translation

1. すきな レストランは 「name of the restaurant」 です。

2. きらいな たべものは 「   」 です。

3. すきな えいがは 「   」 です。

4. きらいな はいゆうは 「   」 です。

Question and answer (sample answers)

1. すきな たべものは にほんりょうりです。
   すきな たべものは おすしと おさしみです。

2. きらいな テレビばんぐみは ニュースです。
   きらいな テレビばんぐみは ありません。

3. すきなところは しずかな ところです。としょかんが すきです。
   きれいな ところが すきです。こうえんが 大すきです。

4. 大きい アパートを さがしています。
   きれいな いえを さがしています。

5. かっこいい かれを さがしています。
   かわいい かのじょを さがしています。

6.　えいごと 日本ごが すこし はなせます。
　　スペインごと フランスごが はなせます。

7.　はい、むずかしいです。
　　いいえ、あんまり むずかしくないです。

8.　はい、とても たいへんです。
　　いいえ、あんまり たいへんじゃないです。

Short dialogue translation

Mr. Deguchi:	You don't look good, Mr. Murata. What happended?
Mr. Murata:	Actually, I got transferred to New York.
Mr. Deguchi:	That's great. When are you leaving?
Mr. Murata:	The 10th of next month. But I don't want to go.
Mr. Deguchi:	Why?
Mr. Murata:	Because I can't speak English.
Mr. Deguchi:	You can't speak at all?
Mr. Murata:	I can just do greetings. I will look for an English teacher in New York.
Mr. Deguchi:	Please do your best.

Reading comprehension translation

Oct. 27th, Heisei 18
To Take chan,
① Thank you for your letter.
② Is a foreign country fun?
③ I became a 3rd grader.
④ My class changed,too. And I made some new friends too.
⑤ I came to like school after I became a 3rd grader.
⑥ Are Take-chan and Sachiko-chan doing well?
⑦ Yuko and I are fine.
⑧ I drew a picture of a dress on the back of this letter.
⑨ Plese take a look.
⑩ Write me a letter again.
From Atsuko

Reading comprehension questions

1.　Who wrote this letter to whom?
　　あつ子ちゃんが たけちゃんに かきました。

2.　What grade is Atsuko in now?
　　いま、三年生です。

3.　Is Atsuko's class same as before?
　　いいえ、ちがいます。

4.　Did Atsuko make new friends after she became a 3rd grader?
　　はい、できました。

5.　Who do you think "Sachiko" is?
　　さち子ちゃんは たぶん たけちゃんの きょうだいです。

6.　Who do you think "Yuko" is?
　　ゆう子ちゃんは たぶん あつ子ちゃんの いもうとです。

7. What is on the back of this letter?
   ドレスの えが あります。

8. Who drew the picture of the dress?
   あつ子ちゃんが かきました。

9. When did Atsuko write this letter?
   へいせい十八年十月二十七日に かきました。

Substitution drill

1. テレビを 見てから、べんきょうします。
   いえに かえってから、べんきょうします。
   手がみを かいてから、べんきょうします。
   ひるごはんを たべてから、べんきょうします。

2. 水が こおりに かわりました。
   しょうわが へいせいに かわりました。
   はるが なつに かわりました。
   みどりが きいろに かわりました。

3. やきゅうが できます。
   りょうりが できます。
   スペインごが できます。
   ピアノが できます。

Question and answer (sample answers)

1. テニスと ゴルフが できます。
   スポーツが できません。すきじゃないです。

2. ピアノと バイオリンが できます。
   なにも できません。

3. いつも テレビを 見ます。でも、きょうは 日本ごの しゅくだいを します。
   いつも、しごとを します。

4. ビールが のみたいです。
   ともだちと かいものに いきたいです。

5. ジョギングを します。
   コーヒーを のみます。

Short dialogue translation

Hiroshi:	Yukiko, where do you want to go for our honeymoon?
Yukiko:	Let's see... how about Italy?
Hiroshi:	Sounds good. Do you want to go right after the wedding?
Yukiko:	No. I want to go after having a night's rest.
Hiroshi:	Okay. Are we going to Italy only?
Yukiko:	I also want to go to France and Germany.

Hiroshi: Well then, I am going to a travel agency after I finish work tomorrow.

And I will ask about package tours to Europe.

Yukiko: I want to go with you.

Hiroshi: Well then, let's have dinner at the usual restaurant after I go to the travel agency.

❑ Lesson 13

Fill in the kanji

1. 車の中で 音がくを ききます。
   I listen to music in the car.

2. 大きい町は でん車や 車の 音が うるさいです。
   Big towns are noisy with train and car noises.

3. 赤い貝を 四つと 白い貝を 五つ 見つけた。
   I found four red shells and five white shells.

4. 百円玉が つくえの下から 見つかりました。
   The 100 yen coin is found under the desk.

5. 五月は 草や 木の いろが きれいです。
   The color of the grass and trees is pretty in May.

6. 青い水玉のシャツは 六千円です。
   The blue polka dot shirt is six thousand yen.

7. 竹林で 竹の子を さがしました。
   I looked for bamboo shoots in a bamboo forest.

Reading comprehension translation

① Amelia is looking for a new job.
② She works at a supermarket now.
③ Since she went to Japan three and half years ago, she started studying Japanese.
④ Since she can speak Japanese, she wants to work for a Japanese company.
⑤ Tomorrow, she is going to have an interview with a computer company.

The interview

Interviewer: You are Amelia, right?
Amelia: Yes, I am Amelia. Nice to meet you.
Interviewer: Nice to meet you, too. Why do you want to work here?
Amelia: When I went to Japan for the first time, I came to like Japan. And I can handle computers. This company is the biggest Japanese company in America, so I thought I would like to work here.
Interviewer: I see. There is a secretary position open. What languages do you speak?
Amelia: I can speak English, Spanish, and Japanese.
Interviewer: How much Japanese can you speak?
Amelia: I can speak daily conversation.
Interviewer: Also, can you write letters in Japanese?

Amelia: I can write a little. I can write hiragana and katakana, but I am still studying kanji.
Interviewer: Where did you study computers?
Amelia: I studied computer programming at college.
Interviewer: That's good. Can you come back here again on the first of next month?
Amelia: Yes, of course.
Interviewer: Well then, please come at eight thirty. We will have a second interview.
Amelia: Yes, I will. Thank you very much.

Reading comprehension questions

1. What is Amelia looking for right now?
   あたらしいしごとを さがしています。

2. Where does she work now?
   いま、スーパーで はたらいています。

3. When did she go to Japan?
   三年はんまえに いきました。

4. What kind of company does she think she wants to work for?
   日本の かいしゃで はたらきたいと おもっています。

5. Why is that?
   日本ごが はなせるからです。

6. Which company is she having an interview with?
   コンピューターがいしゃで めんせつを しています。

7. Why did she think she wanted to have an interview with that company?
   アメリカで 一ばん大きい日本の かいしゃですから。

8. What languages does she speak?
   えいごと スペインごと 日本ごが できます。

9. How much Japanese can she speak?
   にちじょうかいわが はなせます。

10. How much kanji can she write?
    かん字は まだ かけません。

11. Can she handle a computer?
    はい、アミリアさんは 大学で コンピューター・プログラミングの べんきょうを しました。

12. Did she find a job at the computer company?
    いいえ、まだです。らい月の 一日に 二かい目の めんせつが あります。

Substitution drill

1. 先しゅうの 金よう日に さいふを なくしました。
   先しゅうの 水よう日に さいふを なくしました。
   先しゅうの 水よう日に けいたいでんわを なくしました。
   おととい、けいたいでんわを なくしました。

2. このみせで かわいいドレスを 見つけました。
   ディズニーランドで かっこいい Tシャツを 見つけました。
   うみで 貝がらを 見つけました。
   デパートで いいゆびわを 見つけました。

3. けい子さんの 子犬が 見つかりました。
    田中さんの かぎが 見つかりました。
    いい日本ごの じしょが 見つかりました。
    やすい日本りょうりの レストランが 見つかりました。

4. ことしのなつ、あたらしいいえが かえます。
    ことしのなつ、いえに かえれます。
    ことしのなつ、ふるい車が うれます。
    ことしのなつ、しんゆうに あえます。

Question and answer (sample answers)

1. はい、ときどき およぎます。
    いいえ、およぎません。でも、ときどき うみで およぎます。

2. はい、たべられます。まぐろと はまちが すきです。
    いいえ、たべられないです。おすしは きらいです。

3. はい、見られます。
    いいえ、見られません。

4. かん字が 五十こぐらい、かけます。
    かん字が 百こぐらい、かけます。そして、二百こぐらい、よめます。

5. はい、すこし よめます。
    いいえ、よめないです。

Short dialogue translation

Mother	Ken-chan. What are you doing outside? You have a key, don't you?
Ken	No. I lost it when I was swimming in the pool at shool.
Mother	What? You lost it?
Ken	Yes. I looked for it, but I couldn't find it.
Mother	Well then, what are you going to do?
Ken	Do you have one more key?
Mother	Not any more. Go to the Lost and Found center at school tomorrow.
Ken	Okay. Can you make a new one if it is not there?
Mother	All right. But don't lose it anymore, okay?

Particles

1. きょう、 五じに いえに かえれます。
2. 先しゅうの 土よう日に うみで ゆびわを なくした。
3. 山田さんは 三月に 大さかに てんきんに なります。
4. きのう、車の かぎを 学校で なくしました。
5. きょねん、シドニーで ホームステイを しました。
6. 先生が 「もっとかん字をべんきょうして下さい」と いいました。
7. らいねん、とうきょうに いきます。そして、えいごの せんせいに なります。
8. ロサンゼルスに／は 日本の おみせが たくさん あります。
9. お金が ないから、あたらしいコンピューターが かえないです。

The
GLOSSARIES

GLOSSARY Level ③ ———————— **English-Japanese**

GLOSSARY Level ③ ———————— **Japanese-English**

GLOSSARY Level ③ ———————— English-Japanese

English 英語	Japanese 日本語	Kanji 漢字

A

English	Japanese	Kanji
[to be] able to do, can do	できる	出来る
about how long?; how much?	どれぐらい、どのぐらい	どれぐらい、どのぐらい
acorns	どんぐり	団栗
adjectives	けいようし	形容詞
advertisement	こうこく	広告
Africa	アフリカ	アフリカ
after all, in the end	けっきょく	結局
again	また	また
air force	くうぐん	空軍
all	ぜんぶ	全部
all right, safe	だいじょうぶ	大丈夫
almost all, the majority	ほとんど	殆ど
amazing, great, wow (adj)	すごい	凄い
amazing, wonderful, wow	すごい	凄い
anything, nothing	なにも	何も
apartment house	マンション	マンション
appointment book	システムてちょう	システム手帳
arm	うで	腕
armpit	わきのした	わきの下
army	りくぐん	陸軍
army knife	アーミーナイフ	アーミーナイフ
Asia	アジア	アジア
Atlantic Ocean	たいせいよう	大西洋

B

back	うら	裏
back garden	うらにわ	裏庭
backyard	うらにわ	裏庭
ball pen	ボールペン	ボールペン
balloon	ふうせん	風船
bamboo	たけ	竹
bandage, dressing	ほうたい	包帯
basement	ちかしつ	地下室
bat (animal)	こうもり	蝙蝠
battery	でんち	電池
beard	ひげ	髭
to become, be	なる	なる
bell	ベル / すず	ベル / 鈴
best friend	しんゆう	親友
blood	ち	血
body	からだ	体
bomb	ばくだん	爆弾
bone	ほね	骨
booger	はなくそ	鼻くそ
book store	ほんや	本屋
both (items or objects)	りょうほう	両方
bouquet	ブーケ	ブーケ
box	はこ	箱
break	やすみ	休み
breasts	むね	胸
breathe	いき	息
brush	ブラシ	ブラシ
bucket	バケツ	バケツ
buffet	ビュッフェ	ビュッフェ
burp	げっぷ	げっぷ
bus stop	バスてい	バス停
butterfly	ちょうちょう	喋喋

button	ボタン	ボタン
by foot	あるいて	歩いて
by yourself	ひとりで	一人で
alone	ひとりで	一人で

C

caca	うんこ / だいべん	うんこ / 大便
cactus	サボテン	サボテン
calculator	けいさんき	計算機
candle	ろうそく	蝋燭
canteen	すいとう	水筒
car battery	バッテリー	バッテリー
carpet	カーペット	カーペット
cash	げんきん	現金
caterpillar	けむし	毛虫
cavity	むしば	虫歯
ceiling	てんじょう	天井
champagne	シャンパン	シャンパン
to change, turn into	かわる	変わる
check-in	チェックイン	チェックイン
check-out	チェックアウト	チェックアウト
chicken	にわとり	鶏
Children	こどもたち	子供達
Chinese cooking (food)	ちゅうかりょうり	中華料理
Christmas tree	クリスマスツリー	クリスマスツリー
circle	まる	丸
cleaning	そうじ	掃除
clip-on earrings	イヤリング	イヤリング
cold	かぜ	風邪
college student	だいがくせい	大学生
college, university	だいがく	大学
to come to dislike	きらいに なる	嫌いになる
to come to like	すきに なる	好きになる

commuting to work	つうきん	通勤
company	かいしゃ	会社
complex	ふくざつ	複雑
complicated	ふくざつ	複雑
concert	コンサート	コンサート
convenient	べんり	便利
conversation	かいわ	会話
correction fluid	しゅうせいえき	修正液
to cost money, take time	かかる	掛かる
cough	せき	咳
cup ramen	カップラーメン	カップラーメン
curtains	カーテン	カーテン
cutting board	まないた	まな板

D

dangerous	あぶない	危ない
day off	やすみ	休み
denim pants, jeans	ジーパン	ジーパン
dentist	はいしゃ	歯医者
dentures (false teeth)	いれば	入歯
development (picture)	げんぞう	現像
devil	あくま	悪魔
dictionary	じしょ	辞書
diet	ダイエット	ダイエット
[to be] different	ちがう	違う
difficult	ふくざつ	複雑
dimples	えくぼ	笑窪
disagreeable	いや	嫌
Disneyland	ディズニーランド	ディズニーランド
disposable camera	つかいすてカメラ	使い捨てカメラ
divorce	りこん	離婚
to do your best	がんばる	頑張る
doo-doo	うんこ / だいべん	うんこ / 大便

door	ドア	ドア
drawing	え	絵
dress	ドレス	ドレス

E

easy	かんたん	かんたん
electric outlet	コンセント	コンセント
electricity	でんき	電気
elementary school	しょうがっこう	小学校
elementary school student	しょうがくせい	小学生
elevator	エレベーター	エレベーター
emergency exit	ひじょうぐち	非常口
emperor	てんのうへいか	天皇陛下
to end, finish	おわる	終わる
endurance	がまん	我慢
equator	せきどう	赤道
escalator	エスカレーター	せきどう
Europe	ヨーロッパ	ヨーロッパ
evening	ばん	晩
everybody	みんな	皆
everyday	にちじょう	日常
expression	ことば	言葉

F

fan	ファン	ファン
fart	おなら	おなら
feces	うんこ / だいべん	うんこ / 大便
file cabinet	ファイル キャビネット	ファイル キャビネット
film	フィルム	フィルム
film shop	しゃしんや	写真屋
to find (active)	みつける	見つける
fire place	だんろ	暖炉
first time	はじめて	初めて

first time	はじめて	初めて
flashlight	かいちゅうでんとう	懐中電灯
flat	ひくい	低い
flat head screwdriver	マイナス ドライバー	マイナス ドライバー
floor	ゆか	床
flower vase	かびん	花瓶
folder	フォルダー	フォルダー
fool, idiot	あほ	あほ
foreign country	がいこく	外国
foreigner	がいこくじん	外国人
[to be] found	みつかる	見つかる
from now (starting from now)	いまから	今から
front desk	フロント	フロント
front teeth	まえば	前歯
frying pan	フライパン	フライパン

G

garden, yard	にわ	庭
Germany	ドイツ	ドイツ
ghost	おばけ	お化け
girl (usually little girl)	おんなのこ	女の子
to go, come back, return	もどる	戻る
grammar	ぶんぽう	文法
grasshopper	ばった	ばった
grave	はか	墓

H

hall (concert)	かいじょう	会場
hammer	ハンマー	ハンマー
handicap	ハンディキャップ	ハンディキャップ
handy	べんり	便利
hanger	ハンガー	ハンガー

happy	うれしい	嬉しい
to have patience, endure	がまんする	我慢する
headache	ずつう	頭痛
heart	ハート	ハート
heavy	おもい	重い
"Hello?" (telephone only)	もしもし	もしもし
hen	にわとり	鶏
hiccups	しゃっくり	しゃっくり
high heels	ハイヒール	ハイヒール
high school	こうこう	高校
high school student	こうこうせい	高校生
hives, rash	じんましん	蕁麻疹
hole puncher	パンチ	パンチ
to home stay	ホームステイ(を) する	ホームステイ(を) する
hot springs	おんせん	温泉
house work	かじ	家事
how long (time)	どれぐらい	どれぐらい
how many days	なんにち	何日
how many hours	なんじかん	何時間
how many months	なんかげつ	何ヶ月
how many weeks	なんしゅうかん	何週間
how many years	なんねん	何年
how much (money)	どれぐらい	どれぐらい
how; what	どう	どう
hurts	いたい	痛い
husband	だんなさん	旦那さん

I

idiot, fool	あほ	あほ
imaginary company	パナソニー	パナソニー
interview	めんせつ	面接
in the morning time	ごぜんちゅう	午前中

index finger	ひとさしゆび	人差し指
injury	けが	怪我
ink	インク	インク
instead of	より	より
intricate	ふくざつ	複雑
iron	アイロン	アイロン

J

jacket	ジャケット	ジャケット
Japan Sea	にほんかい	日本海
jeans, denim pants	ジーパン	ジーパン
junior high school	ちゅうがっこう	中学校
junior high student	ちゅうがくせい	中学生

K

kettle	やかん	やかん
kind, warm-hearted, friendly	しんせつ	親切
kitchen knife	ほうちょう	包丁

L

L.A.	ロス	ロス
ladder	はしご	はしご
lady bug	てんとうむし	てんとう虫
language		言葉
laptop computer	ノートパソコン	ノートパソコン
large apartment	マンション	マンション
laundry	せんたく	洗濯
lawyer	べんごし	弁護士
letter	てがみ	手紙
library	としょかん	図書館
light	かるい	軽い
little finger	こゆび	小指

to live (in a place)	すむ	住む
long	ながい *(い adj.)*	ながい
long time ago	むかし	昔
to look for, search for	さがす	探す
to lose	なくす	無くす
lot	たくさん	沢山
low	ひくい	低い
lungs	はい	肺

M

Madonna	マドンナ	マドンナ
to make	できる	出来る
many	たくさん	沢山
meaning (of something)	いみ	意味
medicine	くすり	薬
to meet	あう	会う
men's bath	おとこゆ	男湯
Merry Christmas	メリークリスマス	メリークリスマス
Michael Jackson	マイケルジャクソン	マイケルジャクソン
middle finger	なかゆび	中指
miniskirt	ミニスカート	ミニスカート
mixed-sex public bath	こんよく	混浴
molars (back teeth)	おくば	奥歯
most, number one	いちばん	一番
much	たくさん	沢山
municipal (public)	しりつ	市立
muscles	きんにく	筋肉
mushrooms	きのこ	茸
my father	ちち	父
my mother	はは	母

N

nails (for hammers)	くぎ	釘
naked	はだか	裸
national border	こっきょう	国境
navy	かいぐん	海軍
negative	ネガ	ネガ
new car	しんしゃ	新車
normal	にちじょう	日常
North Pole	ほっきょく	北極
not fun	つまらない	つまらない
not interesting	つまらない	つまらない
nouns	めいし	名詞
nuclear bomb	げんしばくだん	原子爆弾
number	かず	数
number one, the most	いちばん	一番
nurse	かんごふ(さん)	看護婦さん

O

ocean	うみ	海
ocean bathing	かいすいよく	海水浴
Oceania	オセアニア	オセアニア
okay	オーケー	オーケー
one-piece dress	ワンピース	ワンピース
one-room apartment	ワンルーム・マンション	ワンルーム・マンション
only	だけ	だけ
ordinary	にちじょう	日常
to originate, start, begin	はじめる	始める
over and including	～いじょう	以上

P

Pacific Ocean	たいへいよう	太平洋

page	ページ	頁
painful	いたい	痛い
paint	ペンキ	ペンキ
painting	え	絵
palm tree	やしのき	椰子の木
paperclip	(ペーパー)クリップ	(ペーパー)クリップ
parking lot	ちゅうしゃじょう	駐車場
part-time job	アルバイト	アルバイト
patience	がまん	我慢
to pay	はらう	払う
pencil sharpener	えんぴつけずり	鉛筆削り
pet shop	ペットショップ	ペットショップ
Phillips screwdriver	プラスドライバー	プラスドライバー
photograph	しゃしん	写真
picnic	ピクニック	ピクニック
pierced earrings	ピアス	ピアス
piggy bank	ちょきんばこ	貯金箱
pilot	パイロット	パイロット
pimple	にきび	にきび
pinky (little finger)	こゆび	小指
pistol	ピストル	ピストル
place	ところ	所
to play	あそぶ	遊ぶ
Polaroid	ポラロイド	ポラロイド
poo-poo	うんこ / だいべん	うんこ / 大便
pool	プール	プール
popcorn	ポップコーン	ポップコーン
potato	じゃがいも	じゃがいも
pots and pans	なべ	鍋
potted plants	うえき	植木
private	しりつ	私立
pretty; clean	きれい	綺麗
probably	でしょう	でしょう

programming	プログラミング	プログラミング
properly	ちゃんと	ちゃんと
puppy	こいぬ	小犬

Q

| quickly, fast; hurry up! | はやく | 早く |
| quiet | しずか | 静か |

R

radio	ラジオ	ラジオ
railroad crossing	ふみきり	踏み切り
to raise an animal	かう	飼う
rap music	ラップ	ラップ
real estate	ふどうさん	不動産
real estate agent/broker	ふどうさんやさん	不動産屋さん
rectangle	ちょうほうけい	長方形
red wine	あかワイン	赤ワイン
reindeer	トナカイ	トナカイ
rifle	ライフル	ライフル
right away, immediately	すぐ	すぐ
right?	でしょう	でしょう
ring (jewelry)	ゆびわ	指輪
ring finger	くすりゆび	薬指
rocket	ロケット	ロケット
roof	やね	屋根
rooftop	おくじょう	屋上
room for two	ふたりべや	二人部屋
room service	ルームサービス	ルームサービス
rose wine	ロゼワイン	ロゼワイン
running	ランニング	ランニング

S

safe (to secure valuables)	きんこ	金庫
safety pin	あんぜんぴん	安全ピン
sandals	サンダル	サンダル
Santa Claus	サンタクロース	サンタクロース
saw	のこぎり	鋸
to say, speak, tell	いう	言う
scary, scared	こわい	恐い
scorpion	さそり	蠍
screwdriver	ドライバー	ドライバー
screws	ねじ	ねじ
secretary	ひしょ	秘書
see you again later	また あとで	また あとで
self defense force	じえいたい	自衛隊
self-control	がまん	我慢
Shinjuku station (train)	しんじゅくえき	新宿駅
shoelace	くつひも	靴紐
to shop	かいもの(を)する	買い物(を)する
short in height	ひくい	低い
short in length	みじかい	短い
shot	ちゅうしゃ	注射
to show	みせる	見せる
shower	シャワー	シャワー
sick	びょうき	病気
sidewalk	ほどう	歩道
silent	しずか	静か
Single, unmarried	どくしん	独身
skeleton	がいこつ	骸骨
slobber	よだれ	涎
sneakers	スニーカー	スニーカー
sneeze	くしゃみ	くしゃみ
snoring	いびき	いびき
snot	はなみず	鼻水

snow man	ゆきだるま	雪だるま
sofa	ソファー	ソファー
someday	いつか	いつか
song	うた	歌
South Pole	なんきょく	南極
speech		言葉
spider	くも	蜘蛛
spring break (vacation)	はるやすみ	春休み
square	しかく	四角
stapler	ホッチキス	ホッチキス
to start, to begin	はじまる	始まる
starting now (from now on)	これから	これから
still	しずか	静か
stomach	い	胃
store	みせ、おみせ	店、お店
straw	ストロー	ストロー
study, studies	べんきょう	勉強
submarine	せんすいかん	潜水艦
summer break (vacation)	なつやすみ	夏休み
sunflower	ひまわり	向日葵
supermarket	スーパー	スーパー
surgery	しゅじゅつ	手術
to swim	およぐ	泳ぐ
swimming pool	プール	プール
Sydney (Australia)	シドニー	シドニー

T

tadpole	おたまじゃくし	お玉じゃくし
tank	せんしゃ	戦車
tape (cellophane)	セロテープ	セロテープ
taxi	タクシー	タクシー
taxi stand	タクシーのりば	乗り場
tears	なみだ	涙

telephone bill	でんわだい	電話代
terrible	ひどい	酷い
test	テスト / しけん	テスト / 試験
that time	そのとき	その時
the other day	このあいだ	この間
therefore, for that reason	だから	だから
thermometer (for body)	たいおんけい	体温計
thing(s)	もの	物
to think	おもう	思う
this morning	けさ	今朝
thumb	おやゆび	親指
tip (for services)	チップ	チップ
toast	トースト	トースト
together	いっしょ	一緒
toilet paper	トイレット ペーパー	トイレット ペーパー
tongue	した	舌
tongue twister	はやくちことば	早口言葉
town	まち	町
transfer (job)	てんきん	転勤
[to be] transferred	てんきんになる	転勤になる
triangle	さんかく	三角
tripod	さんきゃく	三脚
T-shirt	ティーシャツ	ティーシャツ
tulips	チューリップ	チューリップ
two-sided tape	りょうめんテープ	両面テープ

U

um	えーと	えーと
under and including	～いか	以下
unfortunate	ざんねん	残念
United Nations	こくれん	国連
unpleasant	いや	嫌
urine	おしっこ / しょうべん	おしっこ / 小便
used car	ちゅうこしゃ	中古車

| useful | べんり | 便利 |

V

various	いろいろ	色々
vending machine	じどうはんばいき	自動販売機
vitamins	ビタミン	ビタミン
vocabulary, words	たんご	単語
voice	こえ	声

W

to wait	まつ	待つ
wall	かべ	壁
wallet	**さいふ**	**さいふ**
war	せんそう	戦争
war	せんそう	戦争
war aircraft	せんとうき	戦闘機
washing machine	せんたくき	洗濯機
wedding cake	ウエディング・ケーキ	ウエディング・ケーキ
wedding dress	ウエディング・ドレス	ウエディング・ドレス
wedding ring	けっこんゆびわ	結婚指輪
well then	じゃあ	じゃあ
what year of school?		
what grade?	なんねんせい	何年生
wheelchair	くるまいす	車椅子
when, time	～とき	時
which (of two) informal	どっち	どっち
white wine	しろワイン	白ワイン
why?	なんで	なんで
wind	かぜ	風
wine	ワイン	ワイン
winter break (vacation)	ふゆやすみ	冬休み
[to be] wrong	ちがう	違う

women's bath	おんなゆ	女湯
word	ことば	言葉
to work	はたらく	働く
to work part-time	アルバイトをする	アルバイトをする

X

| X-ray | レントゲン | レントゲン |

Y

| yawn | あくび | 欠伸 |
| young | わかい | 若い |

GLOSSARY Level ③ ——————— Japanese-English

Japanese 日本語	English 英語	Kanji 漢字
~		
~いか	under and including	以下
~いじょう	over and including	以上
~とき	when, time	時
あ		
アーミーナイフ	army knife	アーミーナイフ
アイロン	iron	アイロン
あう	to meet	会う
あかワイン	red wine	赤ワイン
あくび	yawn	欠伸
あくま	devil	悪魔
アジア	Asia	アジア
あそぶ	to play	遊ぶ
あぶない	dangerous	危ない
アフリカ	Africa	アフリカ
あほ	a fool, an idiot	あほ
あるいて	by walking	歩いて
アルバイト	part-time job	アルバイト
アルバイトをする	to work part-time	アルバイトをする
あんぜんぴん	safety pin	安全ピン
い		
い	stomach	胃
いう	to say, speak, tell	言う

いき	breathe	息
いたい	painful, hurts	痛い
いちばん	the most, number one	一番
いつか	someday	いつか
いっしょ	together	一緒
いびき	snoring	いびき
いまから	from now (starting from now)	今から
いみ	meaning (of something)	意味
いや	unpleasant, disagreeble (very negative word)	嫌
イヤリング	clip-on earrings	イヤリング
いれば	dentures (false teeth)	入歯
いろいろ	various	色々
インク	ink	インク

う

うえき	potted plants	植木
ウエディング・ケーキ	wedding cake	ウエディング・ケーキ
ウエディング・ドレス	wedding dress	ウエディング・ドレス
うた	song	歌
うで	arm	腕
うみ	the ocean, the beach	海
うら	the back	裏
うらにわ	a back garden, a backyard	裏庭
うれしい	happy	嬉しい
うんこ / だいべん	feces, doo-doo, ka-ka, poo-poo	うんこ / 大便

え

え	a drawing or painting	絵
えーと	um	えーと
えくぼ	dimples	笑窪
エスカレーター	escalator	エスカレーター
エレベーター	elevator	エレベーター

えんぴつけずり	pencil sharpener	鉛筆削り

お

オーケー	okay	オーケー
おくじょう	rooftop	屋上
おくば	molars (back teeth)	奥歯
おしっこ / しょうべん	urine	おしっこ / 小便
オセアニア	Oceania	オセアニア
おたまじゃくし	tadpole	お玉じゃくし
おとこゆ	men's bath	男湯
おなら	fart	おなら
おばけ	ghost	お化け
おもい	heavy	重い
おもう	to think	思う
おやゆび	thumb	親指
およぐ	to swim	泳ぐ
おわります	to end, finish	終わる
おんせん	hot springs	温泉
おんなのこ	a girl (usually a little girl)	女の子
おんなゆ	women's bath	女湯

か

カーテン	curtains	カーテン
カーペット	carpet	カーペット
かいぐん	navy	海軍
がいこく	foreign country	外国
がいこくじん	foreigner	外国人
がいこつ	skeleton	骸骨
かいしゃ	company	会社
かいじょう	(concert) hall	会場
かいすいよく	ocean bathing	海水浴
かいちゅうでんとう	flashlight	懐中電灯

かいもの(を)する	to shop	買い物する
かいわ	conversation	会話
かう	to raise an animal	飼う
かかる	to cost money, take time	掛かる
かじ	house work	家事
かず	number	数
かぜ	a cold	風邪
かぜ	wind	風
カップラーメン	cup ramen	カップラーメン
かびん	flower vase	花瓶
かべ	wall	壁
がまん	patience; endurance; self-control	我慢
がまんする	to have patience; endure	我慢する
からだ	body	体
かるい	light	軽い
かわる	to change, turn into	変わる
かんごふ(さん)	a nurse	看護婦さん
かんたん	easy	かんたん
がんばる	to do your best	頑張る

き

きのこ	mushrooms	茸
きらいに なる	to come to dislike	嫌いになる
きれい	pretty; clean	綺麗な
きんこ	safe (to secure valuables)	金庫
きんにく	muscles	筋肉

く

くうぐん	air force	空軍
くぎ	nails (for hammers)	釘
くしゃみ	sneeze	くしゃみ
くすり	medicine	薬

くすりゆび	ring finger	薬指
くつひも	shoelace	靴紐
くも	spider	蜘蛛
クリスマスツリー	Christmas tree	クリスマスツリー
くるまいす	wheelchair	車椅子

け

けいさんき	calculator	計算機
けいようし	adjectives	形容詞
けが	Injury	怪我
けっきょく	after all, in the end	結局
けっこんゆびわ	wedding ring	結婚指輪
けさ	this morning	今朝
げっぷ	burp	げっぷ
けむし	caterpillar	毛虫
げんきん	cash	現金
げんしばくだん	nuclear bomb	原子爆弾
げんぞう	development (picture)	現像

こ

こいぬ	puppy	小犬
こうこう	high school	高校
こうこうせい	high school student	高校生
こうこく	advertisement	広告
こうもり	bat (animal)	蝙蝠
こえ	voice	声
こくれん	United Nations	国連
ごぜんちゅう	in the morning time	午前中
こっきょう	national border	国境
ことば	speech, language; word; expression	言葉
こどもたち	children	子供達
このあいだ	the other day	この間

こゆび	little finger	小指
こゆび	pinky (little finger)	小指
これから	starting now (from now on)	これから
こわい	scary, scared	恐い
コンサート	concert	コンサート
コンセント	electric outlet	コンセント
こんよく	mixed-sex bath	混浴

さ

さいふ	wallet	財布
さがす	to look for, search for	探す
さそり	scorpion	蠍
サボテン	cactus	サボテン
さんかく	triangle	三角
さんきゃく	tripod	三脚
サンタクロース	Santa Claus	サンタクロース
サンダル	sandals	サンダル
ざんねん	unfortunate	残念

し

ジーパン	denim pants, jeans	ジーパン
じえいたい	self defense force	自衛隊
しかく	square	四角
じしょ	a dictionary	辞書
しずか	quiet	静か
しずか	quiet, silent; still	静か
システムてちょう	appointment book	システム手帳
した	tongue	舌
じどうはんばいき	vending machine	自動販売機
シドニー	Sydney (Australia)	シドニー
じゃあ	long version of じゃ (well, then)	じゃあ

じゃがいも	potato	じゃがいも
ジャケット	jacket	ジャケット
しゃしん	photograph	写真
しゃしんや	film shop	写真屋
しゃっくり	hiccups	しゃっくり
シャワー	shower	シャワー
シャンパン	champagne	シャンパン
しゅうせいえき	correction fluid	修正液
しゅじゅつ	surgery	手術
しょうがくせい	elementary school student	小学生
しょうがっこう	elementary school	小学校
しりつ	private	私立
しりつ	municipal (public)	市立
しろワイン	white wine	白ワイン
しんしゃ	a new car	新車
しんじゅくえき	Shinjuku station (train)	新宿駅
しんせつ	kind, warm-hearted, friendly	親切
じんましん	hives, rash	蕁麻疹
しんゆう	best friend	親友

す

すいとう	canteen	水筒
スーパー	supermarket	スーパー
すきに なる	to come to like	好きになる
すぐ	right away, immediately	すぐ
すごい	amazing, great, wow	凄い
ずつう	headache	頭痛
ストロー	straw	ストロー
スニーカー	sneakers	スニーカー
すむ	to live (in a place)	住む

せ

せき	cough	咳
せきどう	equator	赤道
ゼムクリップ	paperclip	ゼムクリップ
セロテープ	tape (cellophane)	セロテープ
せんしゃ	tank	戦車
せんすいかん	submarine	潜水艦
せんそう	war	戦争
せんたく	laundry	洗濯
せんたくき	washing machine	洗濯機
せんとうき	war aircraft	戦闘機
ぜんぶ	all	全部

そ

そうじ	cleaning	掃除
そのとき	that time	その時
ソファー	sofa	ソファー

た

ダイエット	diet	ダイエット
たいおんけい	thermometer (for body)	体温計
だいがく	college, university	大学
だいがくせい	college student	大学生
だいじょうぶ	all right, safe	大丈夫
たいせいよう	Atlantic Ocean	大西洋
たいへいよう	Pacific Ocean	太平洋
だから	therefore, for that reason	だから
たくさん	a lot, many	沢山
タクシー	taxi	タクシー
タクシーのりば	taxi stand	乗り場
たけ	bamboo	竹

だけ	only	だけ
たんご	vocabulary, words	単語
だんなさん	husband	旦那さん
だんろ	fireplace	暖炉

ち

ち	blood	血
チェックアウト	check-out	チェックアウト
チェックイン	check-in	チェックイン
ちがう	to be wrong; to be different	違う
ちかしつ	basement	地下室
ちち	my father	父
チップ	tip (for services)	チップ
ちゃんと	properly	ちゃんと
ちゅうがくせい	junior high student	中学生
ちゅうがっこう	junior high school	中学校
ちゅうかりょうり	Chinese cooking (food)	中華料理
ちゅうこしゃ	used car	中古車
ちゅうしゃ	a shot	注射
ちゅうしゃじょう	parking lot	駐車場
チューリップ	tulips	チューリップ
ちょうちょう	butterfly	喋喋
ちょうほうけい	rectangle	長方形
ちょきんばこ	piggy bank	貯金箱

つ

つうきん	commuting to work	通勤
つかいすてカメラ	disposable camera	使い捨てカメラ
つまらない	not fun, not interesting	つまらない

て

ティーシャツ	T-shirt	ティーシャツ
ディズニーランド	Disneyland	ディズニーランド
てがみ	a letter	手紙
できる	to be able to do, can do, make	出来る
でしょう	right?, probably	でしょう
テスト / しけん	test	テスト / 試験
でんき	electricity	電気
てんきん	a transfer (job)	転勤
てんきんになる	to be transferred	転勤になる
てんじょう	ceiling	天井
でんち	batteries	電池
てんとうむし	lady bug	てんとう虫
てんのうへいか	emperor	天皇陛下
でんわだい	telephone bill	電話代

と

ドア	door	ドア
ドイツ	Germany	ドイツ
トイレットペーパー	toilet paper	トイレットペーパー
どう	how; what	どう
トースト	toast	トースト
どくしん	single, unmarried	独身
ところ	place	所
としょかん	library	図書館
どちら	where, which and who (polite)	どちら
どっち	which (of two) informal	どっち
トナカイ	reindeer	トナカイ
ドライバー	screwdriver	ドライバー
どれぐらい	how long; how much (time, money)	どれぐらい
どれぐらい、どのぐらい	about how long?; how much?	どれぐらい、どのぐらい
ドレス	dress	ドレス

どんぐり	acorns	団栗

な

ながい	long	ながい
なかゆび	middle finger	中指
なくす	to lose	無くす
なつやすみ	summer break (vacation)	夏休み
なにも	anything, nothing	何も
なべ	pots and pans	鍋
なみだ	tears	涙
なる	to become, be	なる
なんかげつ	how many months	何ヶ月
なんきょく	South Pole	南極
なんじかん	how many hours	何時間
なんしゅうかん	how many weeks	何週間
なんで	why?	なんで
なんにち	how many days	何日
なんねん	how many years	何年
なんねんせい	what year of school?, what grade?	何年生

に

にきび	pimple	にきび
にちじょう	normal, everyday, ordinary	日常
にほんかい	Japan Sea	日本海
にわ	garden, yard	庭
にわとり	a chicken, a hen; a cock	鶏

ね

ネガ	negative	ネガ
ねじ	screws	ねじ

の

のこぎり	saw	鋸

は

ハート	heart	ハート
はい	lungs	肺
はいしゃ	dentist	歯医者
ハイヒール	high heels	ハイヒール
パイロット	pilot	パイロット
はか	grave	墓
ばくだん	bomb	爆弾
バケツ	bucket	バケツ
はこ	box	箱
はしご	ladder	はしご
はじまる	to start, to begin	始まる
はじめて	first time	初めて
はじめる	to originate, start, begin	始める
バスてい	bus stop	バス停
はだか	naked	裸
はたらく	to work	働く
ばった	grasshopper	ばった
バッテリー	car battery	バッテリー
はなくそ	booger	鼻くそ
パナソニー	an imaginary company	パナソニー
はなみず	snot	鼻水
はは	my mother	母
はやく	quickly, fast, hurry up!	早く
はやくちことば	tongue twister	早口言葉
はらう	to pay	払う
はるやすみ	spring break (vacation)	春休み
ばん	evening	晩
ハンガー	hanger	ハンガー
ハンディキャップ	handicap	ハンディキャップ

| ハンマー | hammer | ハンマー |

ひ

ピアス	pierced earrings	ピアス
ひくい	low, short in height; flat	低い
ピクニック	picnic	ピクニック
ひげ	beard	髭
ひしょ	a secretary	秘書
ひじょうぐち	emergency exit	非常口
ピストル	pistol	ピストル
ビタミン	vitamins	ビタミン
ひどい	terrible	酷い
ひとさしゆび	index finger	人差し指
ひとりで	by yourself, alone	一人で
ひまわり	sunflower	向日葵
ビュッフェ	buffet	ビュッフェ
びょうき	sick	病気

ふ

ファイル キャビネット	file cabinet	ファイル キャビネット
ファン	a fan	ファン
フィルム	film	フィルム
ブーケ	bouquet	ブーケ
ふうせん	balloon	風船
プール	swimming pool	プール
フォルダー	folder	フォルダー
ふくざつ	complicated, intricate, complex, difficult	複雑
ふたりべや	a room for two	二人部屋
ふどうさん	real estate	不動産
ふどうさんやさん	real estate agent/broker	不動産屋さん
ふみきり	railroad crossing	踏み切り
ふゆやすみ	winter break (vacation)	冬休み

フライパン	frying pan	フライパン
ブラシ	brush	ブラシ
プラスドライバー	Phillips screwdriver	プラスドライバ
プログラミング	programming	プログラミング
フロント	front desk	フロント
ぶんぽう	grammar	文法

へ

ページ	page	頁
ペットショップ	pet shop	ペットショップ
ベル / すず	bell	ベル / 鈴
ペンキ	paint	ペンキ
べんきょう	study, studies	勉強
べんごし	lawyer	弁護士
べんり	convenient, handy, useful	便利

ほ

ほうたい	bandage, dressing	包帯
ほうちょう	kitchen knife	包丁
ホームステイ(を) する	to stay at someone's house	ホームステイ(を) する
パンチ	hole puncher	パンチ
ボールペン	ball pen	ボールペン
ボタン	button	ボタン
ほっきょく	North Pole	北極
ホッチキス	stapler	ホッチキス
ポップコーン	popcorn	ポップコーン
ほどう	sidewalk	歩道
ほとんど	almost all, the majority	殆ど
ほね	bone	骨
ポラロイド	Polaroid	ポラロイド

ほんや	book store	本屋

ま

マイケルジャクソン	Michael Jackson	マイケルジャクソン
マイナスドライバー	flathead (standard) screwdriver	マイナスドライバ
まえば	front teeth	前歯
また	again	又
また あとで	again later	又後で
まち	a town	町
まつ	to wait	待つ
マドンナ	Madonna	マドンナ
まないた	cutting board	まな板
まる	circle	丸
マンション	large apartment, apartment house	

み

みじかい	short in length	短い
みせ、おみせ	store	店、お店
みせる	to show	見せる
みつかる	to be found (passive)	見つかる
みつける	to find (active)	見つける
ミニスカート	miniskirt	ミニスカート
みんな	everybody	皆

む

むかし	long time ago	昔
むしば	cavity	虫歯
むね	breasts	胸

め

めいし	nouns	名詞
メリークリスマス	Merry Christmas	メリークリスマス
めんせつ	an interview	面接

も

メリークリスマス	hello (telephone only)	メリークリスマス
もどる	to go, come back, return	戻る
もの	thing(s)	物

や

やかん	kettle	やかん
やしのき	palm tree	椰子の木
やすみ	a day off, a break	休み
やね	roof	屋根

ゆ

ゆか	floor	床
ゆきだるま	snow man	雪だるま
ゆびわ	a ring (jewelry)	指輪

よ

ヨーロッパ	Europe	ヨーロッパ
よだれ	slobber	涎
より	instead of	より

ら

ライフル	rifle	ライフル

ラジオ	radio	ラジオ
ラップ	rap music	ラップ
ラップトップ	laptop computer	ラップトップ
ランニング	running	ランニング

り

りくぐん	army	陸軍
りこん	divorce	離婚
りょうほう	both (items or objects)	両方
りょうめんテープ	two-sided tape	両面テープ

る

ルームサービス	room service	ルームサービス

れ

レントゲン	X-ray	レントゲン

ろ

ろうそく	candle	蝋燭
ロケット	rocket	ロケット
ロス	L.A.	ロス
ロゼワイン	rose wine	ロゼワイン

わ

ワイン	wine	ワイン
わかい	young	若い
わきのした	armpit	わきの下
ワンピース	one-piece dress	ワンピース
ワンルーム・マンション	one-room apartment	ワンルーム・マンシ

Japan
日本

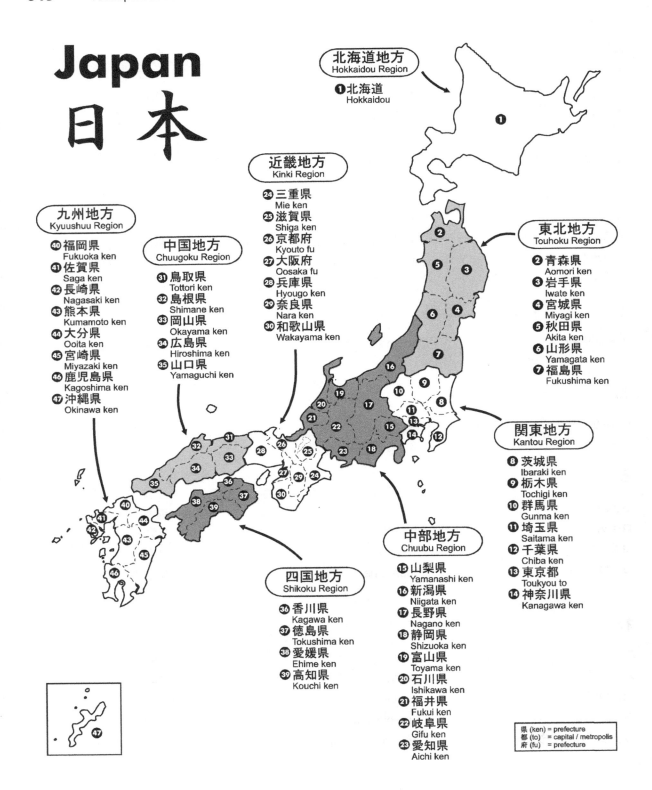

北海道地方
Hokkaidou Region
❶ 北海道
Hokkaidou

近畿地方
Kinki Region
㉔ 三重県
Mie ken
㉕ 滋賀県
Shiga ken
㉖ 京都府
Kyouto fu
㉗ 大阪府
Oosaka fu
㉘ 兵庫県
Hyougo ken
㉙ 奈良県
Nara ken
㉚ 和歌山県
Wakayama ken

九州地方
Kyuushuu Region
㊵ 福岡県
Fukuoka ken
㊶ 佐賀県
Saga ken
㊷ 長崎県
Nagasaki ken
㊸ 熊本県
Kumamoto ken
㊹ 大分県
Ooita ken
㊺ 宮崎県
Miyazaki ken
㊻ 鹿児島県
Kagoshima ken
㊼ 沖縄県
Okinawa ken

中国地方
Chuugoku Region
㉛ 鳥取県
Tottori ken
㉜ 島根県
Shimane ken
㉝ 岡山県
Okayama ken
㉞ 広島県
Hiroshima ken
㉟ 山口県
Yamaguchi ken

東北地方
Touhoku Region
❷ 青森県
Aomori ken
❸ 岩手県
Iwate ken
❹ 宮城県
Miyagi ken
❺ 秋田県
Akita ken
❻ 山形県
Yamagata ken
❼ 福島県
Fukushima ken

関東地方
Kantou Region
❽ 茨城県
Ibaraki ken
❾ 栃木県
Tochigi ken
❿ 群馬県
Gunma ken
⓫ 埼玉県
Saitama ken
⓬ 千葉県
Chiba ken
⓭ 東京都
Toukyou to
⓮ 神奈川県
Kanagawa ken

中部地方
Chuubu Region
⓯ 山梨県
Yamanashi ken
⓰ 新潟県
Niigata ken
⓱ 長野県
Nagano ken
⓲ 静岡県
Shizuoka ken
⓳ 富山県
Toyama ken
⓴ 石川県
Ishikawa ken
㉑ 福井県
Fukui ken
㉒ 岐阜県
Gifu ken
㉓ 愛知県
Aichi ken

四国地方
Shikoku Region
㊱ 香川県
Kagawa ken
㊲ 徳島県
Tokushima ken
㊳ 愛媛県
Ehime ken
㊴ 高知県
Kouchi ken

県 (ken) = prefecture
都 (to) = capital / metropolis
府 (fu) = prefecture

Level 3 Kanji Requirements

(lesson-by-lesson reference)

1. 一 二 三 四 五 六
2. 七 八 九 十 百 千
3. 日 月 火 水 木 金 土
4. 休 上 下 左 右
5. 大 中 小 円 人 目
6. 耳 口 手 足 力
7. 立 男 女 子 生
8. 天 空 気 雨 山 川
9. 林 森 石 花 犬 虫 町
10. 村 田 夕 赤 青 白 見
11. 出 入 先 早 本 文
12. 名 字 学 校 正 年 王
13. 音 糸 車 貝 玉 草 竹

Other From Zero! Books

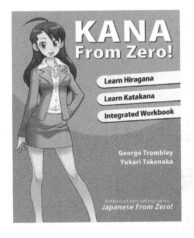